LOVE, SEX & MURDER

IN OLD OREGON

OFFBEAT OREGON HISTORY VOL. II

LOVE, SEX & MURDER
IN OLD OREGON

OFFBEAT OREGON HISTORY VOL. II

By FINN J.D. JOHN

Copyright ©2019 by Finn J.D. John

All rights reserved. However, please note that most stories in this book are edited, revised, and augmented versions of stories that initially ran in the Offbeat Oregon History syndicated newspaper column under a Creative Commons Attribution-Share Alike license. Those earlier versions are still covered under the license, and can be easily found with a Google search.

For information about permission to reproduce selections from this book, write to Ouragan House Publishers, Post Office Box 77, Corvallis, OR 97339, or e-mail permissions@ouragan-house.com.

Softcover Edition
ISBN: 978-1-63591-122-0

Other edition ISBNs:

Hardcover:	978-1-63591-121-3
E-book:	978-1-63591-124-4
Audiobook, retail:	978-1-63591-125-1
Audiobook, library edition:	978-1-63591-126-8
Interactive PDF:	978-1-63591-128-2

Dust jacket design by Fiona Mac Daibheid.

Ouragan House Publishers
An imprint of
Pulp-Lit Productions
Corvallis, Oregon

http://ouragan-house.com
http://pulp-lit.com

This softcover edition comes bundled with the e-book version*.

HERE'S HOW TO ACCESS IT:

Download the E-book in EPUB or Interactive PDF form at http://ouragan-house.com/122.

*Everyone who buys this multimedia bundle edition receives a lifetime non-alienable license to all the e-book editions. **This includes people who buy it secondhand**, and it does not expire if you sell this copy to someone else: you keep your license, and the buyer receives a fresh one of his/her own.

TABLE OF CONTENTS:

Part I: Deadly Beloved 1
  The Dynamite Vamp. 3
      #PussyWillowMurder   #ToDieFor
  The Ax-Murderess. 7
      #SpousalAbuse   #CharityLamb
  The Stalker. 13
      #BadJournalism   #MattieAllison
  The Homesteader. 13
      #Bigamy   #NormanWilliams
  Femme Fatale. 23
      #PortlandHookers   #CarrieBradley
  The Fake Coma. 33
      #SpousalAbuse   #CharlesFiester
  The Triangle Man. 37
      #SecretAffair   #MandyMcDaniel
  The Patsy. 43
      #JudicialLynching   #JosephDrake
  Mesmerized. 47
      #HelicopterParents   #PleasantArmstrong
  The Drywall Contractor. 53
      #FBIsMostWanted   #ThomasJamesHolden
  The Ex-Police Chief. 57
      #FBIsMostWanted   #OttoAustinLoel

Part II: Bonnie and Clyde. 61
The Conjugal Jailbreakers. 63
#CopKiller   #CarlCletusBowles
Gangster and Moll. 69
#SilvermanCase   #JimmyWalker
The Beavercreek Bombers. 77
#Extortion   #DavidHeesch

Part III: Murder, Family Style. 83
The Mother-Son Team. 85
#AxMurder   #RichardMarple
Shotgun Emma. 89
#Boardinghouse   #EmmaFrishkorn
The Housewife and the Bad Seed. 93
#EmmaHannah   #LloydMontgomery
The Bomber. 99
#MatricidePlus   #JackGilbertGraham
The Curse of Gold. 105
#ChildMolestation   #ThomasSmith

Part IV: The Unwritten Law. 111
The "Naked Ladies" Cult. 115
#HolyRollers   #Fratricide
The Loved Dead. 129
#KissTheCorpse   #LuluReynolds
The Family Circus. 135
#ShotgunWedding   #OrlandoMurray
The Manhunter. 141
#Assassination   #JohnBowlsby

A Christmas Carol. 145
    #DysfunctionalFamily   *#OfficerJohnGittings*
The Unwritten In-Law. 155
    #Bigamist   *#AmsterdamJackMurray*
The Gunfight and Bad Timing. 159
    #CharlesPowell   *#JohnBrownsDaughter*
The Time it Didn't Work. 165
    #KillTheWitness   *#RThomasDickerson*
Father of the Year. 169
    #MurderousRampage   *#AlfredBelding*
One for the Ladies. 175
    #ActuallyInsane   *#CarolineBriggs*

Part V: Serial Killers and Deadly Strangers. 179
  The Angel of Death. 181
    #LakeCountySerialKiller   *#RayVanBurenJackson*
  The Trappers. 191
    #ShotFromAmbush   *#CharlesHydeKimzey*
  The Man with the Hook. 201
    #YoungLove   *#LarryPeytonBeverlyAllan*
  The Dark Strangler. 207
    #LandladyKiller   *#EarleLeonardNelson*
  The Railroad Job. 211
    #RobertELeeFolkes   *#UnknownWarHero*

Part VI: Vigilante Murder....................223
The Masked Assassins....................225
#RangeWars #JoeAndLeeLaws
The Prineville Vigilantes....................231
#RangeWars #ColonelBudThompson
Who Got Shorty?....................237
#Sheepshooters #ShortyDavis
Killing Berry Way....................243
#KangarooCourt #JudicialLynching

Part VII: Just Plain Murder....................247
The First Murderer....................249
#LandDispute #NimrodOKelly
The Dead Man's Revenge....................255
#BoxcarMurder #DanCasey
The Bootlegger....................259
#CarSoakedWithBlood #RussellHecker
The Plainview Killer....................265
#ProhibitionRaid #DaveWest
The Prepaid Shanghaiing....................269
#JimTurk #DeadSailor
The Champagne Riot....................275
#CivilWar #ChristmasCheer
The Jackson County Rebellion....................279
#PopulistUprising #LlewellynBanks
The International Murderer O' Mystery....................291
#ShankedInPrison #JamesCook
The Suspicious Gunfight....................297
#LandDispute #KelsayPorter
The Wanderers....................301
#MelmouthTheWanderer #ClaudeBranton

Part VIII: Just Plain Sex. 307
    The Floating Bordello. 309
        #FloatingPalaceOfSin   *#NancyBoggs*
    The Vice Crusade. 315
        #AnyPortInAStorm   *#PortlandHookers*
    The Smutty Anarchists. 319
        #FilthyFirebrand   *#ComstockLaws*
    The Real Meaning of "Bicycle Face." 325
        #PortlandHookers   *#Feminism*
    The Heiress Whisperer. 335
        #MrWickham   *#DiamondBill*

Part IX: Cold Cases. 343
    See Portland and Die. 345
        #BadCompany   *#JosephSwards*
    Balch Family Values. 351
        #ShotgunInLaw   *#ChildMolestation*
    Boneyard Mary. 357
        #AccidentOrMurder   *#ThomasMcMahon*
    The Bordello Murder. 363
        #KlamathFallsHookers   *#MissFayeMelbourne*

PART I:

DEADLY BELOVED.

There's a reason why, in suspense novels and movies, the cops are always trying to pin the job on the victim's husband or boyfriend. It's because they know that, statistically, that's most likely who did it, even if they can't prove it. According to the Department of Justice, in 2011 one out of five murder victims were "done" by an intimate partner; throw in family members and friends, and that figure swells up to four out of five.

In this section of this collection, we've assembled 11 stories of couples for whom passion led, in one way or another, to fatality . . . .

THE DYNAMITE VAMP.

Late on the evening of April 21, 1955, 35-year-old Portland attorney Oliver Kermit Smith left the Columbia Edgewater Country Club and walked to his car. He was probably a little tipsy; there had been a stag party that night, and he was one of the last to leave.

He slipped behind the wheel of his 1952 Buick, turned the ignition switch to "on," and stepped on the floor-mounted starter button.

Two or three seconds later his mangled, lifeless body fell to the ground three feet behind the Buick's rear bumper, amid a shower of broken glass and bits of torn metal.

Someone had stuffed 10 sticks of stumping powder under the driver's seat of Smith's Buick, wired with an electrical detonator to the starter solenoid on the car.

As police would soon learn from the investigation that followed, the killer had rigged the bomb in advance, leaving the circuit open so his victim could drive to the country club without setting off. Then, while Smith was inside playing gin rummy with his friends, the killer had crept up to the car under cover of darkness, opened the driver's door, connected the last two wires together, slipped them under the floormat, closed the door — then scurried back to his own vehicle to speed away into the night.

Portlanders learned about the murder, of course, when they read the front page of the next morning's paper. And if any of them wondered how long it

The wreckage of Oliver Kermit Smith's car after it was blown to pieces by a dynamite bomb in the parking lot of the Columbia Edgewater Country Club. Picture is from the files of Det. Walter Graven. (Image: portlandcrime.blogspot.com)

would take police to find the killer, they weren't kept wondering for long. The crime was more or less solved within 18 hours of Kermit Smith stepping on that fatal starter switch.

The thing was, it wasn't the first time someone had tried to kill Smith. About six weeks before, he had been waylaid outside his home by a shadowy figure wielding a heavy bottle like a club. In the struggle, Smith's nose was broken, but the attacker had gotten away.

When police had asked him, in his hospital bed, if he had any idea who might have done this, he'd said, "Wolf."

Victor Wolf, he told the cops, was a 45-year-old electrician who rented a room in a house owned by Smith's wife, Marjorie. "He kinda likes my wife," Smith added.

There was no evidence, so there wasn't much the police could do; and Smith, as an attorney, knew that — so he told the cops to "forget about him." But, of course, they hadn't, and now they had a far more compelling reason to want to talk to him.

Victor Wolf was literally rousted out of bed and taken into custody within two hours of Smith's death. Of course, he denied any knowledge of either crime. But holes started appearing in his story fairly quickly. He told police he'd used dynamite before, but didn't know how to rig up an electrical detonator... which would be an odd skill for him to be lacking, given that he was a professional electrician.

But then the cops found the extra red-and-yellow wire clipped off the detonator that had killed Smith stuffed in the heater vent of Wolf's brown Mercury. At that point he realized the jig was up — and started talking.

Some of what Victor Wolf confessed to sure sounded like bunk. What he described sounded like it had been ripped straight off from an article in one of the "stag magazines" that were, in those pre-Playboy Magazine years, popular recreational reading for working men.

For one thing, Wolf told the cops that Kermit Smith's wife, Marjorie, had been "using me for a sex slave." Of course, any time a gray-haired 45-year-old man claims an attractive 34-year-old brunette has been literally using him as a sex slave, the chances that he's spilling gospel truth are about equal to the chances that Santa Claus framed him on his last burglary rap.

But maybe, the cops thought, maybe he was dumb enough to *think* it was true. Because a lot of the other things Wolf confessed to turned out to be backed by solid evidence.

Kermit and Marjorie Smith had been married to each other twice. The first marriage had ended in divorce after Marjorie accused Kermit of striking her and being verbally cruel.

It was shortly after that divorce that Victor Wolf had started renting his room from Marjorie Smith. The two of them had started dating, and Wolf said they soon learned they shared a dream in common — a dream of homesteading in the Alaska Territory. This took money, though — more than either of them had.

So, Wolf said, Marjorie had hatched a plan to get that money by having her pretend to reconcile with Kermit and remarry him; after that, Wolf would murder him, and Marjorie would collect on his life insurance policy, and then the two of them would be off to Alaska with the proceeds.

According to a front-page article in the *Oregonian*, Phase One of this plan was implemented forthwith: The Smiths were remarried on Feb. 4, 1955.

"Wolf said that as soon as she was married again to Smith she denied Wolf her favors until he should kill Smith according to the plan," the article continues, with classic mid-century coyness.

Wolf told the cops Marjorie gave him a .38 Special to kill Kermit with, and he lurked in the bushes with it waiting for him on March 10; but at the last minute he "lost his nerve" and tried to murder Kermit with a heavy bottle wielded like a blackjack instead. That, of course, hadn't worked; so he and Marjorie had hatched the dynamite plan. Wolf said he'd wired the bomb up in Kermit Smith's own garage one day while Smith was out, while Marjorie distracted the busybody neighbor by coming over for coffee.

Wolf said he'd bought the dynamite in two different stores near Molalla, and he and Marjorie had traveled to Ridgefield, Washington, to buy the detonators. They'd stopped along the way for a picnic lunch, and he'd cut a bouquet of pussy willows for her.

The detail about the pussy willows made the detectives sit up and take note. They had, of course, searched the house by this time; and there was a vase with pussy willows in it in the house.

Police found more evidence, too. Police, examining the .38 Special that Wolf said Marjorie gave him to kill Kermit with, discovered it was a police service revolver that had belonged to Kermit's father when he was working as a cop. They also found a set of keys to the Smith home in Wolf's pocket. And when he guided detectives to the scene of the picnic he claimed to have had with Marjorie on the way back from Ridgefield, detectives found cut-off pussy willow stems that matched the ones in the vase, and discarded dynamite caps lying around.

Marjorie Smith continued to indignantly deny everything. There was rather a lot of evidence against her — but all of it was circumstantial, and could be explained in other ways. In the end, the jury at her trial didn't find it convincing enough to convict, and she was acquitted.

As for Victor Wolf, he had confessed, and some of the evidence against him — fingerprints, things left in his car, etc. — was far more than circumstantial. In the end, he drew a life sentence, and was probably very happy to get it; in 1954, the gas chamber was a real possibility in a case like this.

Kermit Smith, by the way, was an interesting man, and one we probably would have heard more about had he not been murdered. He was a World War II vet, fought in the Battle of the Bulge, made First Lieutenant, transferred to the Army Air Corps and finished the war as a captain, with a Purple Heart and a Bronze Star on his record. He ran for the Republican nomination for a State Senate seat in 1950.

So, what was the real story? Did Marjorie Smith vamp Victor Wolf to get her husband murdered, like a real-life version of Nicole Kidman's character in the 1996 Gus Van Sant movie "To Die For"? It sure looks that way at first glance. But the jury in Marjorie's case, after digging deeper, didn't agree; and there are aspects of the case that still don't make much sense. It seems likely we'll never know the full story.

Sources and Works Cited:
- "Pussy Willows: The Murder of Kermit Smith," an article by J.B. Fisher published in the Slabtown Chronicle (portlandcrime.blogspot.com) on April 11, 2014;
- Portland Oregonian archives, April 1955

THE AX-MURDERESS.

For many years, the case of Charity Lamb was looked at like a crime-fiction yarn from a pulp magazine like Spicy Detective. It seemed to have it all: illicit sex, a mother-daughter love triangle, conspiracy — and, of course, a brutal ax murder committed by a woman with the most ironically innocuous name imaginable: Charity Lamb.

"Charity Lamb and her seventeen-year-old daughter shared a passion for a drifter named Collins," pop-historian Malcolm Clark Jr. wrote breezily, in his 1981 book *Eden Seekers*. "When [Nathaniel] Lamb, as outraged father and cuckolded husband, strongly protested, Charity cut off his objections with an ax."

The real story, of course, is not only more nuanced, but — well, totally different. In actual fact, the only part of Clark's account that's historically supportable are the names of the involved parties, the words "strongly protested," and the ax. Its original source appears to have been a newspaper article that appeared the week after the killing in the *Oregon Weekly Times* headlined "Revolting Murder," the only sources of which were a gossipy neighbor and a deathbed interview with the bitter and dying Mr. Lamb.

The true story of the Charity Lamb murder will never really be known. But here, as closely as I can pick it out, is the story of how she became Oregon's first-ever convicted murderess:

Nathaniel and Charity Lamb journeyed out to Clackamas County on the Oregon Trail in 1852 and staked a land claim about 10 miles up the Clackamas River from Oregon City. There were few friendly faces in their new home, especially for Charity; they had left all her close friends and relatives behind when they left Missouri.

The Lambs had five children, ranging in age from a newborn baby to a 19-year-old daughter. They also had, according to the later testimony of their older children, a very stormy relationship. The winter after they arrived, Nathaniel knocked Charity down with a punch and kicked her several times for not helping him carry a log. The summer after they arrived on the Oregon Trail, he threw a hammer at her and it clipped her on the forehead, cutting a big gash. He once held her at gunpoint when she was trying to walk out on him.

By the late spring of 1854, things had gotten even worse. In part, that was because of the mysterious Mr. Collins — the "drifter" pop-historian Clark alludes to in his book.

It seems that Mary Ann, the Lambs' 19-year-old daughter, was much smitten with Collins, who had stayed with the family earlier in the season before moving on to California. He apparently quite liked Mary Ann, too, but Nathaniel wouldn't hear of the match and had forbidden her to communicate with him. So Charity helped Mary Ann write him a letter — and then Nathaniel caught Mary Ann with the letter.

This letter brought things to a head. The children testified that Nathaniel was scolding and screaming at Charity all week. And a sinister new element now entered the abuse: death threats.

"He said she had better not run off," 13-year-old Abram Lamb testified in Charity's subsequent trial, "for if she went when he was away he would follow her, and settle her when she didn't know it. I heard her say that morning, before I went out with Pap hunting, that he was going to kill her, and she didn't know what to do."

By "that morning," Abram was referring to the fateful morning which was to end in bloody murder. On that morning, as Nathaniel was setting out on a bear hunt with Abram and a neighbor, Nathaniel stopped at the end of the yard as he walked away from the house. Apparently thinking no one but Charity was watching, he turned, set his rifle down on the top fence rail to steady it, and carefully drew a bead on his wife.

"I was in the house and saw it," 9-year-old Thomas Lamb testified. "When Mary Ann rose up and saw it, he turned away the gun and shot it off at a big tree."

It seems likely that Nathaniel didn't intend to actually kill his wife, even if he wanted to. Theirs was a large family, including a nursing baby who

The Hawthorne Asylum in Portland as it appeared in 1872. The asylum was located just off Hawthorne Boulevard, which was then called Asylum Street, near the intersection with 12th Street. (Image: oregonencyclopedia.org)

would be very hard to keep alive without his mother. But by the time he returned from his hunting trip, having bagged a bear, she appears to have been utterly convinced that he did — and she (and, probably, Mary Ann) had formulated a desperate plan to ensure her survival:

Murder.

And so, when the family was gathered around the table for dinner and

Nathaniel was happily talking about the hunt, Charity excused herself and stepped away from the table, as if to see to something on the fire. Then she returned with an ax — and let him have it.

She hit him twice with it. Even then, Nathaniel was still alive, on the floor, screaming, covered with blood. The ax head had gone two inches into his brain, but the wound hadn't been immediately fatal.

Charity promptly fled the house, closely followed by Mary Ann. She made her way to a neighbor's house a half mile away, and they let her spend the night; meanwhile, Dr. Presley Welch came to do what he could for Nathaniel.

Nathaniel died a week later, probably of an infection. During that time, he gave some fairly damning testimony against Charity to anyone who asked, and the coverage in the local newspapers was very sympathetic. He did not, of course, mention the spousal abuse, and nobody thought to ask.

Naturally, the community was shocked and outraged, and prosecutors threw the book at both Charity and Mary Ann.

But their outrage did not survive Charity's first day in court. Once the Lamb children started testifying about Nathaniel's cruelty, the attitude in the courtroom softened from cold righteousness to a kind of miserable sympathy.

Mary Ann's trial came first, and she was quickly acquitted of all charges. But Charity proved a tough one for judge and jury alike. What she had done did not qualify under any then-existing legal defense. It was sort of self-defense, but not really; Nathaniel been sitting at the dinner table when she did it. It was kind of like insanity, but that didn't fit either; she was clearly not a lunatic. Her defense attorneys made things worse by trying, ridiculously, to claim she'd intended only to stun Nathaniel with the ax rather than kill him.

In the end, the verdict was for second-degree murder, a charge which carried a sentence of life in prison. The prosecution had been hoping for first-degree murder, which would have meant the gallows.

Sobbing and clutching the baby who would shortly be taken away from her, Charity Lamb was remanded to the primitive territorial prison, where she was for many years the only female inmate. Eventually she was sent to the insane asylum on what today is Hawthorne Street in Portland, where occasional visitors found her quietly knitting, apparently contented with her life there. She died in 1879 at the age of about 65.

It **would be many years** before spousal cruelty became a recognized legal defense in murder cases. But the extreme discomfort with which the judge and officers of the court looked on as Charity's case was unfurled before them showed clearly that such a thing was needed, and may have had something to do with some other high-profile murder cases in Oregon — possibly including that of Mary Leonard, who went on after her acquittal to become the first licensed female attorney in both Washington and Oregon.

Sources and Works Cited:
- "The Tragedy of Charity Lamb, Oregon's First Convicted Murderess," *an article by Ronald B. Lansing published in the March 2000 issue of* Oregon Historical Quarterly;
- Eden Seekers: The Settlement of Oregon, *a book by Malcolm Clark Jr. published in 1981 by Houghton Mifflin.*

THE STALKER.

On November 4, 1885, a 27-year-old man was strolling down an Albany street with a pretty 20-year-old brunette woman. He was wearing a disguise — a fake mustache and sideburns, a heavy overcoat. He had introduced himself to the woman as "J. Blankhead." And somehow, he expected her to be fooled by all this.

She was not. She'd recognized him immediately as her ex-fiancé, Charles Campbell. And she'd made arrangements for him to get a lively reception after walking her home.

The reception he got, however, was quite a bit livelier than either one of them had expected it to be. When they reached the front steps of her home, out of the shadows stepped her brother-in-law-to-be, a dark, sinister-looking war veteran named Capt. W. Wirt Saunders. Saunders had a Colt .45 revolver in his hand.

Whether Saunders and Campbell spoke or not is in dispute; the accounts differ. What is not in dispute is that the gun spoke — twice.

The woman, whose name was Mattie Allison, ran to find a doctor and soon found Dr. G.W. Maston.

"For God's sake hurry up," she sobbed. "I never thought it would come to this."

Maston quickly recognized the case as hopeless. He made the wounded man as comfortable as possible and asked him what had happened.

"Mattie and I were coming up the street and Mattie was talking pretty loud," he said. "Just then someone came up and shot me down like a dog without saying a word."

He turned to Mattie. "For God's sake," he begged her, "forgive me before I die."

"I don't know," she told him, "whether I can or not."

The killing galvanized the town of Albany. The popular outrage was enthusiastically boosted by the town's newest startup newspaper, the *Albany Bulletin*, whose editor happened to be looking for a good hobby-horse at the time. The other papers, the *State Rights Democrat* and the *Albany Herald Disseminator*, covered the story fairly evenhandedly, at least at first; but the *Bulletin* went straight to the mattresses.

"A cold-blooded murder was perpetrated in this city a few months ago," the editor wrote. "A young man was shot down without any warning, and leaning on his arm at the time was a woman named Mattie Allison. She put up the whole job, arranged the meeting, and after Charley was shot told people she was sorry she did not do it herself."

District Attorney (and future Oregon governor) George Chamberlain drew up an indictment against both Allison and Saunders. Saunders, who didn't deny the shooting, was promptly indicted on a charge of first-degree murder. But against Mattie Allison, the grand jury did not find enough evidence of her having "put up the whole job," and declined to indict.

Chamberlain tried again. Again, the bill was declined. It looked like Mattie would go free. On his editorial page, the *Bulletin's* editor howled like a blood-mad panther, calling the decisions "an attempt to whitewash the character of a woman whose hands are red with the blood of the innocent." He even called (rhetorically, one assumes) for the arrest and prosecution of the editors of the competing newspapers, whose editorials he deemed insufficiently enthusiastic in asserting Allison's guilt.

"[The *Bulletin*] tore into Mattie Allison like a pit bull defending a butcher bone," historian Diane Goeres-Gardner writes in her book, *Necktie Parties*.

The result was that, when a new grand jury was impaneled later that year and Chamberlain tried for a third time to get charges to stick to her, they finally did.

By that time the waters in Albany had been so thoroughly poisoned by the *Bulletin's* sustained campaign that the trial had to be moved to Salem. This meant that Chamberlain was off the hook for prosecuting the case ... a fact that, given the facts that came out at the trial, may have saved his political career.

Mattie Allison's trial got started in October 1886, just under a year after the killing. And the picture that emerged, as witness after witness took the stand, was at considerable odds with the one the *Albany Bulletin* had painted.

The newspaper reports of this trial were how most citizens of Albany learned just what it was that Charles Campbell had begged Mattie Allison to forgive him for, as he lay dying; and why she so coldly declined. He had been stalking her for three years, starting when she broke off their engagement, back when she was a girl of 17. Knowing her family had no male patriarch to stand up for her, as was then the custom in such matters, he had been very bold, and particularly cruel, in how he went about it.

Witness after witness recounted episodes when Campbell had been caught peering in the windows, the times he'd boasted that he was regularly sleeping with her, the times he got drunk and threatened to kill her. He'd pulled a gun on her at her mother's hat shop; he'd followed her to Eugene when she went to visit her aunt; he'd pulled a pistol on her mother in a jealous rage when Mrs. Allison refused to support his suit for her daughter's hand; and he'd even once drunkenly tried to break into her home while they were inside.

The Linn County courthouse as it appeared about 20 years after Wirt Saunders' first trial was held in it. He was found guilty and sentenced to hang, but the trial was overturned on appeal. (Image: Postcard)

Probably the most damning bit of evidence came from a friend who had spoken to Campbell the night he borrowed the overcoat and fake

The Marion County Courthouse as it appeared about 20 years after the trials of Mattie Allison and Wirt Saunders were held in it. (Image: Postcard)

mustache, who, according to the *Morning Oregonian's* report, said Campbell "had often boasted that he had 'slept with her' and would ruin her that night if it cost him his neck."

Wirt Saunders — who by this time had, a month or two earlier, been convicted in an Albany courtroom and sentenced to hang — testified that she had approached him, her future brother-in-law, several weeks before, to ask if he would protect her from Campbell. She'd told him things were OK just then, but that she expected him to start more trouble soon, and she was afraid he would follow through on his threats to kill or rape her.

Then a letter had arrived from "J. Blankhead," a letter that appears to have been intended as a coyly worded proposition: "I am a stranger in your town and desire to see you and form your acquaintance. I wish you to do me a favor. It will be but a slight task for you to perform, and will afford me great pleasure."

Mattie, not being in the business of doing "favors" for strangers, knew there was only one man who would send her a letter like that. So she'd sent for Saunders — who had promised he would have a little talk with Campbell and, if he would not agree to leave her alone, thrash him for her.

And that's what Mattie Allison had expected him to do that night: give the would-be Lothario the beating of his life and tell him to stay away. But Saunders had brought his Colt with him . . . .

T he verdict was reached very quickly. After about 20 minutes, a "not guilty" verdict was announced, and the entire courtroom burst into applause and cheers.

The *Salem Statesman* lit into the Albany press with surprising savagery, accusing it of having essentially ginned up a lynch mob. Indeed, there had been one particular article in the *Bulletin* that had looked like a coyly worded invitation to form one — an apparently made-up article about Mattie Allison begging the sheriff for protection from angry citizens whom she was afraid might lynch her, and the sheriff telling her she had made her bed and now must lie in it.

Of course, by the end of the trial the Albany residents who would have formed that lynch mob knew the rest of the story, and chances are good that they didn't appreciate the heavy spinning they'd been subjected to. Whether for that reason or some other, the *Albany Bulletin* did not last long after that; although the *State Rights Democrat* and *Herald Disseminator* are still around, having merged into today's *Albany Democrat-Herald*.

As for Saunders, his murder trial, which had been held in the poisoned atmosphere of the Linn County Courthouse in Albany, was overturned on appeal. Retried in Salem, he was convicted of second-degree murder and sentenced to life in prison. Seven years later, Governor Sylvester Pennoyer commuted his sentence. He and Mattie's sister Minnie, who had faithfully waited for him, married after his release and moved to Spokane.

Sources and Works Cited:
- Murder, Morality and Madness: Women Criminals in Early Oregon, *a book by Diane L. Goeres-Gardner published in 2009 by Caxton Press;*
- *Archives of* Albany State Rights Democrat, *July and October 1886, and* Eugene City Guard, *November 1885.*

THE HOMESTEAD MURDERS.

One February day in 1900, a thirty-something man got off the train in Hood River and hired a buggy at the local livery stable. He wanted to be driven to the homestead ranch of a man named Norman Williams. And he wanted to bring along a shovel.

Bert Stranahan, the owner of the livery stable, was happy to oblige. Business was, after all, business. The shovel was a strange request, but he couldn't see any reason to say no.

When they got to the place, it had clearly been abandoned for some time. The visiting man, whose name was George Nesbitt, poked around the buildings with the shovel and then started digging inside a chicken coop in the yard. He dug all day — four feet, five feet, six feet down.

He was looking for his mother and his sister.

Nesbitt's sister's name was Alma, and she had known Williams back in Iowa before he came out to Oregon. They'd probably talked of marriage, because after Williams moved to the Hood River Valley to file his homestead claim, they wrote letters back and forth, and he urged her to come out and file a homestead claim on the adjacent parcel. She finally did, in 1899.

Then her mother, 68-year-old Louisa Nesbitt, came out too, and for a while the three of them wrote happy open-air homesteader letters back to

Iowa, relating how they were all working together to build a house and barn and various other improvements that would make their land productive and homey.

Then, all at once, the letters stopped.

The family wrote to Williams, and he replied that the women had left — that Alma had thrown him over for a younger man. Beyond that, he was very uncommunicative. The family posted notices, contacted authorities, offered rewards. Nothing.

Finally, in desperation, George bought a railroad ticket and came to Hood River.

At the farm, something had seemed to guide him to that half-built henhouse, and kept him going digging into its floor. And at twilight, he finally found something at the bottom of the hole he'd dug: a piece of burlap sacking stained with what looked like blood, and several long silver hairs.

At the courthouse in The Dalles, Nesbitt reported his find and his suspicions. He swore out a warrant for Williams' arrest, and Wasco County Deputy District Attorney Fred Wilson was assigned to the case. Williams, when tracked down in Washington state, was affable and cooperative and apparently unconcerned. In jail, he made no attempt to raise bail. "It'll come out all right," he said with an easy smile.

Unlike all the previous correspondence, Alma's last letter home had been mailed from a boardinghouse in Portland, not from the homestead. So Wilson and Nesbitt went there and talked to the landlord. He learned that the women had stayed there from Feb. 8 to March 8, 1904; March 8 was the postmark date on the letter.

March 8 was also the day a Hood River livery stable rented a buggy and team to Williams and two women, one young and pretty, the other middle-aged and silver-haired. Assuming this was Alma and her mother, that would have been the last time anybody other than Williams ever saw either of them; but the livery stable owner did see Williams again, returning the buggy and team, alone.

Wilson also learned of a possible motive: Williams' house and barn had been accidentally built on Alma's neighboring claim. That would have been a serious problem for Williams if the two of them had ever quarrelled or split up. She would be able to kick him right off her land — out of his house.

Unless, of course, they were married — in which case, under the laws at that time, he'd gain title to all her property . . . .

Acting on a hunch, Wilson crossed the Columbia and checked the public records. At the time, Washington's marriage laws were looser than Oregon's, and many eloping couples ran to Vancouver to get married. Sure

This artist's sketch from the courtroom was published in Portland's Morning Oregonian on May 26, 1904. It shows defense attorney Henry McGinn, Alma Nesbitt's brother George, and, in the inset frame, murderer Norman Williams. (Image: Morning Oregonian)

enough, Wilson found that Norman Williams and Alma Nesbitt had tied the knot before a justice of the peace there — six months before Alma had disappeared.

This was particularly interesting because a record search in Oregon showed he was still married to a woman in Dufur, whom he'd wed in 1898, the year before Alma came out. So the marriage to Alma was bigamous, and therefore void.

There were some other issues, too — skeletons in Williams' closet, as it were. As it turned out, he had been married not just twice, but six times; two of those wives had died of poisoning, and he'd served three years in the Nebraska State Pen for assaulting and nearly killing a sister-in-law.

But Wilson found the real smoking gun at the land claim office. There, he learned that Williams was under indictment for forgery; after Alma's disappearance, he'd brought in a document transferring title to Alma's homestead claim to him, and the clerk had been suspicious so he'd sent back to Washington for a copy of the initial homestead claim forms. The signatures did not match.

To the prosecutors, it all added up: Williams, having discovered the mistake in placement of his house and barn, had talked Alma into marrying him and started making plans to combine the parcels. But before that could happen, Alma learned he'd been two-timing her, and that her marriage was bigamous and void. So she and her mother picked up and left for Portland. Now faced with the prospect of losing not only just her half of their double claim, but his house and barn as well, he found out where they were, went out and sweet-talked them into coming back to the ranch ... then killed them both and cremated the bodies. Having overlooked one piece of bloody burlap, he buried it and built a chicken coop over the spot.

The evidence was all fairly damning, but very circumstantial ... until an expert witness took the stand. This witness was Dr. L. Victoria Hampton, a chemist from Portland, one of the very first female scientists in Oregon and in the U.S.

Hampton testified that based on her forensic analysis, the blood on the burlap was human, and so were the hairs; and that the hairs had been ripped out of the scalp before death.

And on that note, the prosecution rested. But they'd presented enough. Norman Williams was hanged for the murder of his sixth wife and mother-in-law on July 21, 1905, in the last public hanging in Oregon history. He was 48 years old.

Sources and Works Cited:
- Murder Out Yonder, *a book by Stewart Holbrook published in 1941 by Macmillan;*
- "State of Oregon v. Norman Williams," *an article by Diane L. Goeres-Gardner published on March 17, 2018, in* The Oregon Encyclopedia *(oregonencyclopedia.org);*
- Portland Morning Oregonian, *May 1904.*

THE FEMME FATALE.

One of the most enduring and appealing tropes in popular fiction is the "Femme Fatale," like Brigid O'Shaughnessy in Dashiell Hammett's *The Maltese Falcon*. Assertive, sexy, and utterly free from the soft bondage of conscience, she ruthlessly plays the men around her like musical instruments, getting whatever she wants and leaving (or killing) them without a qualm when they're no longer useful.

Usually, in the old hard-boiled pulp stories and noir films, she comes to a bad end — as O'Shaughnessy does, more or less. But occasionally she doesn't, and when the Femme Fatale is done right, it's impossible not to root for her. She's taking on the 1940s "man's world" like a Samurai taking on an enemy army. The odds are always against her; and when she beats those odds, and finishes the story sipping daiquiris on the beach in Togo rather than breaking rocks in the yard at Sing Sing, it's a satisfying — albeit subtly unsettling — outcome.

The Femme Fatale, like most really satisfying tropes in fiction, is based on real life. And arguably, the closest Oregon has ever come to a real-life femme fatale worthy of Dashiell Hammett's pen was in early 1880s Portland, in what today is known as the Tenderloin — in the person of a gorgeous, hard-eyed 28-year-old brunette who called herself Carrie Bradley.

Carrie Bradley was a relative newcomer to Portland in 1881. She'd arrived in the late 1870s, probably from back east, when she was in her early 20s. By 1881 she was running a small bordello in the one-block red-light district that was regularly referred to in the Portland Morning Oregonian as "the Court of Death" — the block bounded by Third and Fourth streets on one side and Taylor and Yamhill on the other.

That block had developed as the preferred location for high-end prostitutes in 1880s Portland. At the time, the majority of Portland's hookers worked out of the old North End, the neighborhood along the waterfront north of Stark Street, known as Old Town today. In the North End, basically, anything went: public drunkenness, open gambling, prostitution, opium smoking, the shanghaiing of sailors, etc. "Respectable" Portlanders tolerated virtually any level of vice so long as it stayed in the North End, where they never had to go and see it and could continue to pretend it did not exist.

Outside the North End, prostitution was tolerated if it was discreet. For instance, Lida Fanshaw, proprietress of the super-fancy whorehouse next door to the prestigious Arlington Club ("the *ne plus ultra* of Portland parlour houses," as Stewart Holbrook memorably put it), had little to fear from Portland's vice crusaders. Neither did Della Burris, whose parlour-house on Park Street was almost as fancy. In part that was due to their client lists — Fanshaw's palace of sin was next door to the Arlington Club for a reason. But the main reason was, Fanshaw and Burris made it very easy for Portland's church-going set to pretend they weren't bordello madams. They did a brisk business, but they were very discreet about it.

This photo of Carrie Bradley appeared in the Morning Oregonian during her trial. (Image: Oregonian)

"Carrie Bradley," historian J.D. Chandler writes with fine understatement in his book, *Murder & Mayhem in Portland, Oregon*, "was not discreet."

But then, perhaps she didn't think she had to be. She was good friends with Portland Chief of Police James Lappeus.

The rest of the "Court of Death" wasn't very discreet either. It was composed of a few bigger whorehouses like Carrie Bradley's, plus a few dozen "cribs" — little cottages just big enough for a bed, a washbasin, and a window seat in which a girl could display herself to good advantage when a potential customer cruised by. These girls would be in their windows, displaying their *decolletages* and occasionally cooing a verbal invitation to an especially oofy-looking passer-by, most of the time; and they were right in the middle of downtown, a block or two from all of Portland's biggest churches, so the "respectables" of the city couldn't pretend *they* didn't exist.

Former Portland police chief James Lappeus as he appeared in around 1890. (Image: Leland John)

Most of the girls had enough sense not to be on display on Sunday mornings, of course; but still, everyone knew what the Court of Death was, whether any girls were visible or not. And pressure was growing to shut them all down.

Carrie Bradley was not helping to alleviate that pressure. Her brothel was a fairly dangerous business to patronize. Drugs and alcohol flowed freely in the downstairs parlour, where piano man "Professor" Otto Jordan tickled the ivories "and carefully minded his own business," as historian Chandler puts it. Customers were plied with good brandy, sometimes spiked with laudanum; and for the really daring, there was chloroform that could be dabbed upon one's upper lip. Customers would enjoy an evening of stimulating conversation and drug use in the parlour, then stroll upstairs with their "dates" for the night.

And, once in a while, they would wake up the next morning in a different part of town, with a splitting headache and empty pockets. Carrie Bradley and her four girls were not above slipping a Mickey Finn to a wealthy customer and lifting his wad while he was sleeping it off.

Which seems to have been exactly what happened to James Nelson Brown, a player in his early 50s who had just moved to town from Freeport, Wash., with money in his poke.

Brown had been working up in southwest Washington Territory as a timber cruiser; but in 1881 he decided to retire, sold some land that he had homesteaded, and headed for Portland to live high on the hog on the $4,000 proceeds (the equivalent of about $105,000 in 2019 currency). Checking into the National Hotel on Front Street at the foot of Yamhill, he set about "making Rome howl," as his contemporaries might have put it — drinking and gambling and, yes, patronizing prostitutes.

Including, of course, one of Carrie Bradley's girls, a 21-year-old bombshell who called herself Dolly Adams. (The previous year, Dolly had called herself "Belle Boyd"; no respectable hooker would ever dream of using her real name with customers. A girl's real name was always a closely guarded secret, and usually the only way the general public could learn it was from newspaper reports if someone murdered her.)

Well, James Brown made the mistake of having $6 in his pocket when Dolly took him upstairs for the night; and when he woke up the next morning, it was gone. This enraged Brown, and he charged off to the authorities to see what could be done about it.

He was in luck. Multnomah County District Attorney J.M. Caples, who had been under pressure for some time to "clean up" the "Court of Death," had been assembling evidence against Carrie Bradley for months. Brown's allegation, he thought, would give him enough to prosecute her successfully; then, after shutting down Carrie's whorehouse, he'd be able to roll up all the cribs with ease — the crib girls were solo practitioners, and had much less clout than Carrie did.

Caples and Brown soon had a deal, and an arrest warrant went out with "Dolly Adams" written on it — and Caples started preparing his case against Carrie and her whorehouse. Brown voluntarily anted up a $25 bond to reassure Caples that he wouldn't run off before trial; and then he waited for the gears of justice to turn, trying — at Caples' insistent

DEADLY BELOVED.

This cartoon was published in The West Shore in 1889 as a criticism of the quality of policing in Portland. The woman in the window on the extreme right is a prostitute negotiating with a prospective customer. It is possible, if not likely, that this cartoon was drawn with the Carrie Bradley case in mind. (Image: The West Shore)

recommendation — to stay as far away from Carrie Bradley's den of iniquity as possible.

Meanwhile, Caples told some of his law-enforcement partners what was afoot, and those partners probably included Chief Lappeus. Chief Lappeus, of course, promptly slipped the word to his friend Carrie that the heat was on. Carrie, after greasing the chief's palm with a $500 bill in exchange for his promise to let her slip out of town if things got ugly, started making some plans of her own ... and the plans she was making were the same ones Brigid O'Shaughnessy would have made, under similar circumstances.

The difference was, Brigid would have executed those plans with her usual supreme competence. Carrie and her friends were destined to bungle things very badly indeed.

On the morning of Nov. 25, 1881, two men were walking to work along the North End waterfront when they saw something incongruous in the river, near a dock at the foot of Everett Street.

It was a pair of bare legs, sticking straight up out of the river, tied together with a piece of wire.

The two of them hurried on to work and reported what they'd seen to their supervisor, who promptly called the cops, and the coroner had to get a rowboat and paddle out to retrieve what was obviously going to be a very dead corpse from out of the drink.

The body turned out to be that of a man in his early 50s, with a trim gray mustache and crescent-shaped scars over each of his eyes. He was wearing nothing but a shirt and collar, and had a hand towel loosely knotted around his neck. And it couldn't have been more obvious that he'd been dumped there — in addition to the wire around his feet, another wire had been used to tie a big rock around his neck to weight his body down.

The coroner soon discovered that the wires binding the feet had been attached to a rock as well, but it had slipped free, leaving the body free to float upright at the top of its tether after decomposition had filled its abdominal cavity with gas. So it had wound up with its feet and legs pointed straight up, sticking out of the river for all to see, like a harbour buoy.

They also found that the man's face had been beaten severely with something heavy and blunt.

Although this sure looked like a murder victim, after the body went unidentified for several days the coroner had it buried — remember, there was no refrigeration technology in 1881, and the body had already smelled pretty ripe upon arrival.

But by the time it was buried, one or two people had come to view the body who knew exactly who it was.

One of those was Portland Chief of Police James Lappeus. If he didn't recognize the vic, he certainly would have recognized his name; this was the body of James Nelson Brown, county prosecutor Caples's star witness as he prepared to prosecute Carrie Bradley.

Which, it looked like, he would not now be doing, seeing as how his main witness, whom he was counting on to sing like a canary in court, was here stinking up the morgue instead.

The other in-the-know visitor was Dolly Adams, and she definitely knew who the man was ... nor was this the first time she'd seen him with his pants off.

Dolly not only recognized Brown, she also recognized the towel that was knotted around his neck. She immediately hurried back to the brothel and told Carrie Bradley — who responded by rounding up all the towels in the house and throwing them into the parlour stove.

Well, Chief Lappeus might have been in on the swindle, but now that there was an obvious murder victim slabbed out in the morgue, there was a limit to how helpful he'd be able to be. The other city cops soon were working the case. Constable Sam Simmons started wandering around asking hotel clerks if they'd had a guest with scars on his forehead, and pretty soon he stopped in at the National Hotel on Yamhill, and then the cat was out of the bag.

The story that Simmons uncovered was remarkably tawdry.

It seemed Carrie Bradley, eager to get her hands on Brown to shut him up, had sent her boyfriend, Pete Sullivan (who was also her "recruiter" of new hookers for her staff), out on the town with instructions to find James Brown and do whatever it took to get him back into Carrie's place. Pete had gone out, accompanied by his young sidekick Asa "Ace" Nisonger (who was dating one of Carrie's girls), and soon found his mark drinking and gambling at one of the other joints downtown — the Grotto Saloon on Morrison Street.

A casual suggestion that they all head over to Carrie Bradley's place for a good time went over with a dull thud. No way, Brown said, was he going back to *that* place. So Pete surreptitiously sent Ace back to the "Court of Death" to fetch Carrie.

Carrie soon arrived, accompanied, for some reason (maybe to identify him?) by Dolly Adams.

Brown, seeing Dolly, said, "That's the girl I had arrested."

Carrie now turned on the charm. She apologized profusely to Brown for all the trouble her girls had caused him, chatted him up, and bought him a drink or two. Soon the four of them were carousing like old friends.

They got a bit loud about it, though, and when the saloon owner asked them to keep it down, Carrie suggested that they go back to her house, where they could sing and dance all they wanted. Brown said he'd rather not go back there, whereupon Carrie Bradley set her femme-fatale-sexiness phaser on "kill" and let him have it: "But tonight, you go with me," she purred, batting her eyes at him.

The upshot was, ten minutes later, Brown walked into Carrie Bradley's house for a second ... and final ... time.

Soon Brown was carousing in the whorehouse parlour, guzzling brandy laced with opium. Professor Otto was hammering away on the piano, as usual, and the other girls were around as well; so if Carrie wanted to put the ice on Brown that night she'd have to be subtle about it. She pulled Ace Nisonger aside and, claiming an attack of rheumatism (surely an odd affliction for a 28-year-old woman), asked him if there was any chloroform around; Ace told her they were fresh out. She handed him a dollar and sent him down to a late-night drugstore to buy two fifty-cent bottles of the stuff.

It took a lot of opiated brandy to do it, but eventually James Nelson Brown passed out. Carrie and Dolly carried him upstairs to bed with a little help from Pete Sullivan, and tucked him in. Then Dolly and Pete left the room ... but Carrie stayed behind. She got out a hand towel and one of the two bottles of chloroform that Ace had brought back for her, soaked the towel in it, and tied it securely around Brown's face.

Then she left him to die in her bed.

Meanwhile, Pete Sullivan and Ace Nisonger had left the house and were off gambling and drinking elsewhere. They hadn't been ready to call it a night when Brown passed out, and apparently they weren't aware of what Carrie had in mind for him; so they'd taken the party down the road for a few hours to finish the night in style. Around 3 a.m. they staggered home, headed off to bed with their respective ladyfriends, and were rudely awakened at around 9 a.m. after Dolly knocked on Carrie's door and said, "He's dead."

Sullivan rushed to Brown's room and, sure enough, there Brown was, dead in bed with a chloroform rag knotted around his face.

Then the door burst open and Carrie Bradly stormed in, a pair of brass knuckles wrapped around her right fist. Straight to the corpse she went, and started savagely pounding its face with the knucks.

Then she rounded on Pete and Ace. "You two are in this as deep as me," she told them. "You have to help me get rid of him."

So Pete went down to the cellar with the fireplace-ashes shovel to try to dig a grave. He got just a few inches into the ground before giving up. Carrie sent Dolly to fetch her ex-boyfriend, Charley Hamilton — they'd split up fairly acrimoniously some time before, and she'd tried to get him arrested for assault and for trying to light her house on fire — but apparently they'd subsequently patched things up.

Hamilton took over corpse-disposal duties. He waited for dark and then, calling in a hack driver he knew, he propped up the dead guy in the back and they took him down to the river, tied him neck and feet to a couple big rocks, and heaved him off the dock and into the drink.

But, of course, he didn't stay there for long ....

The ensuing murder trial held Portland spellbound. Carrie tried to pin the job on Dolly, but nobody believed her.

Dolly turned state's evidence and got off with a few weeks in jail. Carrie was sent up the river for a 12-year stretch on a manslaughter conviction, which she was probably very lucky to get; a first-degree murder rap could have sent her to the gallows.

You might think this would have been the break District Attorney Caples wanted, to shut down the "Court of Death." But it must not have worked out the way he thought it would. The Court of Death was still there in 1885, when one of the "crib girls" there, a 33-year-old French beauty calling herself Emma Merlotin, got brutally murdered with an ax. (See "The Vice Crusade," on page 315.)

In true femme-fatale fashion, Carrie Bradley came to a bad end eventually. Released from prison after five years, she moved with Pete Sullivan to Mt. Shasta, Calif., and set up a new brothel there. They lasted about five years; but eventually Pete was arrested and sent back to prison for enticing girls into prostitution, and when that happened Carrie, who was now pushing 40, shot herself.

Sources and Works Cited:
- Murder & Mayhem in Portland Oregon, *a book by J.D. Chandler published in 2013 by The History Press;*
- Portland Morning Oregonian *archives, February through June 1882.*

THE FAKE COMA.

Charles Fiester really, really didn't want to die.

Fair enough; most of us don't. His wife, Nancy, hadn't wanted to die either; but she'd been trying to leave their 30-year marriage and had taken up with another man, a Mr. Mudd. And, well, one thing had led to another and the next thing anyone knew Fiester was dragging her by the hair to a mud puddle and drowning her in it, while their three youngest children looked on in horror.

As a result, on Sept. 30, 1895, he found himself facing a jury in a Josephine County court. And those jurors weren't turning out to be particularly favorably disposed toward him.

His attorney had pleaded not guilty by reason of insanity. The problem for Fiester was, this was a few years before the great deluge of "temporary insanity" pleas in "unwritten law" murders, and insanity pleas were still very hard to pull off. For a man who's never shown much history of insanity, it was a near-impossibility.

Fiester did have a history of something else, though, something kind of like insanity — but it was something that wasn't helping at all with his case: an anger problem.

He and Nancy had been married 30 years before, when he was around 22 and she a middle-school-age waif of 12 or 13. Since that time, she'd borne him 10 children, who now ranged in age from 6 to 28. Coworkers and acquaintances knew Fiester as a soft-spoken, stoop-shouldered man with a reputation for being a reliable, hard worker, a former officer with the Salem Police Department in the early years before he moved with his family to Kerby and Merlin.

But close neighbors knew better. And the prosecution had talked to those neighbors, and now they were appearing in court testifying to all the times Nancy had turned up at their houses with bruises and injuries and other evidence of his violent temper.

Then, too, the Fiester family was still a little notorious after the events of the previous year, when a Lebanon man had been shot in a fight over Fiester's 21-year-old daughter Jessie "Jet" Black. Jet and her husband, Sam Black, were separated, and apparently Jet Black was seeing a little too much of a man named Jesse Rice for Sam's taste. On the evening of Oct. 3, 1893, Sam unexpectedly showed up at his estranged wife's residence and, finding Jesse Rice there, shot him dead.

Two love triangles turned deadly, in the same family, within the space of a year. Sheer coincidence, surely; but it wasn't a good look.

Finally, the lawyers wrapped up their closing statements, and the jury took just 40 minutes coming to a verdict: Guilty of first-degree murder.

Fiester wasn't too worried at first. He seemed pretty sure that he would be able to get the Supreme Court to overturn the conviction or commute it into a prison sentence.

Sure enough, a few days before his scheduled execution date, the Supreme Court issued a stay of execution to buy it a little time to review his claim of insanity. And it was just after this that Fiester abruptly went into a catatonic state. He lay there on his bunk, neither speaking nor responding to anyone around him, staring straight at the ceiling, all day. And all the next day. And the next.

The psychologist sent in by the court proclaimed him insane. That being the case, of course, he could hardly be executed.

But for some reason — maybe somebody smelled a rat? — the court never got around to declaring him not guilty on that basis. He just stayed there, in the Josephine County jail. Deputies had to feed him, presumably some sort of liquid diet. Deputies also had to help him with other personal-care matters. It's not clear how they did this, since they didn't share the details with the newspapers; but most likely it involved some form of diaper that had to be changed several times a day, as with a baby.

A year slipped by, and most of another one. The sheriff tried at least once to get rid of the huge, bearded baby in his jailhouse; but his requests to get Fiester transferred to the Oregon State Hospital (then called the Oregon Insane Asylum) went nowhere. Most likely Fiester's lawyer's well-meaning attempts to keep his client out of court were the source of the trouble.

In any case, 515 days went by with Fiester apparently catatonic. Then, on May 10, 1897, two of Fiester's sons, 26-year-old William and 18-year-old John, were caught burgling a smokehouse to steal bacon, and lodged in the jail with their "catatonic" father. William was set up in the room with his father, and several other jail occupants heard them whispering together, late in the night.

An engraving of convicted murderer Charles Fiester, published in the Portland Morning Oregonian on June 11, 1898, the day after his hanging. (Image: UO Libraries)

The next morning, the deputy in charge of feeding Fiester walked in with a plate of food and set it down on the table next to him.

"You can eat that, or let it alone," he told Fiester. "I will never feed you again."

He walked out. And upon his return an hour or so later, the plate was empty.

"Old man, you have played your game well," the deputy told Fiester.

"Yes," said Fiester — the first words he'd spoken out loud in nearly two years — "but it has been hard."

Fiester's insanity having been exposed as a ruse, his case was reactivated, and a few months later, on April 21, 1898, he was once again sentenced to hang, the event scheduled to take place on June 10.

On the appointed morning, Sheriff Joseph G. Hiatt found Fiester once again lying on his cot as if dead. He could not be roused; his eyes rolled back in his head, and he seemed to be having trouble breathing. His gasping and rattling sounded so believable that the sheriff postponed the hanging, hoping that he'd die of his own accord before too long and no one would have to burden his conscience with the serving of a death sentence upon him.

But by 1 p.m., nothing had changed, so the sheriff had the still-unresponsive Fiester strapped to a board and hauled to the gallows, where — still unresponsive, and apparently unconscious — he was hanged without incident.

It may have been the only time in Oregon history that an unconscious man was hanged. But, of course, that only goes if he really was unconscious. After his 515-day charade, the sheriff didn't believe he really was, and apparently neither did anyone else.

Sources and Works Cited:
- Necktie Parties: Legal Executions in Oregon 1851-1905, *a book by Diane L. Goeres-Gardner published in 2005 by Caxton Press;*
- Salem Capital Journal *archives, May 1895;*
- Portland Morning Oregonian *archives, June 1898.*

THE TRIANGLE MAN

Of all the variations on the theme of "love gone bad" known to gossips, storytellers and prosecuting attorneys since the dawn of time, the "love triangle turned deadly" pattern has got to be given first place.

And it would be hard to find an example of this kind of story that would top the one that reached its climax with a shotgun blast on a dark Ashland street, a few days before Thanksgiving of 1884.

The story started when a 46-year-old carpenter named Lewis O'Neil rolled into town, three months before the murder. O'Neil had abandoned a wife and six children down in California a couple years earlier and drifted north with the railroad. When he'd arrived in Ashland, he seems to have decided to stay a while and put down some roots — after meeting Mandy McDaniel.

Sarah Amanda "Mandy" McDaniel, 35, was the wife of a prosperous local grocery-store owner, 48-year-old Lewis McDaniel. The McDaniels had married three years before, when she was a pretty youngish widow with a seven-year-old son and he a lonely frontier bachelor. The marriage had soured fairly quickly; when O'Neil rolled into town, the McDaniels were living separately, and Amanda was apparently looking for a new romance. She and O'Neil began a secret affair soon after he arrived in town.

But, of course, "secret" affairs usually don't stay secret for long in a small town like 1880s Ashland.

Two weeks after he arrived, O'Neil took a short vacation from work to go and visit his much-older brother, 72-year-old George, at his mining claim several dozen miles from town. When he returned, he was carrying a shotgun which George had given him to try to sell.

Back in Ashland, O'Neil moved into a room at the Pioneer Hotel and briefly resumed his affair with Amanda McDaniel. Then Amanda approached her husband, reconciled with him, and moved back into their home.

And a few days after that, at 7:30 p.m. on the cold, rainy night of Nov. 20, 1884, someone stepped up behind Lewis McDaniel and shotgunned him in the back of the head. He fell forward, dead, his hands still in his pockets.

The town marshal's night watchman, Charles Miller, was soon on the scene, and, recognizing the corpse, went directly to the McDaniels house to let Amanda know that someone had murdered her husband. With another citizen, he stood on the doorstep and knocked for several minutes as the rain poured down on them; then the two of them retreated to a neighbor's house to figure out what to do next. A few minutes later they decided to wait inside for Amanda to return, and crossed over to the McDaniels house again and — after a little more fruitless pounding on the front door — went inside and lit a candle and settled in to wait.

Then Amanda herself opened the back bedroom door, stepped out, and seemed surprised to see her living room full of people.

Rumors of extracurricular romantic activities spread very rapidly in a small town and are pretty much impossible to keep bottled up. By the time of the murder, everyone — including Lewis McDaniel — knew of O'Neil's affair with Amanda. So when someone murdered her husband, O'Neil was instantly the prime suspect. Almost immediately, the 1880s equivalent of an A.P.B. was out. Town marshal S.D. Taylor found O'Neil around 10 p.m., drinking in a saloon, and arrested him on suspicion.

There wasn't any hard evidence against O'Neil; but there was a lot of the circumstantial kind. For one thing, the shotgun he'd brought back from his brother's mining camp — a distinctive weapon with an alligator carved into the stock — was nowhere to be found. He first claimed he had no shotgun; and then, apparently realizing too many people had seen him bringing it back, he claimed he'd sold it to some guy on the road home. It

The public hanging of Lewis O'Neil, on March 12, 1886, in Jacksonville. O'Neil is the man standing in the middle on the platform. (Image: Southern Oregon Historical Society)

was later found, chopped up into bits, scattered over a vacant lot. The lot had been searched the day after the murder, so someone besides O'Neil had obviously done this. The obvious suspicion was that Amanda had done it, to help him cover his tracks.

It was enough. O'Neil was convicted on March 12, 1885, and sentenced to swing.

A few weeks later, another inmate claimed O'Neil had confessed to him that he'd done the deed under the precise direction of Amanda — who wanted her husband out of the way so that she could formalize her affair with O'Neil and so that she could inherit his grocery store.

On the strength of this conversation, Amanda McDaniel was arrested. But jailhouse confessions aren't very solid evidence, and the jury just wasn't convinced. She was acquitted.

As the hanging day loomed ever closer, a series of remarkable letters started going out from the Jackson County Jail, where O'Neil was being held.

The first and most egregious one went to Amanda McDaniel. It was a proposal, essentially, that she take the rap for him. He prefaced it by assuring her that if her court case had gone badly, he would have "come to your relief and clear(ed) you by taking the whole responsibility on myself, though I am innocent, but ... if you were found guilty you should never hang or go to the penitentiary for I would save you. Now you have been tried and come clear, and it is in your power to save my life."

Since she had been cleared of all charges in her trial, he continued, she could now confess to the murder with total impunity — clearing him. He would then sue the state for heavy damages and split the proceeds with her.

"I hope you will not delay," he wrote, "as I know you can save my life and the disgrace will be no worse on you than it is now."

Amanda did not reply.

Other letters went out as well, to other friends and relatives, with various other schemes for someone else to take the rap for him. The last one went to his brother George, the one who gave him the shotgun; and it was an open request for his brother to "confess" to the killing and take his place on the gallows.

"The most trying feature," the condemned man wrote, "is leaving my six children to the mercy of a world without protection and the disgrace of their father being hanged .... As for you, you have lived to be a very old man, and in the natural course of events you can expect to live but a very few years more and are liable to drop off at any time. If you had one hour to live it would be a hard request to ask you to come and state that you had done the killing and that I had not had any hand, act or part in it or any knowledge of it. That would clear me, and spare me to my children, and only on their account could I ever think of making such a request of you."

Of course, O'Neil hadn't thought so much of the children when he'd abandoned them and their mother four years earlier; but an imminent death sentence does tend to remind one of family and friends. Ironically, the letter never reached the "very old man"; George had, shortly before, died of typhoid fever.

And so, on March 12, 1886, still maintaining his innocence, Lewis O'Neil was hanged.

As for Amanda, after liquidating her late husband's estate and paying off his taxes and debts, she cleared $2,000 (worth about $55,000 in today's dollars). She took this and left Ashland the night before the hanging, settling in Talent, where she opened a café.

And so the story ends. Except, there is just one question still hanging out there in the air, a question that never was fully answered:

DEADLY BELOVED.

Where exactly was Amanda McDaniel, a few minutes after her husband had been murdered, when the town watchmen were pounding on her door?

Sources and Works Cited:
- Necktie Parties: Legal Executions in Oregon 1851-1905, *a book by Diane L. Goeres-Gardner published in 2005 by Caxton Press;*
- Jacksonville Oregon Sentinel *archives, 1884-1886.*

THE PATSY.

On April 1, 1884, an event occurred that probably should have tipped 25-year-old woodcutter Joseph Drake off that bad things were coming his way:

His neighbor, David Swartz, filed for divorce from his wife, Mary, and listed Joseph as the primary cause. Specifically, David claimed Mary had committed adultery with Joseph on March 21, 1884.

With most frontier Oregonians, this would have been cause for some discomfort, whether it was true or not. But for Joseph Drake, it probably should have been his cue to run for his life. That's because Joseph was African-American, one of a tiny handful of Black people living in Salem and the surrounding countryside — and the Civil War had ended less than 20 years before.

Joseph apparently felt safe enough, though. He was boarding with the Swartzes' neighbors, William and Emma Henry, and Delinda Henry, William's mother. The Henrys, although they were good friends with Mary Swartz, had absolutely no use for her husband. So it's understandable that Joseph Drake would feel fairly well protected from any kind of trouble David Swartz might make for him.

Understandable — and dead wrong.

LOVE, SEX *and* MURDER *in* OLD OREGON.

The trouble started on May 3, 1884. On that evening, while Emma Henry and mother Delinda were cooking dinner, William went out to bring the cows in, and Joseph came with him, hoping to do some hunting. When they returned, Mary Swartz was at the house with her son George, and everyone had supper together.

It's what happened after supper that's in dispute.

According to Joseph, he passed the evening quietly, going outside to smoke his pipe and relax. Presently young George ran to fetch him inside, where Mary Swartz asked him if he could take some eggs into town for her. He agreed, and then she and George left, and Joseph went off to bed.

But according to all three of the Henrys, that's not what happened at all.

Delinda and Emma both testified that Joseph Drake and Mary Swartz had an "intimate conversation" in a quiet corner of their house, then left together for the Swartz house, having learned that David Swartz had gone to the mill for a load of lumber and would not be home until very late. Both the Henry women testified that Joseph and Mary were having an affair, and both testified that they had heard Joseph threaten to kill David Swartz, and that the next morning he was openly boasting about having done the job.

And William? William testified that he and Joseph went out that night and waylaid David Swartz as he was coming back home with his load of lumber. William had stepped out to stop David, and then Joseph had shot David from ambush, badly wounding him; then, William said, he had run up and snatched William's pistol away from him and, as David writhed on the ground, shot him in the neck to finish the job.

So, was it true? Was young Joseph Drake a cold-blooded killer — ready and willing, with no particularly strong motive, to murder his alleged lover's ex-husband after filling the ears of three witnesses with the details of his plan and letting one of them witness the actual murder? And after having done this, did he calmly go home, climb into bed, and carry on with his ordinary life, waiting for the sheriff to come slap the cuffs on him?

Yes, the jury decided; that's exactly what happened.

It's impossible not to see the taint of post-Reconstruction racism at work here, both in the Henry family's willingness to throw Joseph under the bus and in the jury's willingness to swallow such a whopper. It's also hard not to look at the details of the case and spin out other possible sequences of events: an angry exchange between David Swartz and William Henry leading to a gunshot, then another one; a hasty retreat to the Henry house to huddle with Emma and Delinda, hashing out a plan to save William Henry from the gallows by pinning the murder on the Black guy now

The city of Salem as it appeared looking west from the dome of the capitol building in the late 1800s. (Image: Salem Public Library)

peacefully sleeping off a long hard workday; and, the following morning, the betrayal.

Delinda nearly blew the whole game, because she couldn't keep her story straight; she testified at the preliminary hearing that Emma was sick and she was up all night taking care of her, and then testified at the trial that she went to bed early. But the jury was, it seems, in a forgiving mood.

Perhaps to his surprise, William Henry found himself in almost as much trouble as Joseph. If he did make up the whole story, he rather overdid it by placing himself at the scene of the murder and giving himself a minor role in the actual killing. Hauled into court for his role in the ambush that he'd essentially confessed to in open court, he was sentenced to life in the Oregon State Penitentiary, and had it not been for Governor Sylvester Pennoyer pardoning him out in 1893 after he'd served nine years, he'd have passed the rest of his life behind bars.

As for Joseph Drake, he went to his fate with bravery and stoicism, if with some obvious trepidation. Although most of Salem had by that time come to believe either that he was innocent or at least that he was not guilty enough to merit hanging, a huge crowd gathered to watch the deed done, and to hopefully hear him finally confess to his crime, now that the scaffold was nigh and eternity near.

What they heard may have made them pretty uncomfortable, because even now, with nothing to gain by dissembling, Drake was not only firmly and quietly insistent on his innocence, but surprisingly gracious toward the people who had apparently played the Judas Iscariot with his young life.

"I am going to be hanged for the company I keep and not for the crime I committed," he told them. "I have not much to say. I am going to be executed for a crime I know nothing about . . . . I lived with William Henry some time and did not think him a very bad man. Henry surely did the work if he knew anything about it. I think it is pretty hard that I have to lay down my life like this. I can't say who did the work, for I was not there. I know I have been rudely dealt with. I thank the people who have tried to help me for their kindness . . . . (Marion County Sheriff) Mr. Minto's folks have done a good part by me and I thank them for it. They treated me kindly and given me all the privileges possible under the circumstances."

Joseph Drake was hanged at 1:48 p.m. on March 27, 1885. His was the first legal execution of an African-American in Oregon history, although the taint of judicial lynching is so strong in this case that the word "legal" kind of sticks in one's throat a bit.

It would be interesting to know what became of the Henry family after the hanging, but I have been unable to learn anything further about them, beyond William's prison sentence.

Sources and Works Cited:
- Necktie Parties: Legal Executions in Oregon 1851-1905, *a book by Diane L. Goeres-Gardner published in 2005 by Caxton Press;*
- Portland Morning Oregonian *archives, April and May 1884.*

MESMERIZED.

Minnie Ensminger, the schoolmistress at Muddy Creek School, was young, smart, and pretty, and nearly everyone in the North Powder area loved her.

Pleasant Armstrong loved her more than most. He was a strong, handsome miner and a gifted fiddle player. He had met Minnie in February of 1900, and the two of them had hit it off very well, and soon were engaged to be married.

But Minnie's parents were not happy about the match at all. Pleasant, though he seemed a very nice man and was popular at all the dances, was not known for his intellect, and was barely literate; and, to make matters worse, he was half Spanish. So when, in the fall of 1902, Pleasant went away for a few months to work at the Maxwell Mine, they started working on Minnie, and persuaded her to break off the engagement.

She wrote him a letter very firmly breaking things off, probably with her parents' help, and posted it to him at the mine. Meanwhile, the parents got the local postmaster to intercept all Minnie's mail so that they could inspect it, to make sure things didn't get started again.

That last bit of interference — technically illegal, although well within the purview of what turn-of-the-century society considered a parent's rights — was destined to have deadly consequences.

> **LA GRANDE, OREGON, WEDNESDAY MORNING, MARCH 4, 1903.**
>
> # ANGRY MOB IS AFTER ARMSTRONG
>
> ## The Murderer of Minnie Ensminger Narrowly Escapes Death at the Hands of a Mob---Her Avengers are Still After Him.
>
> BAKER CITY. March 4, 3 a. m (Special to the OBSERVER)—Pleas Armstrong, the man who murdered Minnie Ensminger, has been on the anxious seat all day and had it not been for the shrewdness of the sheriff he would have been dangling at the end of a rope ere this.
>
> A mob of two hundred angry men yesterday afternoon assembled at the jail doors and ordered the Sheriff to deliver Armstrong over to them but the sheriff had received warning and had spirited the prisoner away to his residence and simply told the mob that their man was not in the jail. The mob did not beleive him and demanded to be admitted to the jail. The sheriff allowed this to be done and much to their surprise, his words were found to be true. The men composing the mob swore they would find Armstrong, and when found his life wou'd not be worth a penny. This happened yesterday afternoon and about dusk it was learned that the sheriff had wired the authorities at the penitentiary at Salem that he would arrive there with Armstrong today, and would deliver him for safe keeping. The mob by this time seemed to have disappeared and it is thought here that they will attempt to board the train and relieve the sheriff of his charge and elevate Armstrong to the top of some telegraph pole.
>
> Since Armstrong pleaded guilty to having murdered Miss Ensminger, her friends in the vicinity of North Powder and Haines have been making threats that he would never live to receive a legal hanging, but little thought was given to their statement, but it seems that there was more than idle talk in their insinuations, and it is not at all unlikely that he will be taken from the sheriff. The Observer called up the telephone operator at Haines and questioned him, but could secure no definite information though he said that there seemed to be something doing "but I am keeping close to the house and not mixing up in anything tonight."

The front-page headline in the La Grande Observer on March 5, 1903, the day after a lynch mob 200 strong tried to storm the Baker County Jail and seize murderer Pleasant Armstrong by force. (Image: UO Libraries)

Upon receiving the letter, Pleasant replied immediately by return mail, begging her to reconsider and in any case asking her to meet with him one last time before Christmas. He knew he would be playing the fiddle at the Redding Ranch Christmas Eve dance in Haines, and she would of course be there, and it would be terribly awkward to see her there "ghosting" him all evening. "I must see you before Dec. 24," he wrote.

There was, of course, no reply. So Pleasant quit his job at the Maxwell Mine and returned to North Powder. And on Dec. 16, he asked a friend to buy a Colt revolver for him. What he planned to do with the revolver is still not known. He maintained, through the date of his execution for Minnie's murder, that he intended to use it on himself, goodbye-cruel-world style, after saying farewell to his erstwhile sweetheart.

Just before the Christmas dance, Minnie got Pleasant's letter; it had, of course, been delayed for her parents' inspection at the post office. She replied right away: "Dear Friend," she wrote. "I did not get your letter until last night, so will reply this morning. I will be at Joe Henner's tonight, and may see you there."

But at the post office, this letter also was set aside for the Ensmingers' inspection, and although Pleasant dropped in several times that day to ask if there was anything for him, the answer he got was "no."

So he loaded the Colt and made ready for the evening.

It was very early on Christmas morning when the dance ended. Minnie had been there, keeping company with another local swain. Pleasant had been sawing away on his fiddle, keeping the couples whirling. The newspaper reports don't say anything about what happened at the dance; but most likely Minnie was waiting for Pleasant to approach her and ask to talk, as she'd invited him to do in her letter, and she must have been a bit puzzled when he did not do so.

As everyone left, Pleasant paused to chat a bit with Minnie's sister Blanche, and then took his leave ... and stationed himself in the bushes near where he intended to stage his Romeo-and-Juliet tableau.

But when Minnie emerged from the building, for some reason instead of presenting himself, speaking his piece, and shooting himself (as he claimed he'd planned to do), he raised the Colt and, without a word to anyone, shot Minnie twice with it. Then he turned the revolver on himself, but the length of its barrel made it hard to commit suicide with; his shot from the long-barreled Colt ricocheted off his skull, gouging a groove in his scalp and stunning him. He was arrested without incident.

Minnie died two days later.

All of Baker County was outraged by Pleasant Armstrong's deed. Sheriff Harvey Brown had his hands full keeping Armstrong from the more vengeful members of the local populace long enough to deliver him for trial. On one occasion, he had to lock the murderer in the county-courthouse vault while a very large lynch mob — 150 angry citizens — trooped through the office and jailhouse looking for Armstrong. Baker County, in 1903, was still a frontier community without a strong law-enforcement presence; residents were accustomed to taking care of themselves, and vigilante action had long been a part of that.

The lynch mob was frustrated that night, but they didn't intend to give up. Brown ended up having to essentially smuggle his prisoner to Portland for safekeeping. He was kept there until the day of his trial, when he was brought back to Baker City, with a substantial and well-armed force of sheriff's deputies on guard, to stand trial.

In court, Pleasant told his story between heavy sobs. There was barely a dry eye in the court after he was done. But, not a single person in the court had any doubt of his guilt, either. He had done it, he told them — he freely admitted he had done it — and he seemed to almost welcome a death sentence, to expiate his crime. He couldn't explain his shooting of Minnie, he said; that had not been what he'd intended to do.

A woman named Cora Rockwell, though, thought she could explain it. Shortly after the trial — which, of course, resulted in a guilty verdict and sentence to hang — she started visiting the sheriff with a startling story. She claimed to be a former agent with the United States Secret Service, and said she was working on a case involving a local gang of murdering hypnotists called the "Blue Beard Family." The idea was, the mysterious hypnotist either impelled Pleasant to shoot Minnie or shot her himself and hypnotically convinced the somewhat-thickish young man that he had. Rockwell added that this gang of hypno-Crips was responsible for three other murders in Baker City, and said she would lead officers to the bodies if they would follow her.

The newspapers don't say if they did so or not; if they did, no bodies were found, but being as there had not been three matching disappearances in Baker City during the time she specified, they may not have bothered. Ms. Rockwell was referred to the Oregon State Hospital in Salem. As for Pleasant, he had no use for her excuses. "Keep that woman out of here with her dope dreams," he said to Deputy Bill Lachner.

Pleasant Armstrong was ready to go, as ready as any convicted murderer has ever been. The last 24 hours of his life almost seemed like a celebration of his coming departure as he dined with relish on a sumptuous turkey dinner, enjoyed a good cigar, and played for his visitors on his violin. Ministers and reporters came to see him and he met them all with forthright good cheer. He had been baptized into the Catholic faith a day or two before, and he spent a lot of time with the local priest, being shrived and preparing himself.

The morning of his execution, Pleasant ate a hearty breakfast of ham and eggs before stepping up onto the gallows platform.

"I had a sweet girl once whom I dearly loved — Minnie Ensminger," he told the watching crowd, standing on the platform with the noose about his neck. "I killed her and I stand ready to die for that crime."

And, a few minutes later, so he did.

DEADLY BELOVED.

Sources and Works Cited:
- Necktie Parties: Legal Executions in Oregon 1851-1905, *a book by Diane L. Goeres-Gardner published in 2005 by Caxton Press;*
- Athena Press *archives, 22 Jan 1904;*
- Corvallis Times *archives, 29 Mar 1903;*
- La Grande Observer *archives, 04 Mar and 22 Apr 1903;*
- Portland Morning Oregonian *archives, 21 Apr 1903;*
- Portland Daily Journal *archives, 29 Jul 1903;*
- Salem Statesman *archives, 28 Dec 1902 and 23 Jan 1904.*

THE DRYWALL CONTRACTOR.

The contractors were getting ready to wrap up work for the day when several visitors arrived at the job site, a house on Scholls Ferry Road near Beaverton. The newcomers were a small group of serious-looking men in conservative, well-fitting suits, accompanied by the workers' boss, Charles Robinson.

Robinson sought out one of his employees, a 55-year-old plasterer named John McCullough. McCullough, although he'd only been on the job for three months, was already one of Robinson's best men. He was quiet, easy-going, hardworking, sober and reliable.

Robinson led his well-dressed visitors to McCullough and introduced them as FBI agents.

The other workers on the job watched with astonishment as the agents arrested McCullough and led him away. They'd been kidding him for days about his uncanny resemblance to a picture that had run in the Portland *Morning Oregonian* a couple days earlier, under the headline, "Accused Murderer of Three Tops FBI List of Wanted Criminals." Maybe there'd been something in that resemblance after all, they thought.

The picture had been identified as Thomas James Holden, and the resemblance to McCullough had been quite startling. Holden could have been McCullough's twin brother. Holden, the newspaper said, was wanted for gunning down his wife and two brothers-in-law during a drunken family argument. He had, apparently, shot each of them once with a .38, and with his fourth shot, grazed the cheek of his sister-in-law. Four shots, three dead. Then he'd fled and disappeared.

The newspaper said Holden was a train robber, serial bank robber and "product of the mad-dog days of gangsterism." The newspaper also quoted the FBI as calling Holden "one man whose freedom in society is a menace to every man, woman and child in America."

That FBI quote may have been hyperbole, but "mad-dog days of gangsterism" was an excellent synopsis of Holden's criminal career.

Holden first came to police attention around 1925, when he made his debut as the senior partner in the Holden-Keating Gang. (You have probably never heard of the Holden-Keating Gang. But if you'd been a Midwestern newspaper reader in the 1920s, you most certainly would have.)

At first, Holden and fellow bandit Charles Keating specialized in jacking up cargoes and bank deliveries. Their most lucrative haul came in 1926, when the gang stuck up an armored truck and got away with $1.3 million.

After that, though, the law started to close in, and finally in 1928 both bandits were captured and sent off to prison at Leavenworth.

In 1930 Holden and Keating escaped from Leavenworth with the help of George "Machine Gun" Kelly, and subsequently helped perpetrate a sensational armed prison breakout in 1931.

Then they'd gone to Chicago and taken up with the notorious underworld characters there. Soon they were back to robbing banks and vaults, in company with bigger and bigger crews of bandits, several of whom ended up dead as a result of disputes and double-crossings among the gang members. On one occasion, the gang took the son of a bank president hostage, then shot him and dumped his body on the outskirts of town.

Finally, in 1932, FBI agents got the drop on the two robbers while they were playing golf in Kansas City, and back to prison they went.

Holden was sent to the federal government's maximum-security facility at that time — Alcatraz. And there he remained for more than 10 years. He was paroled in 1947, whereupon he married his girlfriend.

It had been 18 months later that he'd committed the shocking triple murder for which he was now wanted.

S uch a criminal resume formed quite a contrast with the mild-mannered McCullough that the other men on the plastering crew knew. They never once thought they might be the same man, despite the eerie similarities. But they teased him about it, an activity that was made even more fun by the fact that he apparently had no idea what they were talking about. He had not, it seemed, read Wednesday's paper.

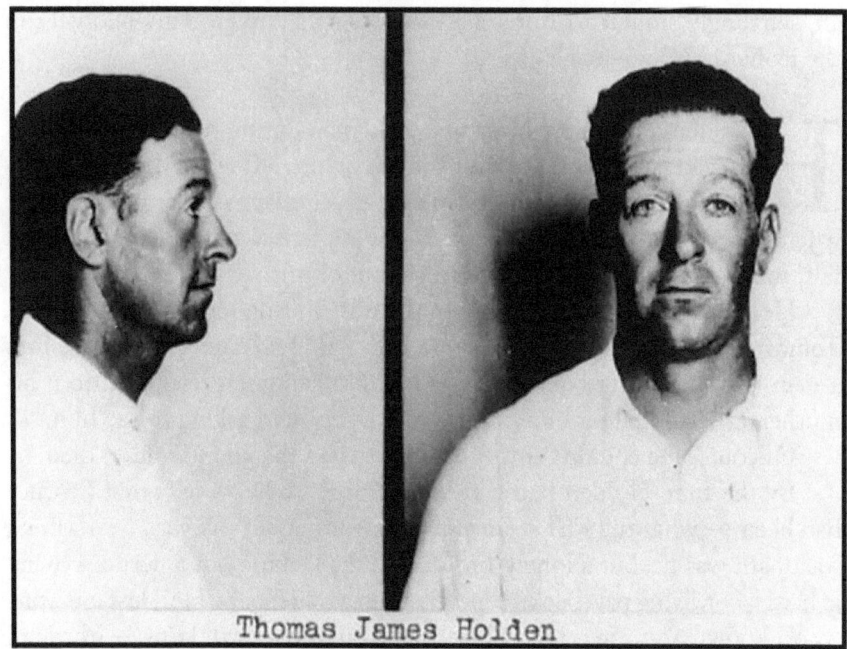

Thomas James Holden

The FBI-supplied booking shot of Thomas James Holden as he appeared in the late 1940s, when he was released from prison, prior to the triple murder for which he was wanted. (Image: Portland Morning Oregonian)

If he had, he would have disappeared immediately, he later told authorities.

"McCullough" at first tried to stick to his story. He was John R. McCullough, he insisted — just a laborer who'd come to Portland three months before from Butte, Mont., to find work. But when they reached the FBI office and he learned how much they knew about him, he broke down and copped to it.

Holden's landlady was shocked by the news. He'd been renting a tiny cabin from her in Sahnow's Motel and Trailer Park since first coming to town.

"He was a model tenant," she told the *Oregonian*. "I suspect a lot of people about being crooks, but not this one. I'm a little shocked. I took his rent every week. He always was happy and singing Irish folk songs. He had a good enough voice to be in opera."

Holden had been the first man ever put on the FBI's Ten Most Wanted list, and he was among the first to be caught. His distinctive appearance made identification an absolute breeze. His mugshot shows a wide and flat forehead, low and straight brow ridge, preternaturally straight mouth — in all, startlingly similar to Boris Karloff playing Frankenstein's Monster in the iconic 1931 movie.

Holden might have been a big, bad man during his younger days as a gangster, but there wasn't much of him left when the FBI finally caught up with him. Karma is a cruel mistress to cruel men. The wife he had shot during that drunken argument was the woman who'd faithfully waited 16 years for him to get out of prison.

He'd also lost his son, Tommy, in the war. During his time on Alcatraz, Tommy had been his only visitor — a U.S. Army private who'd grown into a man with his father behind bars. Then Holden got a telegram from his mother, in 1945, telling him Tommy was dying, and asking to see him.

Of course, he couldn't come. Five days later, the young soldier died.

By the time Holden had arrived in Portland, he wasn't what he once had been — what the FBI seemed to be assuming he still was. No dashing sociopath was he, but a lonely, broken old man, eking out a perilous living at hard labor, living paycheck-to-paycheck in a trailer park. He'd lost everyone who'd known and cared about him, all through his own doing — through murder or through neglect. He was a walking, talking cautionary tale for any young buck thinking of embarking on a life of crime.

So now, caught at last and for the final time, looking tired and resigned to his fate, Holden signed the extradition papers that would send him back to Chicago to stand trial for the triple murder. With his sister-in-law's testimony, it was not a difficult case for the prosecution to win. He was sent to the Illinois State Prison, knowing it would be his home for the rest of his life.

It was. He died there, just two years later.

Sources and Works Cited:
- Alcatraz: The Gangster Years, *a book by David Ward published in 2009 by University of California Press;*
- *http://fbi.gov;*
- Portland Morning Oregonian *archives, June 1951 and January 1955)*

THE EX-POLICE CHIEF.

Back in 1948, the small Oregon town of Sandy had a problem. Its police chief, W.C. Stoneman, had resigned due to illness. And after a search, the city administrators had started to realize Stoneman had been severely underpaid.

Put simply, they could not find a law-enforcement professional who would take on the job of Sandy Chief of Police for the $150 monthly salary they were offering (the equivalent of about $1,550 in modern currency — $8.90 an hour, well below the current minimum wage).

They did find one candidate for the job, though. He was a local fellow by the name of Otto Austin Loel, a relatively recent arrival in town. His only criminal record was a drunken-driving conviction from back east — at that time drunken driving was widely considered to be a minor infraction, like a speeding ticket.

Best of all, outgoing chief Stoneman recommended him. Stoneman had worked with him when the two of them were night merchants' policemen (essentially, security guards) before Stoneman became chief. Stoneman said Loel was a rough-and-ready character and a good fellow, if a little overly fond of an alcoholic beverage or two of an evening.

That was good enough for the city council, the members of which were as loath to part with money as anyone might be. And so, although Loel didn't quite seem to cut the proper figure of a police chief, the job became his.

Three newspaper-clipping mugshots of former Sandy Police Chief Otto Austin Loel, published while the FBI was looking for him to charge him with murder. (Image: FBI)

Regrets came quickly. The new top cop turned out to be a bit unpredictable. Other Sandy residents later recalled that he was cheerful and talkative one minute, and surly and snarling the next. He didn't bother with a uniform, but he often could be found drinking beer in his favorite tavern sporting a leather motorcycle jacket, with a pair of six-shooters slung cowboy-style on his hips and a pair of handcuffs dangling from his suspenders.

The city judge offered the most frank and disdainful analysis of Chief Loel. Loel, he recalled, was "a shifty-eyed, half-shaven roughneck who boasted, bragged and lied."

He was a day-drinker, so he spent a lot of time in the tavern, regaling anyone who would listen with stories of his service in the U.S. Navy during the Second World War and slaking an obviously prodigious thirst with glass after glass of cheap suds.

It wasn't the kind of situation that could last very long, and it didn't. Shortly after Chief Loel was hired, a new mayor was elected, a resident named John Mills. And several months after that, Mills, never much of a Chief Loel fan to start with, happened to be in a tavern with the chief when, nicely liquored up, Chief Loel launched into a spirited denunciation of the personal character of several city council members. Furious, Mayor Mills walked up to him, stripped him of his gun and badge, and fired him on the spot.

Not surprisingly, Loel left Sandy soon afterward. And the town got busy trying to forget about the whole thing.

That wouldn't be so easy, though. Not with the kind of headlines that started popping up in the Portland *Oregonian* just a few years later.

It seems that after leaving Sandy, Loel had ended up in Compton, Calif. There, one January day in 1954, he was drinking in a local tavern and talking about an upcoming road trip to Syracuse, New York, when one of the other bar patrons, 31-year-old Elizabeth Jeanne Henderson, asked him if he'd be willing to take her with him as far as Newark, Ohio, so she could visit her relatives there.

Elizabeth and her husband, both regulars in the tavern, both considered Loel a friend. Soon an expense-sharing deal was struck, and the two of them were on the highway in Loel's snazzy 1947 Buick, headed east.

When they got to Oklahoma City, Loel and Henderson stopped and got a hotel room for the night. By the next morning, Loel had driven on alone. And the maid coming to make up the room got a nasty shock. The room was spattered with blood, and Elizabeth Henderson's body, partially undressed, was wedged under the bed. She'd been beaten, burned with cigarettes and stabbed 19 times.

Loel, of course, promptly vanished. Authorities tracked him as far as Shreveport, Louisiana, where he'd pawned some of his stuff. Then he disappeared from view.

A year went by. The heinousness of the murder caught the attention of the FBI, which put him on its Ten Most Wanted list.

But although the Most Wanted list was generally very effective in catching wanted crooks, Loel wasn't caught that way. Instead, it was his thirst for alcohol that did him in. On Jan. 9, 1955, the cops in Sanford, Fla., arrested a man who called himself Jack McCoy for public drunkenness. McCoy's fingerprints turned out to be a match for Loel's. And how was it that the cops had Loel's fingerprints on file? Because they'd been taken when he was arrested for drunken driving, many years before.

Loel was promptly extradited to Oklahoma and put on trial for the murder of Elizabeth Henderson. His attorney had a tough job trying to represent him, though, because he kept insisting that he'd killed her in self-defense, trying to fend off her sexual advances. Had the situation not been so serious, the jurors would probably have met this claim with scornful snickers. Did this guy seriously expect them to believe that Elizabeth Henderson was so hot for him that he'd been forced to defend himself from her raging nymphomania — by burning her with cigarettes?

It seemed he did. Consequently, the jury took very little time to come back with a unanimous guilty verdict.

And so it was that, following a short series of appeals and requests for clemency (all of which were sabotaged by Loel's remarkably unrepentant

LOVE, SEX *and* MURDER *in* OLD OREGON.

attitude), the former Chief of Police for the city of Sandy, Oregon, found himself strapped into an oak chair in the Oklahoma State Prison, a few minutes after midnight, a black hood over his head and electrodes on his head and legs, waiting for his 2,300 volts.

By 12:07 a.m., he had received them.

By that time, Sandy had learned its lesson. After Loel's firing, the city had promptly raised the city police chief's salary to competitive levels, and the town has enjoyed competent, murderer-free police services ever since.

Sources and Works Cited:
- *"Who's Who in Crime," an article by Wally Hunter in the 30 Jan 1955 issue of the* Portland Oregonian;
- Legal Executions in Nebraska, Kansas and Oklahoma, *a book by Michael R. Wilson published in 2012 by McFarland;*
- Portland Oregonian *archives, May 1954, January 1955, and January 1957.*

PART II:

BONNIE AND CLYDE:

There's something undeniably romantic about the idea of an outlaw couple, drifting around the country surfing on their own crime wave. From Alfred Noyes' famous poem, "The Highwayman," to Bonnie Parker's own "The Ballad of Bonnie and Clyde," to modern country songs like Travis Tritt's "Modern-Day Bonnie and Clyde" — and even in stories in which the sexual coloring is absent or only hinted at, like "Thelma and Louise" — it's an enduring archetype in human storytelling. And, of course, in real life, for most people, few things are sexier than a dangerous member of the opposite sex.

Real Bonnie and Clyde stories are rare in real life, of course, but these four cases come pretty close to filling the bill.

THE CONJUGAL JAILBREAKERS:

This story isn't a "real" Bonnie and Clyde story. It's more like a just-plain-Clyde story in which Clyde got his niece to dress as Bonnie to help him bust out of prison.

Our story starts a few minutes after midnight on May 17, 1974. The Oregon State Penitentiary guard sitting in his car outside the Salem Motel 6 was starting to get nervous.

He was there to supervise a conjugal visit. They didn't call it a "conjugal visit," of course — that term was a little too loaded. The event the guard was there to supervise was officially referred to as a "social pass" — but it involved bringing an inmate to a cheap motel room so that he could meet up with his girlfriend for an unsupervised hour or two before being taken back to the pen. In all but name, it was a conjugal visit.

In this particular case, the conjugal visit was between a convicted cop killer named Carl Cletus Bowles and his fiancée, Joan Coberly. The convict was supposed to have returned to the parking lot by midnight for his ride back to prison. But, midnight had come and gone, and there was no sign of Bowles.

The guard walked up to room 30, knocked on the door. No response.

He went down and used the lobby telephone to call the room. No answer.

Finally the manager used the passkey to let him inside, and he found the room empty — really empty. The bed hadn't even been sat on; the toilet

The formal entry gates at the Oregon State Penitentiary. (Image: Postcard)

bowl still had a paper strap stretched across it (the kind hotels used to use, with the words "Sanitized for Your Protection" printed on in powder-blue ink). Bowles and his "fiancée" were gone — long gone. They had, it turned out, simply walked out the back door of the motel.

It was a jailbreak — quite possibly the most embarrassing jailbreak in U.S. history.

Carl Cletus Bowles was a small, handsome man, charismatic and, before his prison days, something of a ladies' man. He'd gotten into trouble early, before he was a teenager even, and by his late teens he was doing hard time for larceny.

It was in July of 1965, on the run from the law after robbing a bank in Portland just a few days after his release from prison, that Bowles became a murderer. He and fellow bank robber Wilfred Marion Gray were speeding in a red 1958 Triumph TR-3 on Delta Highway north of Eugene when 33-year-old Lane County Sheriff's Deputy Carlton Smith tried to pull them over for a speeding ticket. Bowles and Gray, after pulling the convertible over to the side of the road, turned in their seats with their guns in their hands and opened fire through the windshield of the cop car, shooting across the trunk lid of their open car. Then they sped away, leaving Deputy Smith slumped in his patrol car with six pistol bullets and a charge of shotgun pellets in his body.

Bowles and Gray led the cops on an extensive chase after that. They abandoned the Triumph, took a Eugene woman and her son hostage, forced them to drive them to Marion Forks, and released them there; then they commandeered a camper truck, taking the family camping in it hostage, and forced them to drive to Sacramento. There they invaded the home of the finance director for the state of California, Hale Champion; took him, his wife, and their daughter hostage; and forced them to drive to Nevada. There, they tried to rob a casino, and Champion was grazed by a bullet during the ensuing shootout. Shortly after that, the two desperados released their hostages and surrendered to police.

It was for the murder of Deputy Smith — and for the kidnapping of Champion — that Bowles was in prison at the time of his escape.

Despite the gravity of this crime and the double life sentence it had drawn, prison superintendent Hoyt Cupp knew Bowles would eventually be released — probably at his next Parole Board hearing in 1982. So, Cupp later explained, he was thinking about ways to encourage Bowles to reform himself, so that when he was released, he'd behave himself. To encourage this, Cupp thought a "social pass" — that is, a conjugal visit — would give Bowles a "ray of hope" and encourage him to rehabilitate himself.

Carl Cletus Bowles in 1974.

Bowles had been at some pains to charm Cupp, and it seemed his campaign had worked; Cupp had taken a personal interest in helping this seemingly compliant, positive prisoner to move beyond his sordid past.

Now, it seemed, it had all been an elaborate con. Joan Coberly, as it turned out, was actually Bowles' niece, not his girlfriend. She'd been making visits to the pen posing as his girlfriend, apparently for the express purpose of figuring out a way to bust him out.

This came as a surprise, but it shouldn't have. A teletype letter had come into the state pen six months earlier — just a few weeks after Coberly's first visit — from a detective in Amarillo, Texas, warning that Coberly was

The Motel 6 on Mission Street in Salem, which Carl Cletus Bowles escaped from by walking out the back door during a conjugal visit while a prison guard watched the front. (Image: Postcard)

planning to break Bowles out. Cupp claimed he never saw the letter, and, well, maybe he didn't.

As state and federal law enforcement agencies swung into action, the eyes of everyone were on Hoyt Cupp. What on Earth had he been thinking, people wondered? Why was a man who was doing a life sentence for murdering a cop, who wasn't even eligible for parole for another eight years, getting escorted to a motel room for sex? Wasn't that a bit irresponsible, given what often happens nine months after such an encounter? Why didn't the prison authorities check to see if the Motel 6 had more than one exit? And most of all, why was that Teletype letter ignored?

Governor Tom McCall, who had appointed Cupp and had great faith in him, docked his pay by $1,000 and suspended him for two weeks. Cupp offered his resignation, and McCall refused to accept it — but told him if anyone was hurt before Bowles was recaptured, that would probably change.

Spoiler alert: It didn't.

Meanwhile, Bowles and Coberly were down in the hills near Eugene, hiding out — first at a campsite, later in a commune, and after that on the property of a well-intentioned acquaintance. But authorities soon tracked them down, and moved in.

When FBI agents arrived, Bowles managed to get the drop on them. He shot at an FBI agent at point-blank range and missed, causing the agent to drop his pistol and scramble for cover; Bowles then fled the scene with the agent's gun. Then he went to the nearby home of Earl and Vi Hunter, took the couple hostage, and left town with them in their car.

The felon then picked up where he'd left off the last time he was on the lam, back in 1965 — taking hostages and hijacking cars and just wandering around the west, apparently with no idea what to do.

Eventually he wound up in the Spokane area, where officers found themselves responding to complaints of a man hijacking cars and motorcycles at gunpoint. They found him and chased him into the Spokane River, where, waist deep in the water, he tried to get a shot off at a cop who already had him in his sights. The cop shot him in the stomach.

Surgeons worked for hours to save Bowles' life, and were successful. And authorities badly wanted to talk to him. All the hostages he'd taken were alive and accounted for except two — the Hunters, the couple he'd kidnapped in Eugene. What had happened to them?

Bowles said he released them in Yakima. The cops knew, with that sense that people develop when they're lied to a lot, that he was lying. And this, of course, they found very alarming.

Finally, two bodies were found, about 20 miles south of Spokane in a rural area. It was Earl and Vi Hunter. Bowles had shot them execution-style with the pistol he'd jacked from that FBI agent.

It was now official: The penitentiary's carelessness had cost two innocent lives.

In the months that followed, a number of voices called for Cupp's head to roll. However, Governor McCall decided not to fire him; he served as superintendent there for another 10 years before being promoted to a central administrative position, and retired in 1986.

But Bowles' case had a significant impact on many Oregonians' views on crime-and-punishment issues, especially regarding the death penalty. If anyone deserved the death penalty, it was Bowles, and people found it frustrating that the law wouldn't allow it to be applied. They also found it scary that a man like Bowles had been just a few years away from being paroled. And they felt that the state prison should be more focused on protecting innocent people outside its walls than rehabilitating those within.

Even among folks who didn't agree with that assessment, there was a noticeable hardening of attitudes toward convicts just after this happened. In a 1964 referendum, Oregonians overwhelmingly voted to abolish the death penalty; in 1978, they overwhelmingly changed their minds. This dramatic change was probably at least partly because of this case.

One thing is for sure: Conjugal visits got a whole lot more difficult to arrange, at least for a little while, after this.

As for Bowles, he died in prison in 2005.

Sources and Works Cited:
- *"Oregon Jailbreaks," an episode of the* Kick-Ass Oregon History Podcast *by Doug Kenck-Crispin and Andy Lindberg, first released on July 4, 2012;*
- Empty Promises, *a book by Ann Rule published by Simon & Schuster in 2001;*
- Bend Bulletin *and* Eugene Register-Guard *archives, June 1974, October 1974 and November 2002*

GANGSTER AND MOLL.

Drug addict and convicted robber Ray Moore was in his cheap hotel room on the corner of 12th and Morrison when somebody started pounding on the door. It was Jimmy Walker, a friend and "business associate" specializing in burglary.

Jimmy desperately needed help. He told Ray he'd shot a man, and was sure he'd be "burned for it." He needed to get out of town fast.

Ray said he'd help. He told Jimmy to check into the hotel and wait for him while he made some arrangements. Then he grabbed his hat and he headed out the door.

Soon he was back, and introducing Jimmy to a friend and fellow ex-con — Larry Johnson, the man who was going to get him out of town.

The arrangements were soon made. A friend of Johnson's was going to come by just after nightfall and pick Jimmy up and take him out of town. All he had to do was wait in his hotel room until it got dark.

Then Ray headed back out the door, leaving Jimmy at the hotel. He headed straight downtown, looking for the nearest jewelry store. Bad things, he knew, were going to happen that night. He knew who Jimmy had shot, although Jimmy hadn't told him; but news of that kind of thing travels fast, and it had reached him before Jimmy had. He also knew that, yes, Jimmy was going to be "burned" for it ... and when he was, Ray intended to be safely locked away where nobody could possibly think he had anything to do with it.

He found what he wanted at Zell's Jewelers: a tray of watches behind a plate-glass window. Brazenly he smashed through the glass, grabbed the tray of watches, and hustled off down the street to hail a cab. He was under arrest a few minutes later. The charges were going to be stiff ones, and it probably meant some more prison time — but he didn't mind. The important thing was, his alibi for later that night would be unbreakable.

Meanwhile, Jimmy was on the phone getting word to his girlfriend, Edith McClain, letting her know what had happened. Edith packed a small suitcase and hurried to join him.

Edith was the real source of the problem Jimmy was facing that day. She was, in the lingo of the day, a gun moll, and until a month earlier she'd been the steady girlfriend of an influential but low-key crime boss named "Shy Frank" Kodat.

Shy Frank was an aging safecracker, 50 years old, and he'd spent quite a few of those years doing hard time for plying his trade. For a guy like Frank, that wasn't necessarily a bad thing. Frank was a born networker, and prison was full of guys a safecracker could get to know and network with and make plans for when they got out again. And everybody liked Frank.

His most recent stint in the hoosegow had been a bad one, though. He'd picked up tuberculosis, which was slowly killing him with the help of kidney disease, and on top of that he had bad arthritis.

So Frank, following his release, had announced his retirement: He was going straight, and devoting his remaining years to helping other old crooks get their act together as well. To that end, he opened a boardinghouse, a sort of informal halfway-house for ex-cons, deep in the industrial district of northeast Portland.

Frank's halfway-house was somewhat unusual, as halfway-houses go, in that it apparently offered goods and services that a more traditional halfway house would not — including certain refreshments (remember, Prohibition was still on in '33) and the attentions of friendly ladies.

The beauty of this scheme was soon clear: It offered a convincing explanation for the presence of so many known crooks under one roof. There were always seasoned professionals there — stickup men, cat burglars, box men, pickpockets, you name it. And Shy Frank — who, of course, wasn't really retired at all — could direct their professional activities.

So Shy Frank had a pretty sweet deal, except for the fact that he knew he was going to die soon. The biggest problem with his setup was, sometimes the ex-cons who came to stay at Frank's place were more trouble than they were worth.

Case in point: Jimmy Walker.

This advertisement for the Studebaker President 8, which appeared in *American Motorist* magazine in 1929, shows the size of the car compared with the size of the heads of the people inside it. (Image: *American Motorist*)

Jimmy had come to Frank's place fresh from the state pen, a small-time business burglar with a big-time attitude. Almost immediately he had horned in on Frank's dame, Edith. Soon Jimmy and Edith were spending a lot of time together, and Frank's blood was boiling, and other guys in Frank's place started worrying about how it would end.

Finally one of the other roomers accused Jimmy of stealing his watch — probably looking to give Shy Frank an excuse to kick Jimmy out. Shy Frank seized it eagerly, and the two cons had a heated exchange. Jimmy left, had a few drinks, came back and got into a screaming row with Frank. Frank, who tired quickly because of his T.B., soon retired from the battlefield and stomped off to his bedroom to rest, leaving Jimmy there, apparently alone in an office or den.

The front cover of ADAM Magazine for April 1955 carried this fictitious scene, which — although the car shown is newer — probably looked a lot like what happened when Jimmy Walker and Edith McClain got taken for a ride in April 1933. (Image: ADAM Magazine)

Well, it's no surprise what happens when you leave a burglar alone in a room belonging to somebody he doesn't like. Jimmy apparently got right to work. But one of the first things he found, probably in a desk drawer or something like that, was Shy Frank Kodat's .38 Special — loaded and ready to go.

And then somehow, apparently by accident, Jimmy popped off a round, right there in Frank's house. The bullet zipped through the wall, entered Frank's bedroom and lanced into his back as he sat there on the edge of his bed.

Jimmy's ears must have been ringing, but apparently he could still hear Frank screaming in pain as other boarders ran to see what had happened. Jimmy knew as soon as they figured out he'd shot Shy Frank, accidentally or no, he'd be a dead man. They loved Shy Frank. They did not love him. He dropped the gun and ran for his life.

And that's how Jimmy Walker ended up hunkered down in a cheap motel, Shy Frank's ex-girlfriend by his side, waiting for darkness and a ride out of town.

A factory photograph of the 1929 Studebaker President 8, the car in which Jimmy Walker and Edith McClain got taken for that proverbial ride.

The ride arrived right on schedule. It was a big maroon seven-passenger Studebaker President with two men in it. One, in a wine-colored suit that almost matched the car, helped Edith into the back seat, and then the other one let the clutch out and with a discreet murmur from the luxurious car's straight-eight engine, they glided away into the night.

Early the next morning, logger L.W. Morgan was driving to work on Dutch Canyon Road just west of Scappoose when he saw what he thought was a drunk man passed out in the ditch. He stopped to look.

It was Jimmy Walker. And he wasn't drunk. Neither was Edith McClain, who lay nearby.

Ray Moore had double-crossed Jimmy, and Shy Frank's friends had taken the opportunity to take him and Edith for a ride — gangland style. It had ended with four shots, fired from Shy Frank's .38 Special: two for each of them.

Police didn't have too much trouble putting the pieces together, but hard evidence was in short supply because nobody would talk. Eventually the driver of the big maroon Studebaker, a Jewish hotel operator named Jake Silverman, was arrested for the job, and put on trial for murder.

The trial was a real circus. And, in fact, that trial would become far more important in Oregon history than the murders that prompted it. It would become the pretext for a change in Oregon law that basically overruled the Sixth Amendment to the United States Constitution.

The evidence was copious, but circumstantial. Most damning was the car, which several neighbors had seen driving out toward Scappoose and parking by the road just before the gunshots were heard. Very few people could afford maroon Studebaker limousines in 1933, so the chances that it wasn't Silverman were very slim.

Then, too, a rogues' gallery of seedy underworld characters worthy of a Silver Age Batman comic had been dragged into the trial to testify for and against him, and the overall impression was that he'd almost certainly done the job and that if he hadn't, it wasn't because he wouldn't have jumped at the chance to. And Silverman's gallingly insouciant behavior in court made it even worse.

But one juror just didn't find it convincing enough to send Jake to the gallows for it. Or even to send him up for a life sentence on a second-degree murder rap. So, finally, a compromise was reached: Jake would be found guilty of manslaughter instead. Manslaughter was good for a three-year sentence, which was something at least.

The public, when it heard the verdict, howled with outrage, led by the Portland Morning Oregonian.

"Obviously, Silverman was not guilty of manslaughter," the newspaper opined. "Either he murdered Walker or he was not involved."

Unspoken, but understood by most, was the assumption that the lone holdout had been a fellow Jew, and he or she had held out based not on the evidence, but on tribal loyalties.

And so the *Oregonian* led the charge to "reform the jury system" by making it possible to disregard one or two dissenting votes when necessary.

Now, to be fair, the paper wasn't overtly advocating for the right to suppress minorities. The case they were making was that many fresh immigrants from countries with authoritarian traditions didn't have the right mindset to fully function as an autonomous person in a democracy, and that it needed to be possible to overrule one or two my-compatriot-right-or-wrong types lest millions of dollars be wasted on multiple jury trials.

They were also mindful of the fact that gangsters sometimes try to get to jurors and, through bribes or threats, get them to vote to acquit.

But, as a practical matter, the change radically altered the distribution of justice for minority defendants in Oregon courts. For instance, if a Chinese person was on trial for a serious felony, and the jury was composed of 10 non-Chinese and two Chinese Oregonians — how much more likely would the defendant be to get convicted if the two Chinese jurors could simply be outvoted by the others? And would that be a bad thing, or a good thing? (People in the 1930s would likely have said it was good, because the Chinese jurors would, they'd claim, vote to acquit no matter what. People today would mostly say it was bad, because people naturally empathize more with people who look like themselves.)

It's richly ironic that this painting by Norman Rockwell, titled "The Holdout," was published as the front cover art for The Saturday Evening Post on, of all days, Feb. 14, 1959. That date was Oregon's centennial — the 100th anniversary of the founding of our state — and "The Holdout" depicts a scene that can't happen here unless the defendant is on trial for first-degree murder. (Rockwell, incidentally, appears in this painting; he's the second juror from the right). (Image: Saturday Evening Post)

The entire problem, of course, is nicely illustrated in Normal Rockwell's painting, "The Holdout" — or in the 1957 film "Twelve Angry Men" starring Henry Fonda, in which 11 of 12 jurors are eager to convict a vaguely-ethnic inner-city teen accused of a stabbing and the lone holdout turns out to be right.

Good or bad, it soon became law. Responding to the pressure, the state Legislature drafted a bill and passed it on for public vote using the Oregon referendum system: Except for capital murder cases, conviction could be secured on a 10-2 vote. The measure passed comfortably.

And it remained Oregon law for the next 88 years, despite growing public pressure to repeal it. Over the years, other states that had adopted non-unanimous jury systems — primarily Southern states, which adopted them during the Jim Crow era to make it easier to railroad Black defendants — abandoned them, going back to the Constitutional standard. The last of these was Louisiana, which ended its non-unanimous verdict law in 2018. Oregon soldiered on alone, seemingly maintaining the system out of sheer stubbornness.

Finally, in 2020, the Supreme Court of the United States issued a verdict ordering Oregon to stop.

"Every judge must learn to live with the fact that he or she will make some mistakes," Justice Neil Gorsuch wrote in the verdict. "But it is something else entirely to perpetuate something we all know to be wrong only because we fear the consequences of being right."

He might have been speaking those sentiments directly to the judges and prosecutors of Oregon; indeed, he must have been. By 2020 it was a moot point everywhere else. Oregon was the only state in which a defendant could still be convicted of a felony by a jury vote of 10 to 2 — the most lasting legacy of a silly little love triangle turned deadly, nearly 90 years ago.

Sources and Works Cited:
- Murder and Mayhem in Portland Oregon, *a book by J.D. Chandler published in 2013 by The History Press;*
- Portland Morning Oregonian *archives, April 1933.*

THE BEAVERCREEK BOMBERS.

On a sunny late afternoon, in a remote woodsy area near the base of Mount Hood, five fiery explosions rattled windowpanes in a few farmhouses along Highway 26 near the community of Brightwood.

It was immediately clear what the coordinated blasts had been: an attempt to take down the power grid. The explosive charges had been set at the bases of five of the giant steel towers that carry high-voltage electricity generated at Bonneville and other dams on the Columbia River.

When the smoke cleared, three of the five targeted towers were down, and two of the explosions and subsequent sparking of broken wires had touched off small forest fires. These were quickly brought under control; the power was rerouted around the damaged lines; and Bonneville Power Administration officials started scratching their heads. Who was bombing their power lines? And why?

One thing they now knew for sure: Whoever was doing this was persistent and serious. Three weeks earlier, a helicopter on line patrol had found three heavily damaged towers near Maupin, apparently also targeted with dynamite. This wasn't kids having fun; this bomber was on a campaign.

And if there were any lingering doubts about that, they vanished the very next day, when three more towers went down near The Dalles.

BPA officials still didn't know what the bomber wanted.

But they hadn't long to wait. The answer to that question arrived two days later in the form of a letter sent to the FBI.

"The extent of damages resulting from the demolition of five (sic) of your power-line towers Wednesday night is incidental," the letter stated tersely. "Our primary objective was to impress upon any potential non-believers that we mean business.... We have the men and equipment to keep as many towers down as is necessary to force compliance with our demands."

Those demands were, essentially, one million dollars. And failure to pony up would, the extortionist added, lead to much more than $1 million in damage to other power towers and to companies that depended on the electricity grid for operations.

"If you are entertaining any illusions of apprehending our men, forget it," the letter continued. "An attempt will lead to: Your delivery men will be killed. We will black-out the entire Portland area and vicinity, or both."

The letter was signed by "J. Hawker," an apparent reference to the "Jayhawkers" — the anti-slavery guerilla fighters of pre-Civil-War Kansas. "Mr. Hawker" claimed membership in something called the "R.V.O.V.N.," which stood for "Reorganized Veterans of Viet Nam."

"Hawker" also wrote that the million dollars was not supposed to be seen as an ordinary extortion attempt, but rather as a demand for "just compensation from the government" for Vietnam veterans.

At the urging of the FBI, the BPA immediately and staunchly refused to give "Hawker" a nickel. But the company did immediately offer a $100,000 reward for information leading to the arrest of whoever was responsible for the blowings-up. And, of course, the BPA stepped up patrols of its towers.

The problem was, those towers ran for thousands of miles across the most remote parts of the state. "Hawker" was attaching his charges to the towers using silver duct tape, so they were almost invisible until one got quite close — meaning helicopters were useless as patrol vehicles. Catching "Hawker" planting a charge would be a one-in-a-million shot, no matter how many law-enforcement patrols went out. And if they did find him, he would probably be armed and dangerous.

All they could really do was wait for him to make a mistake.

So the city of Portland hurried to dust off its old gas-turbine backup generators, and everyone waited for the bomber to make his next move.

A week later, "J. Hawker" seems to have gotten impatient. He released another letter in which he threatened to start a forest fire in the Bull Run Watershed, apparently intending to damage the city's drinking water supply, unless that million bucks were speedily forked over. This might have worked OK, had not the skies opened up just after he mailed the letter. By the time "Hawker's" threat to light Bull Run on fire arrived at City Hall, a full half-inch of rain had fallen on it.

BONNIE and CLYDE.

The Bonneville Dam power house as it appeared shortly after it was built, in 1932. This dam and others on the Columbia were the source of the electricity "J. Hawker" sought to ransom. (Postcard image)

Meanwhile, the F.B.I. had received yet another letter from "J. Hawker" — the fourth of a total of six he would send out. This letter included instructions for communicating with him through CB radio transmissions on Channel 9 in Morse Code. In an attempt to avoid having his voice identified, "Hawker" would use a duck call to painstakingly honk out his messages, and the FBI would respond in plain voice. (The FBI wouldn't say, but they were probably pretending to negotiate delivery of the million-dollar ransom.)

In any case, it was this duck-quacking protocol that furnished the FBI with its big break in the case. While monitoring the CB channel for the distinctive sound of "Hawker's" waterfowl honks, an FBI agent just happened to hear a bunch of them while driving behind a blue-and-gray 1968 Plymouth in Southeast Portland. The driver of the Plymouth had his elbow out the window and a walkie-talkie in his hand.

Then, as he watched, the woman in the passenger seat turned, saw his vehicle, and turned quickly to the driver, who instantly threw the radio down on the seat beside him.

Out of the 2 million people in range of the agent's CB radio, what were the chances this one guy was the man he was looking for?

Actually, the chances were excellent. Agents had been communicating with "Hawker" for over a week. Over that time, they had triangulated his CB signal to a small quadrant of Southeast Portland and identified it as a mobile unit. When "Hawker" instructed the agents to contact him via CB radio at 1 p.m. that day, they'd flooded the neighborhood with FBI agents. "Hawker" hadn't stood a chance.

The agent pulled the car over and introduced himself to the couple driving it: David and Sheila Heesch, both 34 years old. They were a ways from home; they lived in Beavercreek, a woodsy rural hamlet about halfway between Oregon City and Molalla.

The radio, when the agent picked it up, was set on Channel 9. There was a duck call on the floorboard. And when the agent honked on it, it sure sounded familiar.

David and Sheila were utterly busted. And once the cops got a warrant to search their home, they found all the evidence they needed: They had found "J. Hawker." And David didn't bother to deny it, entering a guilty plea along with a full explanation to the public. He said he didn't want people worrying that there might still be dynamite out there.

On Nov. 16, 1974 — just one month after the BPA tower blasts that started it all — David Heesch, the "Beavercreek Bomber," was sentenced to 20 years in prison. Sheila drew 10 years as an accessory.

Columnist Paul Keller of *The Gresham Outlook* looked up Sheila Heesch in 2014, on the 40-year anniversary of the bombings. David, she told him, had died eight years previously, from leukemia.

Why had they done it? Sheila told Keller that David had lost his job as a long-haul truck driver and they'd run to the bottom of their resources; so he'd hatched this scheme in a desperate attempt to solve the problem. He told her he was going to do it with or without her help, but added that without her help he'd be much more likely to be caught. So she typed up his ransom notes and drove with him to the remote locations where the towers were to be blown up.

"We were young then," she told Keller. "I suppose we were a little idealistic. I'm sure we rationalized that it would be OK. In a way, I never thought we'd actually do it."

When the two of them were sent up the river, their young children (ages 4 and 7) went to live with their grandparents. But Sheila was released after serving 11 months, and David after four years and eight months.

After their release, David and Sheila's Bonnie-and-Clyde days were over. In 1981 David got a good steady job driving a Tri-Met bus, which he retired from in 2003.

Sources and Works Cited:
- *"Convicted BPA Tower Bomber Accomplice Returns My Call," an article by Paul Keller published 24 Dec 2014 in the* Gresham Outlook;
- *http://fbi.gov;*
- Portland Oregonian *archives, October through December 1974*

PART III:

MURDER, FAMILY STYLE.

One of the signature themes of Mario Puzo's classic novel (and Francis Ford Coppola's movie) *The Godfather* is family. Puzo really showcases the bonds of loyalty within the Corleone family — even for poor hapless Fredo. (Indeed, Fredo's rubbing-out at Michael's behest, in Mark Winegardner's sequel to the story, becomes the one unforgivable sin that more or less ruins Michael's life.)

It makes sense. Since the dawn of organized crime, mobster types have depended on family members in their criminal enterprises. There's a reason for this, of course. Your best friend might be tempted to rat you out to the feds in exchange for leniency, but your sister almost certainly won't.

But of course, that doesn't always work, does it? It certainly didn't for Fredo....

THE MOTHER-SON TEAM.

On November 11, 1887, a 28-year-old convicted murderer named Richard Marple stood on the scaffold in the town of Lafayette and shouted his defiance at the crowd below.

"Murder!" he yelled, as the black hood was fitted over his head. "May God judge you all!"

Marple had maintained his innocence until the bitter end. But his story had changed several times, and every time it changed it got a little wackier and less credible. At one point he was claiming that the real killer of storekeeper David Corker twelve months before was a conspiratorial cabal of prominent members of the local Masons Lodge led by the Yamhill County Sheriff, Thomas J. Harris.

To make matters even worse for him, in the days before the murder, Marple had been overheard joking about how easy it would be to rob Corker, because he was deaf; and Marple was widely suspected of being a thief and a robber. He had moved to Lafayette with his family from Corvallis a year before, and already the family was regarded with considerable suspicion. Marple's mother, Anna, a hard-eyed woman who was believed to be a "gypsy," lived with him and his wife, Julia, and their several children.

In any case, by the time of Marple's trial, most of Lafayette was convinced, for good reasons and bad, of his guilt. The evidence against him was circumstantial, and there really wasn't a whole lot of it, but what there was was serious. The sheriff had noticed blood on his coat the day after the murder.

The Yamhill River near Lafayette, as it appeared in the early years of the twentieth century. (Image: Oregon State University libraries)

Richard explained it as having come from a butchered hog; his wife, Julia, claimed it had come from a child's injury. And Richard also had been found in possession of burglar's tools, which was important because a rear window had been forced to get in and kill Corker.

The real problem for Richard Marple, though, was his mouth. Had he been able to keep quiet and be nice, he likely would have been acquitted for lack of hard evidence; but he seemed utterly unable to keep his trap shut. When he'd first been arrested, he'd first denied involvement and then, with a nasty smile, indulged himself with a series of uncomplimentary remarks about the deceased murder victim. During jury selection he made no attempt to conceal his contempt for everyone in the room, and took obvious pleasure in any display of hostility or enmity from townspeople.

So it shouldn't have been much of a surprise when the jury found him guilty and sentenced him to swing for it — although he himself doesn't seem to have seen it coming.

The judge accidentally scheduled his hanging for a Sunday, so additional hearings had to be convened to make new arrangements, and another court had to study the question of whether the error was grave enough to require a new trial. (It decided that it was not.) Consequently it wasn't until a full year after the crime was committed that Marple was hanged for it.

It wasn't a clean execution. Even by 1880s standards, it was a barbaric and sickening spectacle. The knot slipped up under the condemned man's chin and it took him 18 minutes to slowly strangle to death. Meanwhile,

MURDER, FAMILY STYLE.

from outside the courtyard, the baleful screams of Anna, Marple's "gypsy" mother, arose, calling down curses and maledictions upon the town, screeching that she would see it burn.

By the time the grim spectacle was all over, members of the crowd might have been feeling a little uneasy about it, wondering if all the trouble was a sign — if maybe Marple was innocent after all.

They wouldn't wonder for long.

The very next day, one of Marple's cell mates, William Henry Hess, came forward with a remarkable story. The day before his execution, Marple had pulled him aside and told him he'd give him the truth if he'd swear to keep it secret until after his death.

Here's the story Hess said Marple told him:

Needing money badly, and knowing Corker had plenty, he had collaborated with his wife and his mother to rob him. The plan was that Anna (the mother), who was carrying on a secret affair with Corker, would, after suitably vamping the deaf merchant, fix him a drink with knockout drops in it. Then she'd unlock the door and let Richard in to rob the place.

At the appointed time, Richard found that Anna had forgotten to unlock the door for him, so he had to break in through a window. He found Anna there with the drugged and sleeping Corker, and after a few minutes they had found his wad: $203.75 (worth about $5,600 in 2017 dollars). Only then had they realized that Anna — whose affair with Corker was of course widely suspected — would be the very first suspect hauled in for questioning when the robbery was discovered. Especially if the entire family left town 48 hours later, as they planned to do.

Richard Marple had an idea, though. They'd kill Corker and then set the building on fire.

Anna agreed, then grabbed an ax and aimed a very diffident and girlish blow at her unconscious lover. She missed, but the haft of the ax clipped his head and woke him up.

Now galvanized to action, Richard grabbed the ax and messily finished the job. But the attendant screaming and chopping sounds had spooked both Marples (and had been heard by passers-by), so instead of lighting the place on fire, they hastily arranged the corpse in a ritualistic-looking way, hoping to deflect attention onto the Masons, and legged it.

They still might have gotten away — but Julia, Richard's wife, got sick, delaying their planned exit long enough for the sheriff to develop suspicions and arrest mother and son on burglary and murder charges.

Hess said Richard Marple also told him that he'd killed before, and with an ax too. In 1879, he said, he and three other men had murdered an old lady, a Mrs. Hagar, in Oregon City; they had heard she'd come into considerable money. Mrs. Hagar had turned out to be a savage fighter, and nearly turned the tables on them; but eventually Marple had gotten her with the ax. He showed Hess a ring that he said he'd taken from her.

He also told Hess that he and three other men had killed a French woman in Portland, and that they had gotten quite a bit of money from her. This may have been Emma Merlotin, a French-born courtesan whose brutal ax murder in 1885 in her luxurious "crib" had shocked the city and led to a crackdown on brothels there.

So: was it all true? Jailhouse confessions are notoriously unreliable; it might have been a play by Hess to get out early, or possibly the notoriously cold-blooded Marple just wanted to put a little posthumous scare into the people of Lafayette.

In any case, the people of the town believed it, and likely felt less conflicted about his bungled execution after hearing it.

After the execution, Julia Marple, Richard's wife, moved back to the Corvallis area; less than nine months after the execution, she was remarried and moving on with her life. Anna, his "gypsy" mother, moved to Jackson County and eked out a living on her late husband's military pension; she died at the age of 94.

Sources and Works Cited:
- Necktie Parties: Legal Executions in Oregon 1851-1905, *a book by Diane L. Goeres-Gardner published in 2005 by Caxton Press.*

SHOTGUN EMMA.

From around 1875 to about 1915, the riverfront part of Clatsop County (outside Astoria) was more populated than it is today. The gillnet fishing fleet plied the big waters of the river, hauling in tons of salmon, and the blue-water sailing ships of the grain fleet daily poured in and out of Astoria's ports. Many of the locals who worked as fishermen and net menders preferred to live away from Astoria proper — at the time the town had a reputation, which it sometimes well deserved, as a nest of shanghaiers. When times got really tough in the blue-water fleet, the "boarding masters" had been known to straight-up kidnap people off the streets.

So the net menders and fishermen and sailmakers and chandlers who didn't absolutely have to be in Astoria to ply their trades would row or sail up the great lake-like expanse of the Columbia a few miles, and make their homes in one of the little villages on the riverbank — villages with no roads, whose only connection with the outside world was the river.

Most of these villages are long gone now, all traces having decayed in the relentless dampness of the local climate over the past 100 years. Many of them exist today only as names mentioned in the *Daily Astorian*; you won't even find some of them in *Oregon Geographic Names*, the three-inch-thick reference tome published by the Oregon Historical Society. We don't even know, today, exactly where many of them were.

One such village was called Manhattan, and it was probably a mile or two downstream from Clifton. And it was, in 1887, the scene of a shooting that was unusual in that it was done by a 14-year-old girl.

Here's the story — as much of it as we know:

The Henry and Bertha Frishkorn family had rented a large house in Manhattan. With them lived their two daughters, 14-year-old Emma and 22-year-old Minnie; and two boarders, Norwegian net menders Peter Gunderson, 32, and Julius Udbye, 43.

According to the *Daily Astorian*, the five of them seemed to have worked out an arrangement by which Gunderson and Udbye paid the rent, and the Frishkorn family supplied all the meals. This apparently worked OK, until Gunderson and Udbye started courting Emma and Minnie. Both of them — but Gunderson most especially — seemed to have gotten the idea that the girls' hands in marriage were part of the deal: We pay the rent, and you supply meals — oh yeah, and wives.

Matters came to a head on Jan. 11, when Gunderson got Minnie alone and asked her to marry him. She turned him down.

"He asked her why," the *Daily Astorian* recounted, several days later. "She said she had been told he was cruel, and that he already had a wife and children. He denied it, and asked her who said so; was it her father? She finally told him it was her mother that had warned her."

Gunderson went to bed angry, and the next morning, "he was very abusive to the old folks."

Two days later, the girls were invited to a dance at a neighbor's house — the neighbors, a family called Thompson, lived on one of the islands in the river — and both girls left the house and paddled off to the Thompsons' house.

As soon as they were gone, Gunderson and Udbye turned on the Frishkorns and basically drove them from the house. The two of them fled to the river, climbed into their boat, and rowed to the Thompsons' house for help.

The next evening, with a group of neighbors to protect them, the elder Frishkorns returned to the house to retrieve their things. One of the neighbors rowed ahead to try to smooth the way, telling Gunderson that the "old folks" would be there soon, and just wanted to collect their clothes and personal belongings and leave. Gunderson said that would be fine, and that there would be no trouble.

When the party arrived, Udbye was sitting in a corner playing an accordion and Gunderson was standing by the windows watching them approach. When they entered the house, he shouted, "Who brought all these sons of bitches here?"

"These men will stay here until I get my clothes," Bertha Frishkorn told him.

"Where is my whore?" Gunderson shouted back — meaning, presumably, Minnie. "I am the boss here and will show you. Get out from here!"*

He then picked up a big knife off the table and raised it, yelling for everyone to get the hell out. Udbye put his accordion down and slipped upstairs, returning with a heavy coat draped over his arm.

> **KILLED BY A YOUNG GIRL.**
>
> **Fatal Ending of a Row at Manhattan.**
>
> **Peter Gunderson Shot by Emma Frishkorn Last Friday Evening.**
>
> Coroner J. C. Ross got a telegram from Clifton yesterday morning that an inquest was needed on the body of a man killed near there the night before. Sheriff W. G. Ross got another dispatch about the same time, as follows: "Two men laid in wait for us in our house. We shot one and the other got away. Can you come and arrest him, or have we to make complaint first? Henry Frish-

The newspaper coverage in the Jan. 16, 1887, edition of the Daily Astorian after the shooting in Manhattan several days earlier. (Image: Daily Astorian)

Meanwhile, Minnie, the 22-year-old whom Gunderson had proposed to two days earlier, went to the table to try to calm him down. But instead, once Udbye had reappeared, he gave him what appeared to be a prearranged signal. The arm with the overcoat came up, spat fire. The bullet, intended for Henry Frishkorn, missed. Meanwhile Gunderson was charging straight at Minnie with the knife.

Then a shotgun roared, deafening everyone. Pellets spattered the wall near Udbye's head, and the concussion blew out all the lights in the house except for one bulls-eye lantern.

The shotgun roared a second time, and the top of Gunderson's head flew off and he collapsed, literally dead before he hit the floor. The bulls-eye lantern went out, plunging the house into darkness.

It turned out that while all the adults had been shouting and threatening each other, 14-year-old Emma had slipped into the closet where the shotgun was kept, and quietly loaded it. When Udbye fired at her father, she shot at

---

* *In the original newspaper article, the word "bitches" was redacted and replaced with a long dash. The word "whore," however, was printed intact.*

him, but missed because her mother was standing nearby and she didn't want to pepper the old woman with stray pellets. Then, Gunderson having gotten dangerously close to Minnie with that knife and clearly intending to use it when he got to her, she let him have the other barrel.

The shotgunning, and the subsequent darkness, put an immediate damper on the growing riot. All parties to the conflict separated for the night. Emma, pale and shaking, had already fled to the boat, and she and the rest of her family retreated to the Thompsons' house.

The next day, Henry Frishkorn paddled to the nearby town of Clifton to notify the sheriff of what had happened, and everyone came to Astoria on the sternwheeler *Favorite* so that the sheriff's investigation was held. Emma, not surprisingly, was held to have acted in self-defense; but Udbye drew a one-year prison sentence for assault with a dangerous weapon.

As with so many stories of this kind, there are some unanswered questions here. Chief among those is, why did the Frishkorns come to retrieve their personal effects in the dark of night rather than waiting for morning? And the text of Henry Frishkorn's telegram to the sheriff has a distinctly disingenuous sound to it. "Two men laid in wait for us in our house," he telegraphed from the nearby town of Clifton. "We shot one, and the other got away."

"Laid in wait" . . . playing an accordion?

The real story is probably that this was an old-fashioned group fistfight that got out of hand — that the Frishkorns, reinforced with a large posse of supportive neighbors and perhaps braced with a drink or two, came that night to avenge the insults of Gunderson and Udbye with an old-fashioned thrashing. But regardless of that, no one — especially after Gunderson pulled the knife and Udbye started shooting — could blame the frightened 14-year-old girl hiding in the closet for putting an end to it the way she did.

Sources and Works Cited:
- Murder, Morality and Madness: Women Criminals in Early Oregon, *a book by Diane L. Goeres-Gardner published in 2009 by Caxton Press;*
- The Daily Astorian *archives, January 1887.*

THE HOMICIDAL HOUSEWIFE
— and the —
BAD SEED.

Residents of Linn County probably had a bit of an edgy time over Thanksgiving in 1895. The county jail in Albany had played host, for the previous month and a half, to not one but two of the most notorious murderers in the history of the state.

Linn County's murder season kicked off in the tiny community of Jordan on Sept. 26, when mild-mannered housewife Emma Hannah took a hat, fake mustache and glasses, and a five-shot .32 revolver next door and assassinated a dangerously dishy neighbor, whom she suspected of being overly friendly with her husband.

Then, on Nov. 19, 18-year-old Lloyd Montgomery, black-sheep son of the Montgomery family of Brownsville, flew into a rage and murdered three people (including his parents) with his old man's Winchester hunting rifle.

It has to have been a holiday season to remember in Albany and the surrounding areas, as both of these cases came up for trial and sentencing right around Christmastime.

The Housewife.

Emma Hannah was an ordinary farm wife, or so she seemed. She'd started very late by 1800s standards — she was 29 when she married John, her husband, in 1875 — but she'd filled their farmhouse with four children over the following two decades.

But something seems to have happened in the course of the birth of her last daughter that caused her to be in chronic pain and unable to function sexually the way she felt a wife should. This apparently caused her to feel deeply insecure about her position vis-à-vis John. Her fears, which deepened to the point of outright paranoia, centered around Lottie Hiatt, a younger woman who'd divorced her first husband and now was estranged from her second and living with her mother and three-year-old son a mile or so from the Hannah house.

To Emma Hannah, the fact that Lottie was a divorcée meant she must be a woman of easy virtue, and therefore a threat to her marriage. Jealousy and paranoia simmered quietly inside her until, on the evening of Sept. 19, 1895, she decided she could bear no more. She borrowed her son's hat and her husband's overcoat, put on a fake mustache and glasses, pocketed her other son's five-shot .32 Smith & Wesson, and headed on over to Lottie's place.

When she got there, she knocked on the door. Lottie opened it, and the disguised Emma pushed her way into the kitchen, pulling a leather-bound book out of the pocket of the coat.

"I was wondering if you would be interested in buying a book?" the visitor said, pushing it into Lottie's hands.

"I'm sorry, but I'm really not interested," Lottie replied, handing the book back.

The stranger's response was to pull out the .32 and, muttering, "You should have bought the book," clobber Lottie over the head with it.

Lottie, a little stunned but not badly so, turned and ran. The stranger fired after her, nicking her neck. Lottie's mother, Elizabeth Holman, took advantage of the distraction to clock the strange "man" across the side of the head with a piece of firewood, sending the hat, glasses and mustache flying; the stranger turned and smashed the pistol across her face, sending her flying to the floor, momentarily unconscious.

Then Emma chased Lottie down, put the gun to her temple, pulled the trigger, and left the house.

No one had gotten a very good look at the killer, but Lottie's little boy, Lofa, testified that the killer had had long gray hair done up in a bun. Suspicion naturally fell upon Emma, whose enmity for Lottie was well known; and when the sheriff went to question her, her answers made it clear that although she was denying having killed Lottie, she was very, very glad she was now dead.

During the investigation, it came out that someone in the neighborhood had been leaving little notes on Emma's gate — notes claiming that John had been having an affair with Lottie and would soon be running away with her. No one ever figured out who was leaving them; but whoever it was probably was just making trouble for the sake of making trouble. If John ever did have an affair with Lottie, everyone involved was unusually discreet about it, for no evidence of such a thing was ever found.

The trial started on Nov. 25, and the outcome was never much in doubt. Emma was convicted of second-degree murder and sent to prison, where she was moved back and forth several times between the peniten-

This line drawing of Emma Hannah as she appeared in court was published in the Dec. 13, 1895, issue of the Salem Oregon Statesman. (Image: Statesman)

tiary and the insane asylum until her death in 1930.

By the time her trial had started, though, an even more heinous murder had pushed her case off the front pages of newspapers in Linn Country and across the state: the double-parricide of Lloyd Montgomery.

The Bad Seed.

Loyal "Lloyd" Montgomery was the oldest son of John and Elizabeth Montgomery, who owned a big prosperous farm near Brownsville. Lloyd was their oldest son, and he had just turned 18; he was a hulking, surly youth, very stubborn and with a bad temper. For the previous few years his smaller, frailer father had been afraid to discipline him, and consequently he'd developed an attitude of entitlement and a disinclination to consider the feelings of others. He was, in short, something of a bad seed.

There isn't really any way to know for sure what happened on that day, Nov. 19, when Lloyd shot his parents. Lloyd was a very good shot, and he left no survivors. But the most believable of his several confessions was that his father had slapped him across the face in the presence of a family friend, a mill owner named Daniel McKercher, and he had been so furious that he'd gone back in the house, retrieved his father's Winchester .40-86 express rifle, and shot his father through the head with it.

McKercher had then fled around the side of the house with Lloyd in hot pursuit, trying to take cover by dashing inside. Just as he gained the front steps, Lloyd got a clear shot, and McKercher's body landed with a crash in the middle of the sitting room floor.

This, of course, greatly alarmed Lloyd's mother, who ran for the back door screaming. Lloyd fired twice more: once through the middle of his mother's back, and once in the back of her head.

In the stillness that followed, Lloyd's thoughts naturally turned to the question of how he might avoid being hanged for the crime he had just committed. Laying the rifle down next to McKercher's body, he hustled off to the field that his brother Orville was plowing, hoping to establish an alibi.

This might have worked, but he met his younger sister and brothers on the way. The youngest boy asked him if he knew what all the shooting had been, and he claimed — in front of four witnesses — that he hadn't heard a thing.

Lloyd then followed the other kids back to the house, and when the youngest came out hollering that there was a dead body in the sitting room, Lloyd leaped on McKercher's horse, raced to an uncle's house, and reported breathlessly that someone had murdered his parents and McKercher.

MURDER, FAMILY STYLE.

This image of Loyal "Lloyd" Montgomery ran several times in the Portland Morning Oregonian during the time he was on trial for murdering his parents. (Image: Oregonian)

Suspicious eyes were on Lloyd immediately, and he was promptly arrested. He had lots to say about the murders over the following few months, but he never was able to explain how he'd known his parents were dead when the only body he supposedly knew was in the house was McKercher's.

Also, his reputation as a bad seed didn't help his cause much either. "Be sure and have a strong guard over him," his grandmother told the arresting officers, "or he will be back and murder a lot more of the family."

Probably the most interesting thing about Lloyd's case was his behavior in prison, and the public reaction to it. He first claimed McKercher had murdered his parents and he'd killed McKercher in self-defense — a claim that nearly got him lynched, as he'd seriously misjudged McKercher's popularity in the community. Then he confessed, retracted his confession, re-confessed, and told story after story. When some of his old childhood pals were arrested and put in the cell next to him he had a high old time with them, and seemed to have not a care in the world.

Meanwhile, of course, he had been convicted and sentenced to hang. Each time his story was in the paper, a picture of his strong, boyishly handsome face appeared, and his "fan club" grew. Governor William Lord was deluged with pleas from women around the state begging him to pardon the young rake.

Lord, though a kind-hearted fellow, didn't bite, and just before Candlemas — on Jan. 31, 1896 — Lloyd was hanged for the murder of his parents.

By then, of course, the 1895 holiday season had been over for several weeks. But (with apologies to Dolly Parton and Kenny Rogers) Lloyd Montgomery and Emma Hannah had certainly made this a Christmas to remember for Linn County.

Sources and Works Cited:
- Murder, Morality and Madness: Women Criminals in Early Oregon *and* Necktie Parties: Legal Executions in Oregon, *two books by Diane L. Goeres-Gardner pulished in 2009 and 2005 respectively by Caxton Press;*
- Portland Morning Oregonian *and* Albany Democrat *archives, September and December 1895.*

THE BOMBER.

Stapleton Airfield, Denver, Colorado; November 1, 1955. The killer is sitting with his wife and young son at a little airport coffee shop, chewing on his fingernails, trying to act natural.

No doubt he's going over the numbers again and again in his mind. According to the schedule, United Airlines Flight 629 was supposed to arrive at 6 p.m., and be on its way to Portland at 6:30. That's what the killer planned for when he stealthily stuffed a sack into his victim's suitcase after dropping her off at the terminal at around 5:30 p.m.

The sack was full of dynamite — 25 sticks of it, more than half a case — wired to a timer detonator. He'd set the timer for 90 minutes, so that it would go off 30 minutes into the flight. By that time, he calculated, it would be over some of the most rugged, mountainous country in Wyoming. Everyone would assume the plane had crashed into one of those mountains, and even if they got wise, they wouldn't be able to get to the wreck site until the late-spring thaw — leaving him with plenty of time to cash out his inheritance and collect the payouts from the various life insurance policies he'd taken out on poor dear Mother.

It's a reasonably well-thought-out plan. But the best-laid schemes o' mice an' men, and all that, right? This scheme now looks, to the killer, as if it's about to gang agley. Mother's plane was already 11 minutes late when it finally arrived, and now it's just sitting on the tarmac doing nothing as the minutes drag by.

The scheduled 6:30 departure time comes and goes. Nothing happens. Ten more minutes, then fifteen; Mother's suitcase will explode in less than a quarter of an hour, and still the plane just sits there. The killer sits there too, forcing down sips of coffee, trying to keep his mounting excitement and terror of discovery secret from his family.

As it turns out, one of the other passengers — President Eisenhower's deputy secretary of public health, Harold Sandstead, who's on his way to Oregon State University to give a speech — is running late. Sandstead's connecting flight from D.C. has been delayed, and he's a big enough VIP that they're holding the flight for him.

So there he sits, this killer, with his family, at that little airport coffee shop, trying to eat, occasionally hurrying to the bathroom to vomit his nerves as the clock ticks on and the doomed airliner waits on the tarmac: 6:48 . . . 6:49 . . . 6:50 . . . will the plane be delayed long enough for it to still be on the ground at 7 o'clock? If so, will the blast kill his mother, or will she survive . . . and figure out what he tried to do? Is he about to lose . . . everything?

What a sigh of relief he must have breathed when Flight 629 finally taxied into position and, at 6:52 p.m., launched itself into the night-black Colorado sky.

The airliner was supposed to explode over the mountains, but it never even made it out of sight of the airfield. At 7:03 p.m., the air traffic controllers in the tower saw two bright lights appear suddenly in the sky northwest of the airport, then fall toward the ground. When they reached the ground, the bottoms of the clouds were suddenly lit up with another bright flash. It sure looked like an explosion. Actually, it looked like two.

Controllers got on the air and called for welfare checks from all the aircraft in the area. Flight 629 did not respond.

Meanwhile, telephone calls were pouring into law enforcement agencies from witnesses who had seen it happen. And some of those witnesses were already suspicious. If the plane had exploded in flight, how could it explode again when it hit the ground?

All that night and the next day, local first responders worked to recover the bodies — all 44 of them. The next day, FBI agents arrived. At the time, identification wasn't required to get on an airplane, so the airline didn't know who everyone was; with its extensive file of fingerprints, the Bureau was able to help.

But the Bureau was also looking into the cause, and quickly figured out what had happened. There was explosive residue all over the remains of the

MURDER, FAMILY STYLE.

checked baggage, and the tail had been blown clean off the plane.

They looked at the luggage that was most heavily damaged in the blast; a 53-year-old businesswoman named Daisie E. King was on that list. They checked to see which of the passengers had air-crash insurance, purchased from vending machines in the airport; Daisie E. King was on that list too. Then they looked into her background, and quickly figured out who their number-one suspect would be: Ms. King's lean, squirrely 23-year-old son from a previous marriage, Jack Gilbert Graham.

Jack Gilbert Graham as he appeared just before he was executed for the murder of his mother and 43 other passengers on United Airlines Flight 629. (Image: FBI)

Jack Gilbert Graham was born in 1932, at the height of the Great Depression. When, five years later, his father died, Daisie was forced by poverty to lodge young Jack at an orphanage. And although Daisie remarried in 1941, to wealthy rancher John Earl King, she didn't bring Jack home from the orphanage.

Doubtless that's because new husband King refused to allow it. Whether it was because of abuse suffered in the orphanage, or just a natural baked-in sociopathy, Jack turned out to be the very prototype of a bad seed. He dropped out of school in the ninth grade and embarked on a career as a small-time hoodlum. His rap sheet soon grew to include bootlegging, gun possession, and a serious forgery case in which he stole checks from his employer, cashed

Daisie E. King smiles for a portrait several years before her murder (Image: Associated Press)

43 of them at $100 each, bought a convertible with the proceeds and went on the lam.

But by 1954, he seemed to be doing better. He was married, with two kids. Daisie, his mother, very much hoped he was ready to settle down; and after the death of her new husband, she found herself in a position to help him. So she opened a fast-food restaurant in Denver — a broasted-chicken joint called the Crown-A Drive-In — and set Jack up as manager.

This did not go especially well. Worse, being entrusted with high-value things seemed to have inspired Jack to get into insurance fraud. Soon there was a strange gas explosion at the new restaurant, from which Jack collected $1,200 in insurance money. Shortly thereafter, he turned in an insurance claim for his new 1955 Chevrolet pickup, which he said had stalled on the railroad track just in time to get hit by an oncoming locomotive. Nobody had been able to prove anything, but given Jack's track record, it had seemed funny.

And now he was in a fair way to collect a whole lot more insurance money, wasn't he?

Jack Graham, of course, denied everything when the FBI started asking questions. But after the Bureau searched his home and found bomb supplies there (along with another $37,500 in insurance policies taken out against his mother's life, on which he apparently intended to forge her signature), he confessed.

MURDER, FAMILY STYLE.

In preparation for the trial, federal authorities found, no doubt to their astonishment, that there was no law against blowing up an airliner. Of course, this oversight was quickly rectified; but that didn't help them with prosecuting Jack Graham. The most they could get him for was "sabotage during peacetime," which carried a maximum penalty of 10 years in prison.

Luckily, though, there *was* a law against murder — a state law, not a federal one. So the feds passed on their interstate case, freeing Jack Graham up for prosecution by the state of Colorado — which immediately got busy preparing to send Graham to the gas chamber.

This appears to have been the point at which Graham actually realized how much trouble he was in. Before that, as a *Life* magazine reporter noted, his attitude was sullenly optimistic. "He seems to feel he'll be able to get out," a jailer told the reporter at the time.

But when the case was turned over to the state district attorney, and the phrase "gas chamber" started getting bandied about, suddenly Graham was recanting his confession and exploring the possibility of an insanity plea.

Investigators carefully collected the wreckage of Flight 629 and arranged them in a Denver warehouse. The large piece in the foreground is the airliner's tail section, which was blown clean off the fuselage by the blast; the rudder has been removed so that the piece would fit through the warehouse door. (Image: FBI)

Psychiatrists evaluated him at the state hospital. To them, he said some very odd things; whether they were sincere, or represented him pretending to be crazy, is unclear. "(I) realize that there were 50 or 60 people carried on a DC-6," the FBI file quotes him saying, "but the number of people to be killed made no difference to me; it could have been a thousand. When their time comes, there is nothing they can do about it."

But then he followed up that cold-blooded morsel by adding that it was a great relief to tell the psychiatrist about it, because he had been "quite conscience-stricken."

Unimpressed, the doctors certified him as sane.

After that, the outcome of the trial was never really in doubt. Jack Graham was convicted on one count of first-degree murder on May 5, 1956; prosecutors wanted to reserve the other 43 victims' cases in case the verdict came in as "not guilty" or ended up being overturned on appeal. But this turned out not to be necessary. After the usual round of appeals, he was ushered into the gas chamber at the Colorado State Penitentiary on Jan. 11, 1957. In his final words, there by the gas-chamber door, he doubled down on what he'd told the doctors earlier.

"As far as feeling remorse for these people (the 43 other passengers), I don't," he said. "I can't help it. Everybody pays their way and takes their chances. That's just the way it goes."

And that was just the way it went for Graham as well, about 10 minutes later, at 8:08 p.m.

Sources and Works Cited:
- "Famous Cases: Jack Gilbert Graham," an article published June 12, 2007, at http://fbi.gov;
- "A Case of 44 Mid-Air Murders," an un-by-lined article published in the Nov. 28, 1955, issue of Life Magazine;
- "Justice Story: Son Plants Bomb in Mom's Suitcase . . .," an article by Mara Bovsun published in the May 4, 2013, issue of the Long Island Daily News;
- "Victims en route to varied locations," an article published in the Oct. 30, 2005, issue of the Denver Post.

THE CURSE OF GOLD.

One year after the Civil War ended, a double murder happened in Linn County. It started out grim enough, and the more details were revealed, the uglier it got. This was one of those stories that seem to peel away like an onion, layer by layer, or like one of those Russian nesting dolls. And even today, it's almost certain that the full story isn't known.

Here's how it got started:

On March 9, 1866, a resident of the Brownsville area named James Cunningham saddled up and paid a visit to his neighbors, Sidney and Barbara Presley Smith.

The Smiths were a particularly prosperous pioneer family. Sidney was 42, Barbara 30; the couple had four children, ranging in age from 16-year-old Rhoda Ann to baby Edward.

They were especially prosperous just then, because it was the height of the Idaho gold rush of the early 1860s, and Sidney had just returned from the gold fields — where he had been very successful.

Sidney had been able to go to the gold fields because his brother Thomas had been around, to stay behind and run the farm while he was gone. Thomas had lived on the farm, taking care of business, until Sidney's return, at which time he'd moved out to stay with a neighbor.

Upon his return, Sidney had hidden his gold on the farm — banks were few in 1860s Oregon, and those that did exist weren't always trustworthy.

So, with a successful farm and a big stash of cash, the extended Smith family seemed to have it made.

Which was just one of the reasons Cunningham was surprised to learn, from Thomas Smith, that Sydney had suddenly gone nuts, pulled a revolver, murdered his wife, then shot himself — all in front of Thomas and the kids.

The sheriff was called in, and took everyone's statements. The kids, understandably, were terrified — having just witnessed what they had.

But then one of the two older girls overcame her terror and asked the sheriff a simple question: "How could Papa kill Mama when he was dead already?"

The implication that she knew more about the sequence of the murders than she had previously said was not lost on the sheriff. He questioned all the kids again, closely and by themselves, and a new story emerged:

It turned out that Thomas and Sydney had had an argument earlier in the day. This had been an increasingly common thing since Sidney had returned from the gold fields, which was probably why Thomas had moved out of the house.

It was about the gold. Remember, Thomas had stayed behind to run the farm while Sidney went to the diggings, and Sidney had come back with a lot of gold. Thomas felt, not unreasonably, that some of that gold should belong to him, since without him it would not have been possible for Sidney to go dig it up; Sidney disagreed. It had become a source of some tension.

Today, that tension seemed to have come to a head. In the account given by the children, Thomas, snarling "This will not do me," stormed out of the house. And then, several minutes later, Rhoda Ann, sitting with her back to the door, was startled out of her chair by the roar of an indoor gunshot, and saw a dark spot appear on her father's forehead, right between the eyes. Sidney Smith fell forward, dead.

Thomas fired again, and this time the bullet sped past the baby's head and hit Barbara in the chest. Barbara, wounded badly but not fatally, carefully laid the baby on the floor and ran out of the house; Thomas followed, caught her up at the woodpile, dragged her into a smokehouse, and stabbed her to death.

Then he came back into the house and promised to kill all the kids if they didn't swear that their father had shot himself and killed their mother.

The terrified children did as instructed — but at least one, probably 10-year-old Leora, didn't fully understand what Thomas was asking them to do; hence the inconvenient (for Thomas) question about how Papa could have killed Mama when he was already dead.

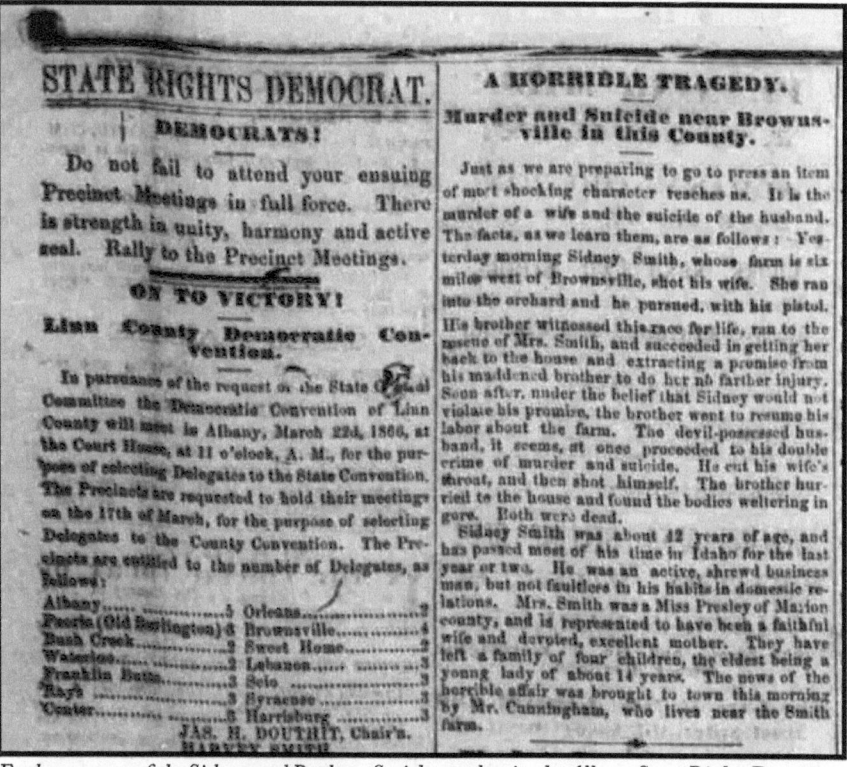

Early coverage of the Sidney and Barbara Smith murders in the Albany State Rights Democrat took Sidney's brother Thomas at his word. By the following week's issue, though, the story had changed. (Image: UO Libraries)

But by the time this question was being asked, the sheriff was already suspicious. He'd noticed an absence of powder burns around the hole in Sidney's forehead, which absolutely ruled out the suicide theory. He had already decided maybe Thomas ought to be questioned again.

Thomas was — and when he confessed, a third layer of this awful onion was exposed.

Thomas told the sheriff that the whole thing had come about because he had been having "an affair" with his oldest niece, Rhoda Ann, then 16. Rhoda Ann had, he said, "confessed the affair" to her mother, who had told Sydney about it shortly before the murder. Her father, furious, had staged a confrontation. Rhoda Ann had refused to cooperate, so Sydney had started beating her; and Thomas, in defense of his incestuous "lover," had murdered her father, after which he'd gone ahead and murdered mother Barbara too.

Obviously, this left a few questions unanswered. The peculiar savagery with which Thomas attacked Barbara — slashing her face and hands before fatally stabbing her in the neck — argued for more personal feeling than he was admitting to.

A modern reader can hardly fail to draw certain conclusions from Uncle Thomas's story, especially in Oregon in the aftermath of the Neil Goldschmidt case. It's clear that the "affair" was child molestation, started by Thomas after Sidney left for the gold fields and left the Smith women and children in his care.

(Knowing this, it's hard to avoid the suspicion that the reason for Thomas's savagery in cutting up Barbara with the knife was that he had tried to make a move on her, and been rejected.)

Then Sidney had returned, and learned what he'd done. Now both his victim's parents knew what he'd done . . . and what he was. So he'd murdered both of them so that they could not expose him. Then, when he'd been exposed anyway, he'd tried to paint poor Rhoda Ann as a "scarlet woman," a teenage temptress who had seduced him.

It's hard to say from the newspapers' accounts whether or not anyone bought this. It seems likely they did not. But, it would be nice to know what became of Rhoda Ann after all her family's dirty laundry was aired in the newspaper and she was publicly accused of seducing her uncle.

Regardless of whether people understood the true nature of the "affair," there was widespread agreement that Uncle Thomas needed to die, and the outcome of the trial was never in doubt. A hanging was scheduled for May 10, 1866.

On that very morning, the newspapers carried the word of the death of Thomas Smith's other brother, Calvin, who was still in the gold fields of Idaho. He had, apparently, committed suicide. Thomas was the only surviving Smith brother.

That changed a little later that day, just 62 days after the double murder — it's still a speed record in Oregon history. Then, nattily dressed in frock coat and leather boots, Thomas Smith dropped through the gallows trap door into eternity.

There is a postscript to this story, by the way. Sometime after the execution, the orphans were out playing on the Smith farm, and one of them found a leather bag with $25,000 in gold dust — obviously the proceeds from the gold prospecting trip that had taken Sidney away from his farm, his wife, and his daughter. In 1866, $25,000 was a tremendous fortune; but it's surely safe to say that if Sidney could have turned back time, knowing what it would cost him to acquire it, he would have turned that money down.

Sources and Works Cited:
- Necktie Parties: Legal Executions in Oregon 1851-1905, *a book by Diane L. Goeres-Gardner published in 2005 by Caxton Press;*
- Albany State Rights Democrat *archives, March 1866;*
- Portland Oregonian *archives, March and May 1866.*

PART IV:

THE UNWRITTEN LAW.

A century ago, the entire country was in the grip of a sort of lethal mania. You can sometimes catch references to it in old novels and stories by nonplussed Britons like P.G. Wodehouse — a sense that the U.S., unlike England or France or Germany, was not really a country of laws. Oh, laws were fine for things like train robbery and pickpocketing and claim jumping, but when it came to transgressions involving "honor," nothing but cold steel or hot lead would expiate the offense.

The concept was popularly known as "The Unwritten Law." It was, essentially, a social sanction for honor killings.

The idea was that when a man caught another man making time with his wife, or moving in on his sister, not only was he justified to seek out the perpetrator and murder him, he was morally obligated to do so. Of course, he was taking quite a risk in answering this call, since murder was punishable by hanging. He had to commit his deed openly with head held high and shoulders back, as one who has merely done his moral duty and trusts that "no jury in the land" would allow the law to punish him for doing so.

That's "his moral duty," not "his or her moral duty." This "right" was essentially for men only; nationwide, there were a few cases of women claiming the protection of The Unwritten Law after gunning down their husbands' mistresses, but with one or two special exceptions, they were not successful.

The case for The Unwritten Law is articulated beautifully in a sympathetic 1890 editorial in the Portland *Morning Oregonian*:

"There are certain gross offenses against persons, against the family relations, against woman, against virginity and domestic chastity, against reputation and the finer sense of moral shame, too impalpable to be measured by the coarse standards of formal law; too dependent upon circumstances to be defined by any general code; too profound and far-reaching in individual cases to be punished adequately by any penalties prescribed by the law for all cases alike," the editor wrote.

The editorial goes on to make the case that the very illegality of honor killings was the best guarantee that the "Unwritten Law" would not be abused.

"Herein lies the salvation of the principle from abuse," the writer gushed. "Written only in the moral sense of society and never given even the popular sanction of an open jury verdict, it has never been erected into a precedent or established as a permanent general rule. No homicide ever dares plead this principle in defense ...Whether he shall come out of the court room a criminal or a rightful executioner of justice depends upon no formal statute of general principle, but only upon the workings of an unconfessed sentiment in the human mind."

There is, of course, a flaw in this logic. Most murders aren't committed in cold blood. For a homicide who, for example, whips out a revolver and guns down a fellow poker player after being accused of cheating, the very next topic his mind turns to is how he might escape being hanged. For literally thousands of hot-blooded killers, The Unwritten Law offered a ray of hope: could they but convince a jury that they thought the deceased was surreptitiously getting busy with a female relative, they might walk free.

And so it was that, in the course of the 1890s, The Unwritten Law went from a long-shot throwing of oneself upon the mercy of a jury, to a habitual claim of "temporary insanity" for murderers who had killed in anything less than ice-cold blood. By 1897 or so it was beginning to become a serious problem in the Beaver State.

This is almost certainly why, just a few years after publishing that friendly editorial, the *Oregonian* had completely reversed its position on The Unwritten Law.

The UNWRITTEN LAW.

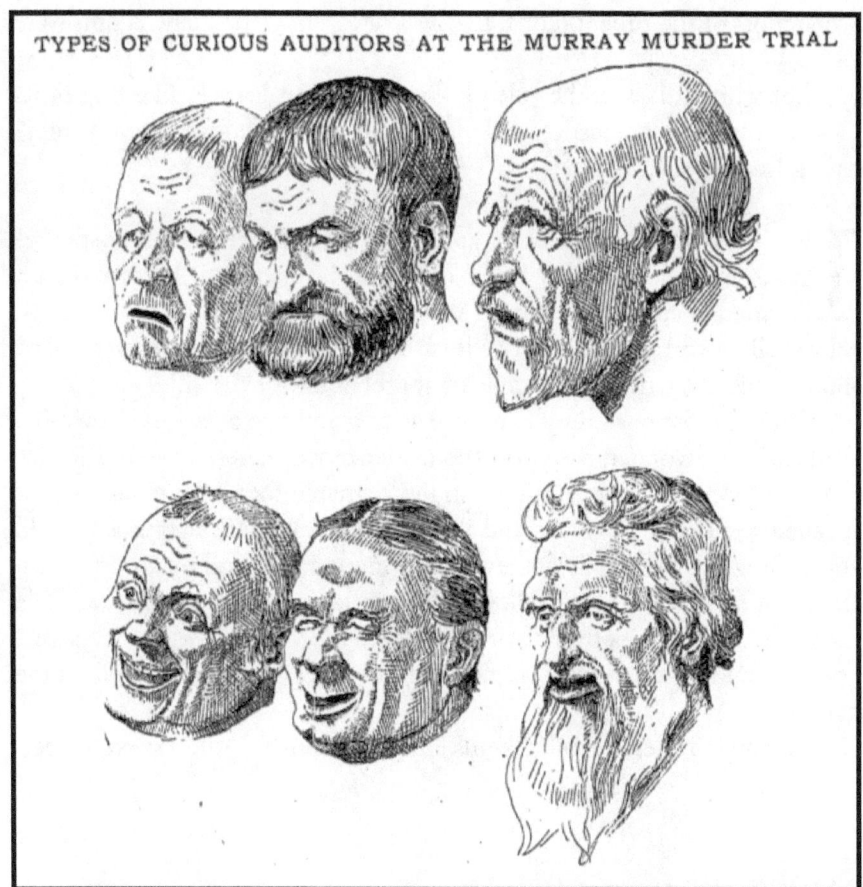

The Portland Morning Oregonian's sketch artist, at the 1906 trial of Orlando Murray for murdering the seducer of his sister, captured these images of some of the faces he saw in the crowd of very interested spectators. Public interest in and enthusiasm for the trials of "Unwritten Law" murderer/executioners was always very high. (Image: Oregonian)

"In America we make a bloody burlesque of justice by saying that any man may safely slay his fellow if he can make a jury believe that he believed his victim was criminally intimate with his family," the paper scoffed in 1898. "Of course, on this plea any malignant wretch might cunningly contrive suspicious circumstances and situations and do murder on his pretended conviction of guilt."

This implication was almost certainly accurate. But regardless of whether or not any murderer successfully dressed his crime up as an honor killing and got exonerated on that basis, the period from about 1896 to 1911 saw a stunning rise in the number of Unwritten Law killings. Sometimes, the killer's claim was of "temporary insanity"; sometimes they invoked the Unwritten Law directly. Most of the time, it worked — until the day came when most of the time it didn't. By the 1920s, "unwritten law" claims were rare.

But while it lasted, the rule of The Unwritten Law — like that of its close cousin, vigilante justice or "Judge Lynch" — made for some very interesting frontier history.

In the following pages, we're going to explore some of the most egregious examples of "Unwritten Law" cases in Oregon. They make for fascinating study. They can be shocking and tawdry, and they're almost universally awful — although at least one of them will leave even many modern readers with a grim smile of approbation for the killer's act.

But the most rewarding part of revisiting any one of these century-old scandals is to wonder, based on the evidence we see today — did justice miscarry? Was the jury so caught up in the mania for vigilante justice that it failed to notice the cracks and flaws in the defendant's argument? Did some Oregonians literally get away with murder, and end up covered with laurels by their enthusiastic fellow citizens celebrating them as brave, noble men who did not shirk from their terrible and bloody duty, when their actual crime should have earned them nothing but shame and a short walk to the gallows?

In many of these cases, it seems almost certain that the answer is yes.

THE "NAKED LADIES" CULT:

In the years after onetime Corvallis resident F. Edmund Creffield died, his legend got weirder and weirder. But then, it was pretty weird to start with, and it was not the kind of story that mellows with age.

By 1951, 45 years later, it reached something of a high-water mark in a story/article in *Startling Detective Magazine* headlined "Nemesis of the Nudist High Priest."

Pulp fans will instantly recognize the "Startling" part of "Startling Detective" as the telltale hallmark of a hard-boiled pulp magazine. And indeed, for the true fan of wild and shameless sensationalism, this article does not disappoint.

The article paints a fantastic picture of a lascivious con artist posing as a holy man, sharking up a flock of the town's comelier ladies and preying upon their weak, feminine minds with a diabolical message: "Clothing is vanity — let's all get naked and roll on the floor!"

It gets worse. The article goes on to relate how the "prophet" Creffield, calling himself "the new Joshua," convinced the lucky ladies that one of them was to be the new Mary, mother of the next Jesus, and that he himself would be standing in for the good Lord in making the necessary carnal arrangements so that could happen.

So, this thoroughly untrustworthy account continues, Creffield started a selection process in which the brainwashed beauties were, if you will,

Startling Detective magazine's two-page spread giving its own pruriently augmented version of

auditioned (naked, of course) behind closed doors, in a process that sometimes involved whips.

No, really.

The whips were a nifty addition to a yarn that was first set to paper by legendary Oregon writer Stewart Holbrook in 1941. Holbrook, delightful though he is to read, simply can't be trusted not to augment a story like this

the Bride of Christ Church story drew extra scandal-mongering power from some fanciful artwork.

with a made-up detail or two, and to sometimes pass on especially juicy rumors without examining them too closely. Holbrook's article was clearly the primary source for the Startling Detective story.

The real story of Creffield's cult, which came to be known as the Bride of Christ Church, is quite a bit more believable, and more nuanced. It certainly relies a lot less on the once-prominent myth that women are naturally gullible, stupid and (absent the steadying hand of a man) easily led into promiscuity and sin.

In other words, if you're female, you'll find the real story a lot less insulting. But the real story is, if anything, even more disturbing than the augmented ones, because it lacks the comforting feel of stereotype and fantasy. It's a story of good-hearted, well-meaning people who, in the name of goodness and holiness, opened the door to evil and chaos — the story, if you will, of how the saintly can become the tools of Satan.

The story starts in 1903, when Creffield, a thirty-ish native of Germany burning with religious fervor, left the Salvation Army because he thought they weren't sufficiently serious about holiness. He then settled in Corvallis and started preaching, building a flock of super-strict believers.

Creffield's followers were like the most hardcore in-tongues-speaking Pentecostalists you can imagine; at the same time, their extreme simplicity made the plain-dressing Quakers look like French royal courtiers by comparison. They prayed face down on the floor, occasionally rolling over in a sort of power-grovel; hence the pejorative term "holy roller," which may actually have started with this very group, in Oregon at least. Their church services were loud, sincere and disruptive to the neighbors, full of wailing and gnashing of teeth, and lasted for hours on end, dragging on into the night until the small hours of the morning.

Corvallis residents at first got along reasonably well with their new, freakishly hyper-holy neighbors. But things started going sour within a few months. The main reason was, Creffield taught that believers were to have nothing to do with unbelievers. That meant if a man or woman joined the group, he or she was to cut off contact with any family members who had not also joined: wives, husbands, children, parents — whatever.

Here's how that worked out in practice: A married couple would join the church. After a while, the husband would get tired of the extreme self-denial and subjugation to the will of Creffield, and start drifting off.

For the wife, though, self-denial and subjugation to the will of another was a less unfamiliar situation. In 1903, that was the most common vision of her role in marriage. So the restrictions of the church would bother her much less than they would bother him; she would see no reason to leave. He, however, would find it intolerable, and would stop going to services.

At some point, then, she would identify him as a non-believer and cut off all social contact with him. If there were children involved, they would either stay in the church and be cut off from their father, or leave the church and be abandoned by their mother. It was not a healthy dynamic, no matter how it played out.

Soon Creffield had a reputation for breaking up homes, and a flock consisting largely of women — women who actively avoided their "infidel" family members.

It also bothered the rest of the community that Creffield's cult members were living in a communal house, women and men together. Moreover, their "simple" clothing consisted of a plain cloth wrapper which, one source recounts, was similar to a bathrobe; the outsiders felt it was inadequate to protect female modesty, and in any case it looked entirely too easy to take off.

By itself, the communal living arrangement would have been bad enough. But Creffield's followers combined it with a mania for secrecy that all but invited other community members to fear the worst. Members vanished from their families' lives into a locked house with barred windows, supervised only by the cult leader and his cronies.

Edmund Creffield as he appeared in the early 1900s, when he was leading his flock in Corvallis. (Image: Portland Morning Oregonian)

Things got worse. Following yet another pattern that would become all too familiar to the world in later decades (think David Koresh and Jim Jones), the lack of contact with the outside world and the unstinting adoration of his flock started doing things to the mind of the cult's leader. His message got increasingly un-Biblical as he claimed he was receiving instructions directly from God Himself. He promoted himself from "the second Joshua" to "the second Elijah," which, if you know your Old Testament, is rather a big step up.

Finally, the men of Corvallis organized a group of vigilantes, calling themselves the White Caps, for the express purpose of ridding their town of Edmund Creffield. Getting the drop on him one night, they marched him and his sidekick (a man named Brooks), to the edge of town, stripped them naked, painted them with pine tar, covered them with feathers, and ordered them to get out of town and stay out.

Creffield responded by appearing the very next day at the courthouse in Linn County, his skin bright red from scrubbing and reeking of the turpentine used to remove the tar, and marrying one of his followers — Maud, a daughter of the Hurt family of highly respected Corvallis pioneers.

A few months later came the pivotal incident in our story — the incident that would doom Creffield and much of his flock: A man named Burgess Starr filed charges against Creffield for adultery, accusing Creffield of sleeping with his wife, Donna Starr (who was, by the way, his new wife's aunt).

Creffield promptly went into hiding. Weeks later he was found, naked and filthy, hiding in a coffin-size hole under a follower's home in Corvallis.

Hauled into court, Creffield unhesitatingly admitted guilt. It had been part of a vital, God-ordered purification ritual, he explained.

This development electrified Corvallis. All over the area, people started making the same connections. They thought about all these women, refusing the speak to their husbands and fathers, praying and rolling around in somebody's house or on the sect's encampment on a secluded island in the Willamette — under the supervision of an avowed adulterer who saw nothing wrong with having sex with someone else's wife. Could it be Donna Starr wasn't the only one? Perhaps "God" was ordering Creffield to "purify" other women too. Really, given the evidence, it would be hard to think otherwise.

It was probably at this time that the rumors got started about Creffield's alleged plan to impregnate a selected follower on behalf of God Almighty. It's possible that this rumor was true, but I've found no solid evidence to back it up and neither have Phillips and Gartner, who spent a lot more time looking than I did. There certainly were plenty of newspaper stories about it, though, at the time.

This also is almost certainly the point at which cult members' ostracized male family members started thinking seriously about assassination as a solution to the Creffield problem. They'd have some time to think about it, and to get ready; Creffield was, of course, found guilty, and was now on his way to prison.

The UNWRITTEN LAW.

F. Edmund Creffield in prison, to which he had been sent for a two-year sentence after being convicted of adultery with a follower in 1904. (Image: Oregon State Archives, penitentiary records)

The sentence was two years. As a practical matter, though, it might as well have been death. When Creffield emerged from prison after serving his term, it was a completely different world that waited for him outside.

By the time of his release, the newspaper stories about Creffield and his flock had gotten extraordinarily sloppy, and the many rumors swirling around the case got earnestly presented to the public as factual. Some of them, no doubt, were; others seem less likely. For instance, the Corvallis Times announced that Creffield was now representing himself as Jesus Christ,

Maude Hurt Creffield, the Corvallis woman the prophet married the day after being tarred and feathered, as she appeared around the time of Creffield's imprisonment. (Image: Portland Morning Oregonian)

having "risen from the dead" by emerging from the state pen; and that he had claimed to be personally responsible for the San Francisco earthquake. Either or both of these claims may be true, but some skepticism is definitely warranted.

But it's an incontrovertible fact that Creffield told the court his sex with Donna Starr was part of a God-ordered purification ritual. That's in the court records.

It still isn't known for sure if he thus "purified" any other women in his cult. But everybody outside his secretive little group instantly assumed he had.

And remember, the cult was rumored to believe in staying naked all the time. This rumor was almost certainly groundless and based on the perceived inadequacy (by Edwardian-era standards) of the "simple garment" believers wore, but people believed it.

To outsiders, Creffield's flock was looking more and more like a harem, and less and less like a congregation. The husbands of women in Creffield's flock now considered themselves not just cut off from marital relations, but cuckolded to boot. Older brothers assumed their little sisters had been sexually initiated. Men — at least three, probably more — started buying guns and making plans to use them.

The UNWRITTEN LAW.

The first attempt on Creffield's life happened in Yaquina City, near Newport. Creffield had returned to Corvallis just long enough to collect his scattered flock back together and lead them out of town. (According to the by-now-thoroughly-untrustable *Corvallis Times*, this was because he had prayed for God to destroy Corvallis with another earthquake like the one that had leveled San Francisco, and wanted to be out of town when He did.) As had Moses so many years before, he was going to lead his people into the wilderness — a patch of unimproved woodland near Waldport, on the coast — and God would take care of them there.

Among the women in Creffield's flock at the time he went to prison were Cora Hartley and her daughter Sophia. When Creffield was locked away, the two of them came home to Cora's husband, wealthy mine owner Louis Hartley, with whom they'd had nothing to do after joining the church — he was, after all, an unbeliever, and believers were not supposed to consort with the damned.

Louis obviously was not happy when Creffield, fresh from the slammer, strolled into town and called for his former flock to come follow him into

This .32-caliber Smith & Wesson pocket pistol is of the style and vintage used by Louis Hartley in his attempt to assassinate F. Edmund Creffield in Newport. Around the turn of the century, small and weak five-shot pocket revolvers like this one were very common and made by numerous gun manufacturers; many Americans carried one habitually, like we do cell phones today. (Image: smith-wessonforum.com)

the wilderness. Cora and Sophia answered the call immediately and started packing to go.

When the two of them left town on T. Edgenton Hogg's railroad line to Yaquina City and Newport to join their prophet by the sea, Louis secretively followed.

When he arrived in Yaquina City, Louis realized he'd lost their trail. (The two women had spotted him en route, and got off early at Toledo to shake him.) So he hopped a ferry to Newport and tried to find a judge who would order Creffield's arrest. None would.

So Hartley went to a sporting goods store instead. And with a brand-new .32-caliber revolver in his pocket, Hartley now started searching not for his family, but for Creffield.

Eventually, not finding his quarry in Newport, Hartley boarded the ferry and returned to Yaquina City. And as the ferry he was on was docking, he saw another ferry just getting ready to depart — and his wife and daughter were standing on the stern.

With Creffield.

Hartley leaped from his ferry and raced to the other just as it pulled away from the slip. He drew his revolver and opened fire on Creffield, who stood on the ferry facing him, a few yards away.

Five clicks rang out. The bullets Hartley had bought with the pistol were the wrong type for the gun; it probably was made to fire .32 Smith & Wesson Short rimfire cartridges, which are the same size and shape as .32 Colt Short centerfire shells — but obviously a rimfire pistol won't shoot centerfire cartridges.

Apparently when Hartley burst into the Newport sporting-goods store, gasping for breath and demanding to be sold a pistol, the store clerk, realizing he was probably being asked to furnish someone with a murder weapon, "accidentally" sold him the wrong bullets.

Although he put a good face on it at the time, and represented his deliverance as evidence that God was looking out for him, Creffield seems to have taken this lesson to heart. From then on he was a hard man to find, always on the move. He led his flock to the "wilderness" camp, but didn't stay long; when Hartley returned with a Winchester rifle to try again, he found his prey long gone.

Over the following few months, Creffield's itinerant lifestyle frustrated at least one other would-be assassin, and probably more.

But eventually Creffield ended up in Seattle. And it was in that city, at 7:10 a.m. on May 7, 1906, as he was walking down the street with Maud, that a fellow named George Mitchell walked up behind him with a pocket pistol and put a bullet into the back of his head.

The UNWRITTEN LAW.

The Salem Capital Journal also reported Esther Mitchell's killing of her brother in the railroad station after he was acquitted of murder charges for gunning down Creffield. (Image: Univ. of Oregon Libraries)

George Mitchell was Creffield's relative by marriage, and brother of two of Creffield's most devoted followers: Esther Mitchell and Donna Mitchell Starr. The latter, you'll remember, was the woman he was convicted of adulterously "purifying." The former, according to some highly questionable testimony offered at the subsequent trial, was supposedly Creffield's final nominee for "The New Mary," whom he supposedly (according to the rumors) planned to impregnate, as a sort of blasphemous avatar for God the Father, with the reincarnate Jesus.

Mitchell, after the police arrived, quietly handed over his pistol to them and was taken into custody. "I have only done my duty," he told the officers, according to police reports. "I came here to kill that man, as he ruined my two sisters, and I have completed my work."

The trial was something of a landmark for Seattle. There was widespread sympathy for Mitchell. For all practical purposes, his defense rested on The Unwritten Law, although it does not appear to have been specifically invoked in the proceedings.

The trial was rich with a kind of dark irony. Mitchell may have intended to address the ruination of his sister's reputation by killing Creffield; but in order to use that as a defense, his legal team had to sell it to the jury as a legitimate fear. To do that, they utterly trashed her reputation, calling up witnesses who repeated and augmented all the ugliest rumors that had coalesced around the case — that she'd been weighed in Creffield's balance and been found not to be wanting, and was destined to become his "New Mary," and would have been an unwed mother had her brave, noble brother not saved her from this "fate worse than death" with a pistol shot.

It may have been hard on Esther, but it worked. When the trial concluded, the jury found Mitchell not guilty — this in spite of the fact that he had admitted, in open court, to an action that fit the definition of "premeditated murder" with remarkable precision. Mitchell was a free man.

In finding this way, without invoking an insanity defense that would result in Mitchell spending some time in an asylum, the members of the jury no doubt thought they were doing him a favor. They were gravely mistaken.

A few days later, Mitchell met up with Esther in a railroad depot for what other family members hoped would be a reconciliation of sorts. Instead, it turned into another execution. Esther shot her older brother in the back of the head with a pocket pistol, in exactly the same way he'd gunned down Creffield.

In the aftermath of this shocker, the newspaper reporters really wanted Esther to tell them God had told her to avenge Creffield's death, or that somehow a religious frenzy had made her do it. Instead, she told them two things:

First, she said, she was doing exactly what her brother had done. The law was inadequate to the task of punishing a murderer, as evidenced by the fact that he'd been acquitted despite having admitted in court that he did it. This was pretty similar to George's courtroom defense that he'd had to shoot Creffield because the law wouldn't keep him away from his sisters.

Secondly, she pointed out that George had done exactly what he'd accused Creffield of doing: branded her as a fornicator. She insisted that Creffield had never had sex with her. By making the statement that he had killed Creffield because he'd "ruined" his sisters, and leaning so hard on the lascivious rumors to sell the story at trial, George had, in effect, "ruined" his sisters.

At her trial, Esther Mitchell refused to try to claim insanity. The state forced it on her anyway, and committed her to an asylum. A few years later, out of the asylum and staying at a family friend's place, she took a massive dose of strychnine and died — following the example of the widowed Maud Hurt Creffield, who'd killed herself in the same manner shortly after the trial.

The UNWRITTEN LAW.

Even water, in excessive quantities, is a deadly poison. Perhaps the same is true of what Creffield and his followers would call the Water of Life.

Sources and Works Cited:
- Murdering Holiness, *a book by Jim Phillips and Rosemary Gartner published in 2003 by the University of British Columbia Press;*
- Wildmen, Wobblies and Whistle Punks, *a book by Stewart Holbrook edited by Brian Booth, published in 1992 by Oregon State University Press;*
- "Nemesis of the Nudist High Priest," *an article by Lewis Thompson published in the March 1951 issue of* Startling Detective *magazine.*

THE LOVED DEAD.

On June 20, 1907, a retired military man named Charles Reynolds was hurrying home as fast as he could — with a .38-caliber revolver in his pocket.

Charles was an old U.S. Cavalry man in his 50s who had moved to Portland with his wife, Lulu, and his two grown children from a previous marriage. Charles had married Lulu in Colorado five years before, when she was just 25 years old.

In Portland, the Reynoldses were part owners of a bathhouse on the corner of Second and Washington, and lived in a large house about 15 blocks away that Lulu managed as a boardinghouse.

They'd moved to Portland from Milton-Freewater, where they'd owned and operated a hotel. Lulu, with a powerful interest in music and a dream to become a great songwriter someday, had met a music teacher and band leader there named George Herbert Hibbins — whose stage name was "Professor Herbert." Lulu and the "professor" had rather hit it off.

Professor Herbert was a tall, handsome man with a striking mustache and a reputation for moving on the ladies early and often. He was married to a musician from Seattle, but they were estranged and living apart. Shortly after the Reynolds family left Milton-Freewater for Portland, he'd moved to Walla Walla, where he was orchestra leader for the Keyler Grand Hotel band.

But before everyone left town, Professor Herbert tried his very hardest to initiate an affair with the pretty, young, musically oriented Lulu. He didn't get her into bed, not yet; but they did start writing letters to each other, very frequently. And Lulu was hiding them from Charles by picking them up directly from the General Delivery desk at the post office.

At first, these letters were nothing out of the ordinary for a teacher and his pupil: friendly talk, song lyrics, suggestions for making a particular melody better. But by early 1907 they must have been getting a little racier, because when Charles found one it was necessary for Lulu to lie to him about whom it came from. She told him it was from an old admirer from Colorado who didn't know she was married and therefore unavailable, and that she had set him straight. And he seems to have accepted this — at the time.

But by spring, Professor Herbert's letters had gotten positively torrid, and Lulu's replies not much less so.

Although the Portland Morning Oregonian's editor was initially supportive of "The Unwritten Law," by the time the Reynolds case came up the paper had gotten much more skeptical, as illustrated by this cartoon published during the trial. (Image: Morning Oregonian)

The UNWRITTEN LAW.

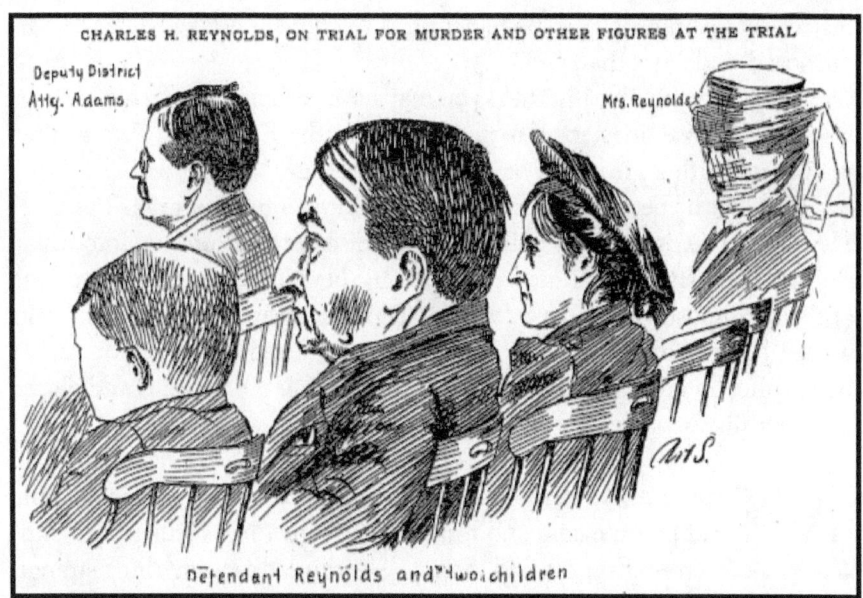

A drawing of the Reynolds family in court during Charles Reynolds' murder trial. Reynolds sits flanked by his 16-year-old son John and his 19-year-old daughter Etta; their stepmother Lulu, heavily veiled and apparently weeping (as she was throughout most of the trial), sits some distance away. (Image: Portland Morning Oregonian)

Meanwhile, Professor Herbert had been making plans. He had bought a small farm near San Diego, upon which he proposed to build for his Lulu a honeymoon home. Now he planned to come to Portland so that, in person, he could convince her to elope thither with him. The two of them would divorce their respective spouses, move to San Diego, and live a dreamy life of peace, harmony, music and marital bliss. What could go wrong?

Professor Herbert launched his campaign by sending Lulu a letter in which he claimed his wife had run off to New York with, of all people, Larry Sullivan — the ex-prizefighter who had been Portland's top-dog shanghai boardinghouse operator a couple years before. Now, he told her, was the time for her to divorce her husband and run away to San Diego with him. And he would be moving to Portland immediately to help guide her through this out-with-the-old-and-in-with-the-new scheme.

Lulu promised to ask for the divorce, but begged him not to come to Portland. The fact was, Lulu was much less serious about taking their affair to the next level than he was. It was one thing to exchange torrid and steamy letters with a romantic man who lived far away; it was quite another to actually burn all one's bridges and run away with him.

She tried to put him off. But he would not be deterred. He pointed out to her that, in several of her letters to him, she had declared herself to be his; as, that being the case, he had a right to come and take her, and so he purposed to do just that.

She was wise to be afraid. As you may have gathered, Professor Herbert was one of those "masterful" men with whom the Edwardian Age seemed to abound, with a great deal of self-confidence and force of will.

Making the best of the situation, Lulu found a nice room for Professor Herbert to rent, in a nearby building with a discreet side entrance into which she could sneak to spend time with him while her husband was away working at the bathhouse. She started regularly slipping away to see him. There he wooed her ardently and shamelessly, and she started to come around. He bought her an engagement ring worth well over $100, kissed it and placed it on her finger.

Meanwhile, Charles was growing increasingly suspicious. Lulu had become cold and distant. And when he asked his two children — Etta, 19, and John, 16 — if they'd seen anything strange, John told of a strange man who was visiting regularly while Charles was away. He'd actually seen Lulu with her arms around that strange man's neck, kissing him.

Then, about two weeks into June, Lulu finally worked up the courage to ask for a divorce. Charles, greatly alarmed, launched a campaign to win her back. Nothing seemed to be working. Finally, he took her up to the Council Crest Amusement Park for a day of fun ... and interrogation.

"He tried to treat me kindly, and asked for one of his old-time kisses," Lulu later testified later, in court. "Then when Mr. Reynolds continued to question me I got angry and threatened to go home. Then he noticed the ring. He asked where I got it. I told him, because I was angry, that maybe he would know some day."

Subtlety was not, it seems, one of Lulu's strong points — a fact that became even more clear a day or two later, when Charles noticed a strange picture on Lulu's bureau — a picture that looked a lot like a certain music teacher he'd met once or twice back in Milton-Freewater.

It all came to a head on a Wednesday afternoon, when Charles called Lulu on the telephone to ask her to come down to the bathhouse and she refused to come.

But then, as he was arguing with her, Charles heard over the telephone line the faint but distinctive sound of a man's voice in the background.

"Don't talk to him any more, sweetheart," the voice said.

Charles said not another word. Onto the hook went the telephone receiver, and out the door went Charles, his right hand wrapped tight around the butt of his .38.

It takes some time for a fifty-something man to run 15 blocks up hill, so Professor Herbert certainly had plenty of time in which to stage a strategic retreat. But it doesn't seem to have occurred to him. He and Lulu continued their leisurely preparations for a stroll in the park, and just as they were about to step out, the master of the house arrived, gun in hand.

"I'm onto you," Charles shouted at Professor Herbert, and opened up on him. Three shots; three hits. Charles was good with a pistol.

Professor Herbert ran down the street to a drugstore, where he was put in a bed and tended to; but one of Charles' bullets had cut through his intestines. In 1907, that meant guaranteed sepsis. By 1 a.m., he was dead.

Charles was utterly unrepentant when the police arrived and arrested him. Assuming a "dramatic attitude," as the Oregonian's reporter put it, and pointing to a photograph of himself in the uniform of an 1870s U.S. Cavalry scout, he declaimed, "Do you see that picture there? I was with General Custer for a long time as a scout, and do

> **BETRAYED BY KISS ON LIPS OF DEAD**
>
> Mrs. C. H. Reynolds Reveals Guilty Secret in Presence of Lover's Corpse.
>
> **MAKES FULL CONFESSION**
>
> Tells Coroner's Jury Every Detail of Her Intrigue With Professor George H. Herbert, Whom Her Husband Killed.
>
> Lulu M. Reynolds, wife of C. H. Reynolds, the slayer of Professor George H. Herbert, betrayed herself by a kiss Thursday evening when she viewed the corpse of the musician who was shot and fatally wounded at her home Wednesday. Unable to conceal the love she bore Herbert, she cast herself upon his lifeless body and kissed his cold lips passionately. Realizing

The headline in the Portland Morning Oregonian on June 22, 1907, announcing the dramatic events that ensued after Lulu saw the lifeless body of her lover in the coroner's office. (Image: Portland Morning Oregonian)

you think that now, when my home was in danger from a despoiler, I would show the white feather? I will stand by my home."

But, Lulu claimed, there'd been no danger and no despoiler, just an innocent musician collaborating with an equally innocent wife to write a piece of music — a wife whose good name he himself had despoiled by assuming, in his jealous rage, that she was an adulteress. Professor Herbert, with his last dying breaths, concurred. And authorities were disposed to believe them.

Until, that is, Lulu was asked to come to the coroner's office to identify the body.

Now, the Portland *Morning Oregonian* was one of the most prestigious newspapers in the West, and over the years its readers have been plied with the fruits of the finest pens in the world. But frankly, none of them have ever been able to offer a single morsel that matches the un-by-lined account of Lulu Reynolds' reaction to seeing the body of her dead lover, lying there on that cold mortuary slab:

"Unable to conceal the love she bore Herbert, she cast herself upon his lifeless body and kissed his cold lips passionately," the article recounts. "Realizing then that she had laid bare the secret of the tragedy, she made a complete confession before a Coroner's jury, denying the ante-mortem statement of Herbert, who had lied with his last breath to shield her name."

The ensuing murder trial held Portland enraptured. Lulu's love letters were published in the newspaper for all to see. She spent much of the trial with her head down, audible sobs coming from behind her heavy veil.

Charles' defense was distinctly sketchy — as his statement on the day of the killing indicates, he was relying almost entirely on the Unwritten Law for exoneration.

And he was not disappointed. The jury — all men, of course — took just half an hour to declare Charles not guilty.

Charles, asked what his plans were, said he still loved Lulu and intended to stay married to her. And, so far as I've been able to learn, he did. The couple moved to Hawaii shortly after the trial, doubtless feeling the need for a fresh start somewhere where everyone in the community hadn't been let in on their most intimate secrets.

Sources and Works Cited:
- Murder and Mayhem in Portland Oregon, *a book by J.D. Chandler, published in 2013 by The History Press;*
- Portland Morning Oregonian *archives, June through September 1907.*

THE FAMILY CIRCUS.

Early in November 1906, 21-year-old Orlando Murray went to pay a call on a 22-year-old acquaintance named Lincoln C. Whitney.
The main subject of their conversation was to be Murray's 16-year-old sister, Mary. Secondary topics for the two men's tete-a-tete included wedding bells and a baby shower — preferably, but not necessarily, in that order — and, last but not least, a .38-caliber revolver.

The conversation did not go well.

Lincoln Whitney had met Mary Murray when she'd traveled from her Portland home to Hubbard, where Whitney lived, to work in the hop fields for a week. Whitney had, Orlando Murray said (and, later, testified), sweet-talked the cute young out-of-towner into bed with fair promises of marriage, then disappeared as thoroughly as he could. Meanwhile, several weeks after their brief liaison, Mary discovered that Lincoln's disappearance had left her in a decidedly awkward position — or, at least, a position that would become decidedly awkward in nine months.

"My sister told my father that she was threatened with disgrace unless Whitney could be induced to make good his promise and marry her," Orlando Murray told a *Morning Oregonian* reporter. "My father and Mary went to Hubbard. Father talked it over with the elder Whitney and then called the young man himself. Whitney laughed in my father's face and said he would not marry my sister. Mrs. Whitney then came out, called my sister a vile name and insulted my father."

The younger Mr. Murray said that when he learned about the situation the following week, he decided to settle the matter one way or another. So, once he tracked Whitney down, he gave his best shot at persuading the young Lothario to, as the saying goes, make an honest woman of the maiden he had seduced. This Whitney steadfastly refused to do. Murray said he pleaded with him, appealed to his moral sense, to no avail. He tried offering him money — that didn't work either.

So he pulled the .38 and offered him lead.

Not even then would Whitney agree to marry the girl, Murray claimed. So Murray let him have it. Three shots, all lethal hits.

Then Murray hurried to the sheriff's office and turned himself in. And the next morning, newspaper readers across the state read the details with breathless avidity.

It was the opening act in yet another drama made possible by The Unwritten Law.

If Orlando Murray had hoped his conversation with Whitney would save his sister from public shame and humiliation, its outcome was rich with irony. Murray's subsequent murder trial bore a more than passing resemblance to a circus, with a main attraction (the trial); sideshows (including a fistfight involving the defense attorney and the county sheriff); and numerous clowns and jokers, both on the witness stand and in the crowd of onlookers. The whole sordid story — replete with insanity, sex, alcoholism, hysteria, and of course murder — was unpacked before capacity crowds of very interested spectators. Mary twice suffered hysterical breakdowns and had to be removed from the court.

Murray, of course, pleaded not guilty by reason of temporary insanity — the classic Unwritten Law plea. In entering it, his attorney claimed that "when he saw all chance and hope of Whitney's making right by marriage the wrong he had done the young woman, (Murray) was suffering from emotional insanity, and not responsible for his murderous act," the *Oregonian* reported.

The defense's moral case was bolstered by widespread accounts of Whitney having boasted of his "conquest" of Mary Murray. Its case for the insanity plea was bolstered by the bizarre sideshow spectacle of Orlando Murray's aged mother testifying that insanity ran in Murray's family; her brother-in-law, she told the riveted onlookers, "died a maniac at Salem, while another brother served a term in the Salem asylum," the newspaper reported. She further testified that Murray's father (who was in court, although the newspaper never names him) was compelled to give up his medical practice three years earlier because of "mental incapacity, brought on by excessive use of alcoholic stimulants."

The UNWRITTEN LAW.

Courtroom sketches of accused murderer Orlando Murray and his father. (Image: Oregonian)

Perhaps it's not much to be wondered at that Lincoln Whitney didn't want to marry into the Murray clan.

Others, however, did. Murray's attorney's office was soon flooded with marriage proposals for Mary, from all over the state — most of them probably coming from lonely bachelors working in logging camps. It's not clear whether any of these offers were actually passed on to their object of long-distance affection, though.

As the case continued, the two opposing attorneys fell into some eyebrow-raising interpersonal acrimony. The fireworks seem to have started when Murray's attorney, John F. Logan, used his opponent, W.T. Vaughn, as a case study in personal disreputability.

"To give point to his contentions, Mr. Logan suggested that Mr. Vaughn might possess an excellent character, but that a considerable interval would elapse between the date of his death and the hour when people would be saying good things about him," the newspaper recounted.

This poke drew a rebuke from the judge, but the pugnacious Mr. Logan doesn't seem to have taken the hint, for on the last day of the trial Logan punched one of Whitney's relatives in the ante-room. In the ensuing scuffle, a wild punch landed on the chin of the Multnomah County Sheriff, who was helping to restrain the would-be combatants.

From the perspective of the scandal-hungry newspaper readers of Portland, it was over all too soon. When the verdict came in, it was an open-and-shut victory for The Unwritten Law: Not guilty.

The crowd in the courtroom was overjoyed. "Thank God for it!" quavered an old woman from the front row of the gallery. Spectators rushed to congratulate Murray, who was clearly the hero of the hour — the righteous avenger and defender of his sister's honor.

But even the *Oregonian* reporter, who was clearly on Murray's side, seemed a little uncomfortable with his reaction to the verdict:

"He took his mother in his arms," the reporter recounts. "She commenced weeping hysterically, and he began laughing, both exhibiting the same emotion in a different way."

So, what really happened? As with most "unwritten law" cases, the trial generated far more heat than light; it's likely that we'll never know. Murray's account — that Whitney looked down the barrel of a .38 revolver and refused to say he'd marry Mary — is very improbable. It seems most likely that Murray's conversation with Whitney escalated from accusations to insults to threats of violence, and then Murray simply got so angry that he whipped out his revolver and started shooting.

Another subject we know nothing about: How did Mary feel about the

The UNWRITTEN LAW.

way things turned out? She spent most of the trial either in a hysterical breakdown, or recovering from one at home in bed while other members of her family laid out the most intimate and personal details of her nascent sex life (not to mention three generations of her family's dirty laundry) for all the world to gawk at and judge. Were her hysterics a reaction to that? Or was she, in part, grieving for the father her child would never know?

Questions like that are, of course, like a handful of gravel in the comforting balm of mob justice. No one in the audience really wanted to know. It was enough that Woman had been Wronged and Man had Avenged.

The day after the trial ended, Lincoln Whitney's bereaved father was also in the paper. The spectacle of seeing Orlando Murray hailed as a brave hero and champion of virtue for the act of murdering Whitney's own son was apparently too much for the old man. After going home from the courthouse, he'd suffered a heart attack and died.

Sources and Works Cited:
- Portland Morning Oregonian *archives, November and December 1906.*

THE MANHUNTER.

It was a little after 6 a.m. on June 14, 1907. Dawn was just brightening the decks of the passenger steamer *Alliance*, docked at the pier in Astoria, when John Bowlsby saw his prey step aboard. He fingered the big .44 revolver in his pocket and tried to stay out of sight, waiting for a chance to make his move.

His chance came almost immediately. The marked man was moving away from the crowd of people, and soon he stood in a spot where Bowlsby felt he could get in a good shot without risking hitting any bystanders. Carefully he steadied the big wheelgun against the side of a deckhouse — and pulled the trigger.

Bowlsby's target, a fellow North Bend man named Cleve Jennings, died in a hospital eight hours later. Meanwhile, with his head held high, a triumphant John Bowlsby quietly submitted to arrest and handed over his revolver.

Hard as it is for a modern person to believe, this cold-blooded assassination met with widespread approval. It was about as close to a pure example of "The Unwritten Law" in action as Oregon would ever see.

"It was the outcome of one man alienating the affections of another man's wife and was the result of a manhunt in which the hunter finally found his game," wrote the *Morning Oregonian's* Astoria correspondent the next day.

Bowlsby was, or at least considered himself to be, a wronged husband. The man he had stalked and gunned down was Cleve Jennings, a former co-worker of Bowlsby's wife; Jennings and Mrs. Bowlsby had both worked in a cheese factory in North Bend for a time. Bowlsby had grown suspicious of Jennings, and determined to run him out of town. This he apparently did; Jennings left North Bend sometime in early 1907.

Some time later, Mrs. Bowlsby (the newspaper never mentions her name) had journeyed to Astoria to visit her brothers; after her departure, Mr. Bowlsby had somehow heard a report that she had secretly met up with Jennings at a lodging house in Astoria prior to going to her brother's house. Immediately Bowlsby had journeyed north to pursue — and, of course, to avenge.

He found his wife easily enough; but Jennings, he learned, had traveled on to Portland. Bowlsby followed, but was unable to find his rival in Portland after several days' search, so he booked a ticket back home to North Bend — via Astoria — on the steamer *Alliance*.

It had been during the passenger loading at Astoria that Bowlsby had spotted his rival, who apparently was also journeying home to North Bend.

And that is how the two of them came to be on the deck of the *Alliance* that morning, taking part in a dramatic tableau of assassination and revenge.

From the very start, Bowlsby openly based his defense on The Unwritten Law. He told reporters he regretted nothing. "I believe I did no more than any other man would do under similar circumstances, as there appears to be no law to protect a man's home and family unless he does it himself," the unrepentant assassin told the *Oregonian's* correspondent the next day. "The only regret I have is the disgrace to my son and daughter. For myself I do not care."

He blamed the affair on Cleve Jennings' aged mother, who, he claimed, encouraged the affair, and on another "meddlesome old woman"; both of them, he said, "were constantly urging my wife to leave me."

The picture Bowlsby painted clearly resonated with the coroner's jury, which not only ruled the killing justified, but excoriated its victim at the same time.

"The evidence shows that the defendant and his wife had lived together in peace and happiness for a period of over 15 years until the serpent entered their household in the shape of Cleve Jennings and destroyed their home," the jurors wrote. "We are furthermore of the opinion, on account of the lack of statutes covering crimes of this character, that said Bowlsby was fully justified in shooting the said Jennings."

The district attorney nonetheless filed charges against Bowlsby. But one

BASE VERDICT ON UNWRITTEN LAW

Slayer of Despoiler of Home Acquitted.

WIFE ADMITS HER GUILT

Testimony Before Coroner's Jury Shows Home Ruined.

SHOOTS ENEMY ON A BOAT

After Hunting Several Days, Bowsley Fires Deliberately and Kills Cleve Jennings, Which Action Jury Says Was Justifiable.

ASTORIA, Or., June 19.—(Special.)—The Coroner's jury summoned to investigate the circumstances surrounding the death of Cleve Jennings, who was shot by J. H. Bowlsby on the steamer Alliance last Friday morning, returned a verdict this evening that is rather a remarkable document, in that it not only exonerates Bowlsby, but also "roasts" the deceased.

Bowlsby admitted the shooting, said he had been hunting for Jennings for several days, but asserted that he killed Jennings because the latter had been intimate with his (Bowlsby's) wife. Mrs. Bowlsby in her testimony admitted the intimacy and the Coroner's jury, consisting of J. N. Laws, J. Strauss, P. Lawler, A. L. Steele, E. A. Coe and A. C. Jeffers, placed its stamp of approval on Bowlsby's act by a verdict which reads as follows:

"We, the undersigned jurors, sworn to inquire into the cause of the death of Cleve Jennings, on oath do find: That said Cleve Jennings came to his death at Astoria, Clatsop County, Or., on June 14, 1907, at St. Mary's Hospital; that his death was caused from a gunshot wound in the body, inflicted by a weapon in the hands of J. H. Bowlsby. We further find that, after fully considering the evidence submitted to us, the shooting was justifiable, and therefore recommend that the defendant be released from custody.

Broke Up Happy Home.

"The evidence shows that the defendant and his wife had lived together in peace and happiness for a period of over 15 years and until the serpent entered their household in the shape of Cleve Jennings and destroyed their home. We are furthermore of the opinion, on account of the lack of statutes covering crimes of this character, that said Bowlsby was fully justified in shooting the said Jennings."

An information charging Bowlsby with the crime of murder is on file in the Justice Court and the defendant is confined in the County Jail awaiting a hearing, which Deputy District Attorney McCue says will be held as soon as he can summon the witnesses.

The headline in the Portland Morning Oregonian on June 20, 1907, announcing the coroner's jury verdict in the case of John Bowlsby's murder of Cleve Jennings. (Image: Portland Morning Oregonian)

gets the distinct impression that this was done as a courtesy, to secure for him a record-clearing acquittal and an official declaration of innocence. Certainly the outcome was never for a moment in doubt. Mrs. Bowlsby had confessed to having been intimate with Jennings, and although it's possible that she was lying to keep her husband out of prison, that seems fairly unlikely. To that jury in 1907, the case for acquittal seemed as clear and obvious as the case for conviction would be to a jury today.

The Unwritten Law was actually discussed by name in court during this case, until the judge interjected that there was no such thing as The Unwritten Law, and ordered the jury to give it no consideration in the verdict. Nevertheless, a rose by any other name is still a rose, and when the verdict came in after just 30 minutes of deliberation, it was a clear victory for The Unwritten Law: "Not Guilty on Account of Insanity."

But the headline the *Morning Oregonian* chose to apply to its final article on the Bowlsby-Jennings affair nicely sums up the growing ambivalence the newspaper was feeling about The Unwritten Law: "ANOTHER SLAYER ACQUITTED."

It was an ambivalence that would ripen into full-blown revolt later that same year, in an event involving a jealous wife-beater, a philandering policeman, a saloon and a gunfight. We'll talk about that case in the next chapter.

Sources and Works Cited:
- Portland Morning Oregonian *archives, June and October 1907.*

A CHRISTMAS CAROL.

When the story first hit the newspapers, just a few days before Christmas, it all seemed very clear and simple:

An Albina man got drunk and beat up his wife. Her brother went looking for him to teach him a lesson, and brought along a friend who happened to be a police officer. The wifebeater, tracked down and challenged to fight at a local saloon, came out shooting, and moments later the innocent, luckless policeman lay dying on the sidewalk as the wife-beating murderer fled into the night.

For newspaper readers on the morning of Dec. 19, 1907, it was like a Vaudeville stage tragedy come to life. There was a good guy — brave, valiant Joseph P. Sivener, on a mission to deliver a much-deserved thrashing to his no-good, wife-beating brother-in-law; a bad guy — Melville Bradley, the aforementioned brother-in-law, whose surly, shifty-eyed mugshot appeared next to the story in the paper; the fair damsel — poor, battered Mrs. Bradley; and an innocent victim: the poor policeman, who was just doing his job when sudden and undeserved death came and bore him away from his devastated wife and four tiny children.

But those newspaper readers would have just one day in which to savor that comfortingly familiar storyline. The very next day, the first of a series of revelations started peeling away layers that eventually revealed a drama that seemed to take every convention of the clean-cut crime-story genre and turn it inside out. When all was revealed to the increasingly appalled and jaded readers, there was not a single adult in the entire story that most Portlanders could respect or relate to in any way — except, perhaps, in some small way, the murderer.

But the greatest loser in the whole affair seems to have been Portland's formerly growing infatuation with "The Unwritten Law."

Here's the story police got on the night of the murder:

Melville Bradley had gotten into a fight with his wife, Kate, earlier in the day — a fight that ripened into "a beating administered to Mrs. Bradley by her husband in a fit of drunken jealousy," according to the *Morning Oregonian's* report.

After that, Bradley stormed off to a saloon, where he apparently had several more drinks. Meanwhile, Kate had gone to her brother, Joseph Sivener, and told him what had happened.

Sivener, as brothers are wont to do when such news reaches their ears, rolled up his sleeves, stuck out his chin and stalked off to the saloon, intending to serve his brother-in-law a few hand-crafted knuckle sandwiches along with a side order of free advice about how his sister should be treated.

A Portland policeman named John W. Gittings accompanied Sivener to the saloon, and stood on the sidewalk nearby as Sivener entered.

Once inside, Sivener soon found his man. "Come outside," he growled. "I want to see you."

"You do, do you?" Bradley shot back. "Well, I can't see you any too damned quick." And he followed his brother-in-law to the door.

Sivener wasted no time. As soon they were both out the door, he hauled off and punched Bradley in the face. Bradley's response was to pull a revolver out of his pocket and fire point-blank at Sivener. It was a clean miss, as was a second follow-up shot. Sivener turned and tried to flee, but tripped and fell into the mud by the street. There he lay, petrified with fear.

Meanwhile, Bradley had seen Gittings, and Gittings was probably already drawing his service revolver. Bradley turned his pistol on the policeman and fired his other four shots straight into the officer. Gittings managed to get off several shots of his own before collapsing to the sidewalk. None of Gittings' shots, apparently, touched Bradley.

Bradley immediately took to his heels. After a few moments, Sivener picked himself up out of the mud and went to see to Gittings, who was still alive — but barely.

"I'm afraid I'm done for," the fallen policeman said. "Send for a doctor at once. Here is my gun. There is only one shot left in it. Take it and get him if you can."

The UNWRITTEN LAW.

The mugshots of Officer John Gittings and his killer, Melville Bradley, as they appeared on the front page of the Portland Morning Oregonian on Dec. 19, 1907. (Image: Oregonian)

He then struggled to his feet, tottered a few steps, then collapsed into Sivener's arms and died.

Meanwhile, Bradley was running for home, where he got his hat and vanished. Authorities assumed he'd hopped a freight out of town. They angrily vowed to bend every possible effort to catching him.

The very next day, though, this nice, clean morality-play narrative was already starting to show a few spots of tarnish. First off, it soon became clear that Gittings was more than just some random beat cop sucked into someone else's domestic drama.

"There is plenty of evidence to show that there was very bad feeling existing between the two men," the *Oregonian* reported; "that Gittings was friendly with Mrs. Bradley; that Gittings was friendly to and in sympathy with the members of Mrs. Bradley's family, who were on bad terms with Bradley."

Just how friendly Gittings was with Bradley's family — and with one member in particular — became obvious at the policeman's funeral, held the following day. The funeral service was a fairly short one, and just as it was ending, a closed carriage raced up to the funeral home and three heavily-veiled women burst forth. It was Kate Bradley (the wife whose abuse at the hands of Melville Bradley had touched the whole thing off) with her sister, Aggie Vanders, and one other woman whom the reporter didn't identify.

"My God, are we too late?" sobbed Aggie Vanders noisily. Upon being told that they were, Kate Bradley asked where the interment would be held. Then the three ladies bounded back into the carriage and raced away.

The carriage caught up with the funeral procession, then passed it and raced on to the cemetery, where the three ladies installed themselves at the open grave to await the arrival of the casket. When it did come, they made a tremendous scene with noisy sobs and wails of anguish, as the dead policeman's widow stood at the head of the grave, ashen-faced and trembling, quietly weeping and obviously trying to ignore them. Remember, these intruders were her husband's murderer's wife and sister-in-law. They were clearly the last people poor Mrs. Gittings wanted to see.

If their arrival was unexpected, it shouldn't have been. The funeral director told the *Oregonian's* reporter that Vanders, in particular, had visited the funeral parlor twice before to view the body — the first time on the day after the murder, a Thursday, on which occasion she "cried over the body until requested to leave."

"Friday she called again," the article continues. "She threw herself across the casket, her sobs being audible throughout the building. After this scene she was not allowed to view the remains again."

The reporter then puts the pieces together — almost — with the next paragraph:

"Mrs. Vanders has long borne the bitter hatred of Mrs. Gittings," he wrote. "She lived next door to the Gittings shanty on Humboldt Street and Gittings spent much of his time in her company."

And if that weren't enough to clue Portlanders in on what was really going on, there was this small item, run as a sidebar to the main story:

"Last night it was learned that Mrs. Aggie Vanders ...demanded of the policeman's widow that she surrender certain papers, said to be in Gittings' pocketbook. The woman also asked for the dead man's watch and revolver .... Mrs. Gittings refused to give up the belongings."

The story was already starting to smell more than a little bit sordid.

For the average Oregon newspaper reader, this was the first inkling that something about Officer John Gittings' murder was not as it appeared.

By itself, the alleged affair wouldn't seem to change much. The facts, as Portlanders knew them, were still pretty black-and-white: Melville Bradley beat his wife, Kate; Kate's brother, Joseph Sivener, went looking for him to thrash him, and brought Gittings along; Bradley came up shooting and Gittings caught a bullet. The fact that Gittings was Kate Sivener's sister's boyfriend, rather than just some random innocent beat cop helping out a citizen, didn't really change much.

But it had a significant effect on Officer Gittings' posthumous reputation. It soon became clear that not only was Gittings married with three small children (and one more on the way), but that he neglected his family shockingly.

The *Oregonian's* reporter called the Gittings family manse "a deplorable little shack, cold, forbidding, leaky, un-paid-for."

"The wind whistles uncomfortably through the cracks where the boards fail to meet," he continued. "The shack stands three feet from the ground and

WOMEN INTRUDE AT GITTINGS FUNERAL

Wife of Murderer and Her Sister Stand Unabashed at Policeman's Tomb.

DREARY GRAVEYARD SCENE

Widow and Children of Dead Officer Huddle Shivering at One End of Coffin, While His Female Friends Sob at the Other.

WOMAN MAKES DEMANDS ON WIDOW.

Late last night it was learned that Mrs. Aggie Vanders, sister-in-law of the murderer of Patrolman Gittings and the woman who was an unwelcome visitor at the funeral yesterday, demanded of the policeman's widow that she surrender certain papers, said to be in Gittings' pocketbook. The woman also asked for the dead man's watch and revolver, putting her request to Mrs. H. C. Schellhorn, who is taking care of the prostrated widow. Mrs. Gittings refused to give up the belongings.

This headline and sidebar ran atop the Oregonian's follow-up article on Officer Gittings' funeral, the overall tone of which is perhaps best described as nonplussed. (Image: Oregonian)

LOVE, SEX *and* MURDER *in* OLD OREGON

This tear-jerker cartoon by Oregonian cartoonist Harry Murphy motivated a flood of Portland residents to contribute to the relief of Officer Gittings' widow and orphan children. (Image: Oregonian)

by way of a front stoop two earthen jars do service .... Gittings got $100 a month from the city, but his family did not get so much from Gittings. There is no evidence that they ever got anything. The widow is miserably clothed, the three little children actually look cold."

Gittings' brother officers now rose gallantly to the occasion, and started taking up a collection to take care of the widow and orphans.

"The sentiment seemed to be that whatever discreditable there might have been in the affair ... the widow and the children were innocent of it and eminently deserving of assistance," the *Oregonian* reported.

Under the cops' leadership, with the full moral support of the newspaper, and in the spirit of the Christmas season, the community rallied around poor Mrs. Gittings. Soon she and the kids were living in a fully paid-for, upgraded home, with a cow and chickens in the back to supply milk and eggs.

Time passed. There was no word on the murderer — a man for whom public animosity was already starting to die down. Meanwhile, his wife, whose beating had started the whole spectacle, had moved on with her life, as had her brother, Joseph Sivener. Both were back in the headlines just a few months later, both under rather unfortunate circumstances.

First, in March of 1908, Sivener was picked up by police and tossed in the city pokey. It seems he had acquired the habit of swindling small amounts of money by forging checks drawn on the accounts of East Side saloonkeepers and cashing them. In the grand scheme of things, it was a minor offense, but it didn't play well with the public's image of him as the righteous, avenging brother of the poor wronged wife, charging forth to call her wife-beating no-good husband to account.

Speaking of the poor wronged wife — well, perhaps it's best to just quote from the newspaper directly. This article hit the papers a little over a year after the killing:

"Mrs. Kate Kakarous, the wife of a Greek bartender and formerly the wife of Melville Bradley, the murderer of Policeman Gittings, was arrested last night as a streetwalker by Patrolman Stillwell, at the corner of Third and Everett streets."

Third and Everett, by the way, is right in the middle of the old North End — the rough-and-tumble waterfront district, down by the wharves and sailors' boardinghouses, brothels and shanghai joints, exactly where one would expect to find a prostitute on the prowl.

If anyone was surprised, he or she probably shouldn't have been. By this time, the avid newspaper readers of Portland had learned a few more details about the Gittings killing. For one thing, they'd learned that the party whom Bradley had suspected of being intimate with his wife (the pretext for the beating) was Gittings himself. This suggested a whole new theory of the crime — one in which Bradley, called out of the saloon by Sivener, saw Gittings waiting for him in uniform and wearing his service revolver. Gittings, as he would have known, was a crack shot. Thinking the whole thing a setup with Gittings the trigger man, he drew and emptied his revolver at him.

This theory, of course, doesn't quite square with the earlier impression that Gittings and Kate Bradley's sister, Aggie Vanders, who had made such a dramatic commotion over his corpse, were lovers. But by then, most Portlanders had concluded that everyone involved in the whole affair was some sort of dangerous looney. And there was such a dramatic flair in Aggie Vanders' grief; could it have been a put-on?

So, if you're keeping track — at this point in the story, every single character in our crime drama had been revealed to be some sort of unlovable freak. The Good Guy — Sivener, who went forth to avenge his sister's beating — turned out to be a petty swindler. The Damsel In Distress — Kate Bradley — turned out to also be a prostitute and bigamist. The Innocent Bystander Policeman turned out to be a serial philanderer, homewrecker and worst family man in the city, and to also have possibly been intending to murder Bradley.

And for anyone tempted to conclude that Bradley had been right to do as he did — beat his wife and murder her maybe-lover — there was the testimony of his brutality to his family to deny even that.

"Friends and neighbors of the Bradley family said that he not only abused his wife, but that his children, too, came in for a share of his cruelty," the *Oregonian* reported.

That last remark was delivered in the *Oregonian* article that announced, in July of 1909, that the fugitive murderer had at last been caught in Idaho and was on his way back to Portland for trial. It also suggested that Bradley would try to invoke the Unwritten Law at his trial, since the man he was accused of killing had been his wife's home-wrecking lover — or so he claimed to have supposed.

But it scarcely mattered any more. The story had utterly subverted the clean morality play that lay behind every Unwritten Law honor killing.

As for the final denouement of Bradley's case, I haven't been able to learn it. It wasn't in the paper. Toward the end, it was clear that people were weary of it and just wanted it all to go away.

There is one final chapter, though, in this sordid drama. The news was published in March of 1909 — just over a year after the murder. It seems Policeman Gittings' widow — whose first name is never mentioned — had plunged once more into desperate poverty.

"They have had nothing to eat but cornmeal and water for some time," the *Oregonian's* reporter noted. "At the time of Gittings' death, the police of Portland made a fund out of which was purchased a home, and private citizens and philanthropic people furnished the house, purchased a cow and chickens and sent provisions and wood.... The cow has since died, the children are too young to assist and the mother cannot leave them to secure employment."

Many a jaundiced eye was probably cocked at this assertion, since most Portlanders knew the oldest Gittings boy was now 10 — plenty old enough for babysitting duties. Also, not mentioned was the fact that the Police Officers' Social and Aid Society had been sending Mrs. Gittings monthly support payments of $11 each month — not a lot, but plenty enough to buy food other than cornmeal mush.

The community rallied around once again to relieve the need and succor the children, who were clearly getting the brunt of their mother's lack of overall competence.

Then the helpful community members did something that likely wasn't what Mrs. Gittings had in mind:

"As a result of investigations made into conditions existing in the family of J.W. Gittings ... steps have been taken to place the children in the Children's Home, and to send the mother either to the Home for Feeble-Minded Persons or to the County Poorhouse," the paper announced.

And so the whole affair ended, with a clear demonstration of a credible motive for Policeman Gittings' actions in neglecting his family.

But there did seem to be one clear take-away from the whole sordid mess: Life was just not simple enough for The Unwritten Law to be any kind of true justice.

It was a lesson that seems to have taken hold in Portland, for even as the honor killings continued elsewhere in the country, Oregon, after this, saw very few of them.

Sources and Works Cited:
- Portland Morning Oregonian *archives: December 1907, January 1908, February and March 1909 and July 1909.*

THE UNWRITTEN IN-LAW.

The Unwritten Law didn't come out of nowhere, of course. Although the widespread enthusiasm for it wouldn't appear until the mid-1890s, it was being used to justify homicide throughout the 1800s and even before — with a disturbing degree of success.

But in order to successfully claim the protection of the Unwritten Law, there were some requirements that a man had to meet. Those requirements constituted a fairly low bar; a fellow might be a wife-beater and/or a philanderer without worrying too much about ruining his chance of being acquitted after murdering his wife's boyfriend.

But he did have to make sure that the man he murdered was not his brother-in-law. And also, it was pretty important that he not be a bigamist who had abandoned a wife and several children back east to slink away to the West Coast and start a new family.

In early 1884, John W. Murray failed to clear both these bars, and in consequence, on Feb. 13, roughly a year later, he found himself standing on the gallows scaffold ready to answer for his crime.

The trouble started on Jan. 5, 1884, at the Foresters' Ball, held at the Masonic Center in Portland. Murray, dressed to the nines, arrived and spotted his estranged wife, Annie, there with her brother, Alfred Yenke.

John and Annie had been married for four years, and had a three-year-old daughter. But the marriage had been stormy, and three weeks earlier — just

This panoramic, from an 1888 edition of The West Shore magazine, shows the city of Portland as i t

before Christmas — Annie had taken the baby and moved back in with her parents. A divorce, on the grounds of excessive cruelty, was probably in the offing.

John seemed to be in the mood to smooth things over now. He approached Annie and pleasantly asked if she'd like to dance.

She turned him down cold. "I do not think we should be seen together," she told him. "I would prefer not to associate with you any longer."

John was instantly furious. "I'm going to watch you," he raged. "If you go home with anyone I'll have you both arrested."

Annie turned her back on him, leaving him still further incensed. They didn't speak again that night; and at around midnight, when John returned to the boardinghouse where he now lived alone, he was still simmering. He had probably had a lot to drink as well.

His landlady was still up, and had also been at the dance. John got out his shotgun and threw it down on the table. "Here is the old gun," he raged. "I am going to shoot any damned man that goes home with Annie, and then I am going to shoot her."

The landlady pleaded with him not to do it — for his daughter's sake. "Why do you want to kill her away from your beautiful little girl?" she said.

John seemed chagrined by this thought, and seemed to agree. But when he left the building a few minutes later, he took the shotgun with him.

The UNWRITTEN LAW.

appeared around the time of John W. Murray's shotgun murder of his brother-in-law.

Some time later, John spotted Annie. She was visiting with one of the other couples outside the dance. Then a man joined them, and the couple left going one way while Annie and the man strolled down the street toward Annie's parents' home.

They made it about two blocks before John caught up with them. "Now I've got you!" he shouted. The man turned — and caught the full charge from both barrels square in the chest. The blasts knocked him off the plank sidewalk and into the mud of the street.

That seems to have been the point at which John realized he'd just murdered his brother-in-law. It was Alfred Yenke who was lying there in the mud looking up at him with fast-glazing eyes.

At the murder trial, John's attorney tried very hard to demonstrate that he was crazy — that, having already had some insanity in the family, the prospect of having his home broken up had driven him over the edge and out of his right mind. Granted, a terrible mistake had been made in thinking his wife's brother was a marauding Lothario, but that mistake had led to temporary madness which should not be punished with death.

Against that, the prosecution brought forward some credible evidence that John might have actually intended to murder his brother-in-law all along, and that all that posturing and fuming about Anna "going home with someone" was intended to give him cover for the deed. He had asked his landlady's daughter to keep his dog indoors that night, something he had never done before; the implication was that he feared the dog would run to greet Anna and Alfred and alert them to his presence, at which point they might see the shotgun in time to escape.

There were also a couple witnesses to whom John apparently spoke too freely at the dance, one of whom remembered John pointing out Alfred and saying, "I'll get even with the [expletive redacted from original newspaper article] tonight. I'll show him how the work is done."

The verdict, when it came in, was guilty of first-degree murder.

John's attorney appealed to the state Supreme Court, resulting in a nearly year-long delay of the execution. During this time, word filtered back from Amsterdam, New York, that John was a bigamist.

"He was known there as Amsterdam Jack, and he fled that part of the country about eight years ago, leaving a wife and two children," the Portland *Evening Telegram* reported. "She is working for the support of herself and children in one of the knitting mills at that place."

Although the news arrived too late to affect the outcome of the trial, it may have had some impact on the decisions of the appellate courts and the Supreme Court. Eventually the Supreme Court denied the motion for a new trial; the judge re-sentenced John Murray to be hanged; and on Feb. 13, it was done.

As a side note, the gallows used to hang John W. Murray was equipped with an electrically-controlled trap door, which was sprung open with the push of a button. It was the first use of electricity in an execution in Oregon history, and possibly in American history as well.

Sources and Works Cited:
- Necktie Parties: Legal Executions in Oregon 1851-1905, *a book by Diane Goeres-Gardner published in 2005 by Caxton Press.*

THE GUNFIGHT
— and —
BAD TIMING.

By 1908, most Oregonians' views on the Unwritten Law were hardening into suspicious disapproval.
    Just one year earlier, citizens had burst into spontaneous applause in the courtroom when Orlando Murray was acquitted of murdering his sister's ex-boyfriend. Since that time, though, suspicions had been growing that things were getting out of hand. The newspapers found the trend rather frightening, and didn't hesitate to say so. Defendants were still getting acquitted because of the Unwritten Law — but it was getting noticeably harder for cases to qualify for its protection.

The Gunfight.

Take, for example, the case of Charles J. Powell's trial in Linn County that year. Powell was a prosperous and well-respected farmer near Brownsville and a grandson of legendary pioneer preacher "Uncle Joab" Powell. He had a 15-year-old daughter, Leah, who had attracted the attentions of a 22-year-old Lothario named Homer Roper.
    Powell didn't favor the match, so he barred young Homer from the

Portraits of Homer Roper and the girl with whom he'd eloped, Leah Powell, as they appeared in the Portland Morning Oregonian after Roper was shot. (Image: Oregonian)

house. In good Romeo and Juliet style, therefore, Homer secretly met up with Leah and the two of them eloped to Pilot Rock, out in Eastern Oregon.

Things must not have gone well, because after they had been living together there for a week, Powell learned where the young couple was — probably because she contacted him, although the newspapers don't specify — and traveled to see them. When he arrived, the two were still not married, so Powell was able to collect his daughter and bring her back home.

But then Homer came back to Brownsville and renewed his attentions to Leah. He was persistent and furtive. Powell complained to the police, who tried in vain to help. This went on for several weeks.

Finally, on the evening of Jan. 28, Leah went with her brothers to a party, and Homer crashed it. He managed to catch her eye while avoiding her brothers, and coaxed her into coming outside with him. When her brothers realized she was missing, they raced for home, fearing there had been another elopement. In response, Charles Powell grabbed an old Winchester .44-40 cowboy carbine, mounted up, and galloped toward the house.

When he got there, he dismounted from his horse, and at that moment, he heard Homer Roper's voice coming from a nearby shed. It shouted, "I've got the drop on you!"

Powell whipped around in the direction of the voice and fired into the shed. Homer, apparently panicking, ran out of the shed where Powell could see him. Powell fired two more shots. Both of them passed through Homer Roper's head.

The young man's last words, they soon learned, had been a bluff. He'd been unarmed.

The resulting murder trial was the first in 13 years at Linn County. In the end, after a short deliberation, the jury acquitted him, and once again the newspapers got the chance to shout of another victory for The Unwritten Law. But the obvious element of self-defense was not an insignificant part of Powell's story; after all, when a man yells from cover that he's "got the drop on you," he can't really complain if the fellow he's shouting at assumes he's about to get shot at and reacts accordingly. Moreover, this killing occurred in defense of a daughter's safety rather than the "sanctity of a home."

So although it was what might be termed "Unwritten Law-adjacent," the Powell case didn't quite fit the model.

Bad timing.

The same was true, even more egregiously, in the 1908 case of a farmer from the Malheur County town of Ironsides named John Brown.

Brown was having a rough year. His wife had left him five months before, leaving their five young daughters in his care; the oldest of these was Bessie, who was just 13 or 14 years old.

About five months after Mrs. Brown left the family, Bessie came to see her father. She told him a family friend, Bill Wisdom, had been sexually molesting her since she was 11 years old.

"At first, she did not know what it meant," Brown told a newspaper reporter later. "When she got older, he made her do worse, and she began to realize more as she grew older what he was doing. Finally he got so brutal and unnatural that she made up her mind that she could not stand the life any longer, and she came and told me."

John Brown was momentarily at a loss. He came to town to talk to another friend, Ike Whitely. Whitely's advice was very sensible: The damage was done, he pointed out, and any publicity would further traumatize the innocent girl. He urged Brown to leave the matter to him. He, Whitely, would confront Wisdom and tell him to leave the area and never return. Brown accepted this offer with thanks.

The next day Brown was in town again, and saw that a flock of ducks had settled in a pond near town. Quickly he made his way to the general store and asked the owner, Ike Nichols, if he might borrow a shotgun. Nichols got one out, loaded it up and handed it over.

Just then the door opened and Bill Wisdom walked into the store.

John Brown found himself standing face to face with the man who, posing as a trusted family friend, had been secretly molesting his daughter for the previous two years. And he just happened to be holding a loaded shotgun.

> **FATHER AVENGES CRIME ON CHILD**
>
> Malheur Farmer Slays Man Who Blights Life of His Little Girl.
>
> **TRAGEDY NEAR IRONSIDES**
>
> John Brown, Goaded by Daughter's Awful Story, Kills W. K. Wisdom on Impulse of Moment as Latter Enters Country Store.

The shotgun was loaded with bird shot. But from 10 feet away, it scarcely mattered. The news accounts don't say if Brown stayed long enough to help clean up the mess he left on the floor and walls of Nichols' store — just that he quietly went home to be with his daughters and to wait for the sheriff to come arrest him.

The March 18, 1908, headline on the story about the shotgun slaying of William Wisdom. (Image: Oregonian)

Several weeks later, the grand jury met and — to the surprise of absolutely nobody — decided not to indict him. And afterward, not even the Portland *Morning Oregonian* — which by that time was on a virtual crusade against The Unwritten Law — vouchsafed a single word in disapproval.

That wouldn't be the case with another high-profile Unwritten Law case, though, which was coming a few months later in Portland. It would be another case of a jilted husband gunning for his rival, and it would fairly definitively put the would-be honor killers of Oregon on notice that they could no longer expect The Unwritten Law to protect them. That story is in the next chapter.

Sources and Works Cited:
- Portland Morning Oregonian *archives: March and May 1908, January and March 1909.*

LOVE, SEX *and* MURDER *in* OLD OREGON

The UNWRITTEN LAW.

THE TIME IT DIDN'T WORK.

The Unwritten Law had quite a run in Oregon during the first decade of the twentieth century. But by the time R. Thomas Dickerson made his attempt to claim its protection, the signs of it having worn out its welcome were there for those who looked.

It had certainly worn out its welcome at the city's newspapers. Probably the best demonstration of the *Morning Oregonian's* attitude toward The Unwritten Law was the lead sentence in its story about Dickerson, after he did his bit of Unwritten Law killing:

"Charged with the commission of a cold-blooded murder," the reporter writes, "closely guarded in a cell in the county jail, believing his act will be excused by a jury of his countrymen through invocation of the Unwritten Law, R. Thomas Dickerson, a street contractor, of 512 Patton Road, Portland Heights, his voice shaking with vindictive rage, openly told the story while in the custody of officers of a tragedy yesterday morning shortly before 6 o'clock, which ended in the death of Harry A. Garrett, one of his teamsters, and disclosed to the world a shocking scandal of an allegedly faithless wife and the punished wrongs of a home destroyer."

What's most noticeable about this sentence (other than its astonishing length — 106 words!) is the clear hostility it shows toward both Dickerson and the Unwritten Law.

The Oregonian's article goes on to detail the full story, or as much of it as was known at the time. Dickerson was inside a stable when he caught sight of one of his teamsters, Harry A. Garrett, walking out in front of the building. Dickerson immediately exited the stable, pulled a revolver out of his pocket, and fired five shots into Garrett.

Garrett then fell to the ground and died, and Dickerson went to surrender himself to the police.

He freely admitted what he'd done, telling them he'd done it because Garrett had wrecked his happy home by getting frisky with his wife, Martha Messner Dickerson — who had, in consequence of Garrett's depredations, moved out of the family manse with the couple's 7-year-old daughter, Pearl, and sued for divorce.

He also claimed Garrett had threatened to kill him as soon as the divorce case was concluded and then run away with Martha, and added, "I have heard of his breaking up other homes. He boasted of this, and some of my wife's folks said, so I heard, that she told them she was going to leave with one of my men as soon as the divorce hearing was over."

But Martha stoutly denied that there was anything going on with Garrett, and suggested another possible motive for her husband's actions — one that was easy to document: Garrett was to have been the lead witness in her suit for divorce.

And there was another thing, too: This was the Dickersons' second marriage to each other. The first one had ended when little Pearl was 5 years old, when Martha had sued for divorce on grounds of physical cruelty and verbal abuse. The court had not only granted her a divorce, but had given her sole custody of little Pearl.

They'd been separated for a little over a year when they reconciled and remarried. This time, though, Dickerson got his wife to sign a pre-nuptial agreement to the effect that if the marriage failed again, he would get custody of Pearl.

The new marriage lasted just a few months before Martha was once again suing for divorce. But this time, she needed more than just her freedom. She needed to make a strong enough case to the judge for her pre-nuptial custody contract to be set aside. And this was where Garrett came in. As one of Dickerson's more trusted employees, he'd seen and heard a lot — and Dickerson mentioned in his testimony that he had asked Garrett for advice on the case. Clearly Garrett knew, and was preparing to reveal on the witness stand, something that might very well take Pearl away from Mr. Dickerson, contract or no contract.

This didn't prove anything, of course. But it did establish another possible motive for Dickerson's shooting him. And it also created some

This sketch of the murder scene appeared in the Portland Morning Oregonian the day after the shooting. (Image: Oregonian)

problems with the story Dickerson tried to tell in court.

"She begged me to take her back," he testified. "I told her I would take her back if she had learned her lesson, and would treat me right, as I had always treated her."

Dickerson then tried to paint a picture of the happily remarried couple before the arrival of the interloper Garrett, apparently keen to make sure the jury knew a contented, happy home had been wrecked by his predations.

It was clearly a tough sell — especially considering that the couple's plans for re-divorce had been covered prominently in the *Oregonian* less than a month before. As every newspaper reader knew, the divorce had been precipitated by Dickerson coming home drunk, accusing his wife of infidelity, firing a rifle shot through the roof of the house and threatening to kill her. All of this was a matter of public record, along with the testimony of drunkenness and abuse that had resulted in the couple's first divorce.

On the other hand, there were some letters that had been found in Garrett's trunk, which Martha had written to him, which made it very clear that she was quite fond of him. There was nothing to support Dickerson's claim that they'd had an affair, but plenty to suggest that Garrett planned to woo Martha after the divorce was finalized. It wasn't much — but for Dickerson's defense team, it was all they had to go on.

In closing arguments, Deputy District Attorney Fitzgerald unleashed a rhetorical broadside that clearly resonated: "When a man goes out in broad daylight and shoots his victim down like a dog he has to get his lawyer to concoct some sort of a defense for him," he said. "If there ever were any criminal relations between Mrs. Dickerson and this poor devil Garrett, Dickerson never knew anything about them except by idle rumors. Dickerson never saw those letters written to Garrett by Mrs. Dickerson until after the murder was committed."

Against this, defense attorney Seneca Fouts had little to offer besides the usual Unwritten Law exhortation: that, in the *Oregonian's* words, "the verdict of this jury (would) be watched by all the libertines in the country" and "the verdict ought to be such that it would be a warning to such men."

Dickerson's other defense attorney was even less subtle: "I do not think you men will declare by your verdict that the seducer of women and the smasher of homes can ply his wicked vocation unrebuked right here in Portland."

It wasn't looking good for Dickerson as the jury retired to think on his fate. Seven of the twelve were for throwing the book at him with a conviction of first-degree murder — which would have meant a hanging — against five who favored acquittal. But over the subsequent 11 ballots, compromises were suggested — first second-degree murder, and then manslaughter — and the jury finally decided to convict him of manslaughter.

When the verdict was read, Dickerson was visibly shocked. "He evidently expected acquittal," the reporter wrote. "He paled a little as he stood while the verdict was read."

He was sentenced to three years in the penitentiary — a sentence which, although not as stiff as it could have been, sent the first clear message out that The Unwritten Law could no longer be relied upon to justify murder.

Sources and Works Cited:
- Portland Morning Oregonian *archives: May, June, and September 1909.*

FATHER OF THE YEAR.

Alfred Lester Belding may have intended to try to claim the protection of the "Unwritten Law" when he made his plans for revenge. But, reviewing the historical record, it seems more likely he didn't give a single thought to anything beyond the four murders he had planned.

It would have been a long shot anyway. The Unwritten Law didn't have much to say about murdering mothers-in-law, fathers-in-law, and/or the wife herself.

Belding and his wife, Sylvia Maude, had been married for seven years — long enough to produce one son, Eddie, now 6. Their marriage had been, to use a euphemism of the day, a stormy one, and by July 11, 1902, everyone knew it was over. Sylvia, after at least five years of everyone in her family urging her to do so, was finally suing him for divorce; moreover, she had been seen with another man, George "Gyp" Woodward. Belding was convinced that they were having an affair, cuckolding him. He himself had been carrying on an adulterous affair with a younger woman named Cora Dawson for a number of years, but that, of course, was different.

So, Gyp Woodward had to die. And Sylvia had to die, because if Belding couldn't have her, nobody could. And her mother and father, who had urged her to leave him and then taken her in when she finally had — they had to die, as accessories to the crime of home-wrecking.

And now, as the evening of July 11 wore on, it looked like Belding was going to get his chance. He had learned that Gyp Woodward had come over to the in-laws' house for a visit. All four of them were there. The only way it could be better would be if her brother and sister were in the house too, but one couldn't be too picky. Four was enough.

So after bracing himself up with a generous measure of liquor, he armed himself with a pair of revolvers, which he "borrowed" from his employer — he worked as a bartender at a saloon at 14th and Marshall. He didn't know it, but the wheelguns — a Colt and a Smith & Wesson — weren't fully loaded; there were only nine shells between the two guns, a fact that would quite possibly save at least one life that night.

Then he headed over to Sylvia's parents' house, on the corner of Fifth and Flanders.

Out on the porch Belding found his son, young Eddie. He paused for a few minutes to talk to the boy, then gave him a kiss goodnight and told him to go inside to bed.

Just then, Gyp Woodward stepped into the doorway. Belding lifted the Colt and let him have it. One shot, right through the head. The curtain had gone up.

Belding stepped past Eddie and over the dead body of his "rival" and walked into the house. Startled by the noise of the shot, Sylvia now stepped into the hall, met his eyes. The Colt bellowed again, and Sylvia Maude McCroskey Belding died in her tracks.

The murderer now started down the hall, knowing his in-laws were both still alive and in the house somewhere. He found his mother-in-law, Deborah McCroskey, first. Again he fired one fatal shot.

Belding was obviously quite a good shot when his victim was standing there waiting to be murdered. But his skills weren't nearly as good when his

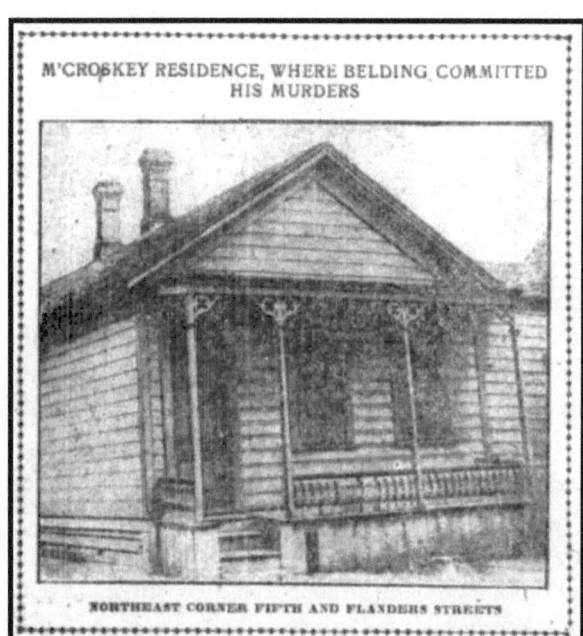

The McCroskey home, at Fifth and Flanders, where Alfred Belding staged his shooting spree, as shown on the front page of the July 13, 1902, edition of the Sunday Oregonian. (Image: UO Libraries)

Portraits of three of Alfred Belding's victims, published in the Sunday Oregonian on July 13, 1902: his wife, Sylvia Maude McCroskey Belding; his mother-in-law, Deborah McCroskey; and his father-in-law, Lemuel McCroskey. No portrait of George "Gyp" Woodward was published. (Image: UO Libraries)

victim was shooting back, as his next victim, Lemuel McCroskey, was. Lemuel had had plenty of notice as to what was going on, and he'd gotten his own pistol out. When Belding found him, he was charging, firing as he came.

Luckily for Belding, Lemuel wasn't a very good shot; none of his bullets touched their mark. Belding had better luck; of the three shots he fired, all three hit. The first one nicked his neck; the second one inflicted a minor flesh wound in his arm; and then the older man clinched with him. Belding got one more shot in, and this one did the trick — it would have been fatal had it not been deflected by the old man's pocket watch. As it was, it put Lemuel out of commission for the night.

Knowing the house was now empty of targets that could shoot back, Belding now turned and opened fire on little Eddie, who was apparently still on the porch.

"Pa fired three times at me," Eddie testified at the subsequent trial. "Once at my right foot and then at my left, but the third time it did not come near me. I was across the street."

Leaving one of the now-empty pistols lying on the floor where he had dropped it wrestling with Lemuel, Belding now strolled leisurely across the street to the Lake Charles Saloon, throwing the other pistol down in the street as he did. Then he telephoned the police to let them know what he'd done, ordered a drink, and waited for the cops to arrive.

At trial, Belding's attorney didn't have much to go on; but he tried to argue his client had been temporarily insane, driven thence by the sad news that his wife was moving on and his happy home was lost and gone. This proved to be a really tough sell. For one thing, when Belding had learned that his fourth victim — Lemuel McCroskey — was still alive, he'd become visibly enraged. That didn't strike the jurors as consistent with a claim that the crime had been done in hot blood during a temporary bout of insanity. It was, however, very consistent with the prosecution's claim that Belding was a cold-blooded monster who had tantrums when he didn't get what he wanted.

Another blow came from a police detective, who testified to having seen Belding smoking in opium dens several times. Opium was legal in 1902, but in mainstream Portland society, indulging in it was regarded in much the same way injecting methamphetamine is viewed today: as the *ne plus ultra* of trashiness and dissipation.

The most damaging bit of testimony, though, came from young Eddie Belding, Alfred's six-year-old son.

"He talked to me and kissed me, and said I had better go in the house," the little tyke testified. "Then he shot the man on the porch, and went inside and shot some more. I saw him shoot Mamma and heard Grandma say 'Oh!' Then he wrestled with Grandpa and shot at me."

And it was lost on no one that, having murdered (or, in Lemuel's case, tried to murder) Eddie's entire family, he had coldly crossed the street for a drink in a bar, leaving his six-year-old son to deal with the loss of his "mamma and grandma" in whatever way he might.

Even today, in far less bloodthirsty times, even a stellar lawyer would be hard-pressed to keep a defendant like that from drawing a death penalty. In 1902, it was a no-brainer. Prosecutor George Chamberlain (the future governor and U.S. Senator) had only charged him with one of the three murders, holding the other two in reserve in case something should go wrong with the case. But he need not have bothered. The jury was out for less than an hour before coming back in and declaring the young rake guilty.

While waiting in jail for the inevitable appeals to be heard, Belding's blood finally started to cool, and his bravado slipped away. In desperation he hatched a scheme to escape. His young mistress, Cora Dawson, had been coming to see him frequently, and the jailers had started to get a little careless about searching her. She could, he figured, smuggle all sorts of things into the joint for him.

The UNWRITTEN LAW.

So he slipped a note to a fellow prisoner who was about to be released, to be given to a friend. It asked the friend to buy about $50 worth of guns and bullets and hide them in a place where he could get to them; then, to give Cora a package containing ground cayenne pepper and two heavy blackjacks. The friend was to ask Cora to blow the pepper in the guards' faces to blind them, grab the keys, let Belding and his cellmate out, and give

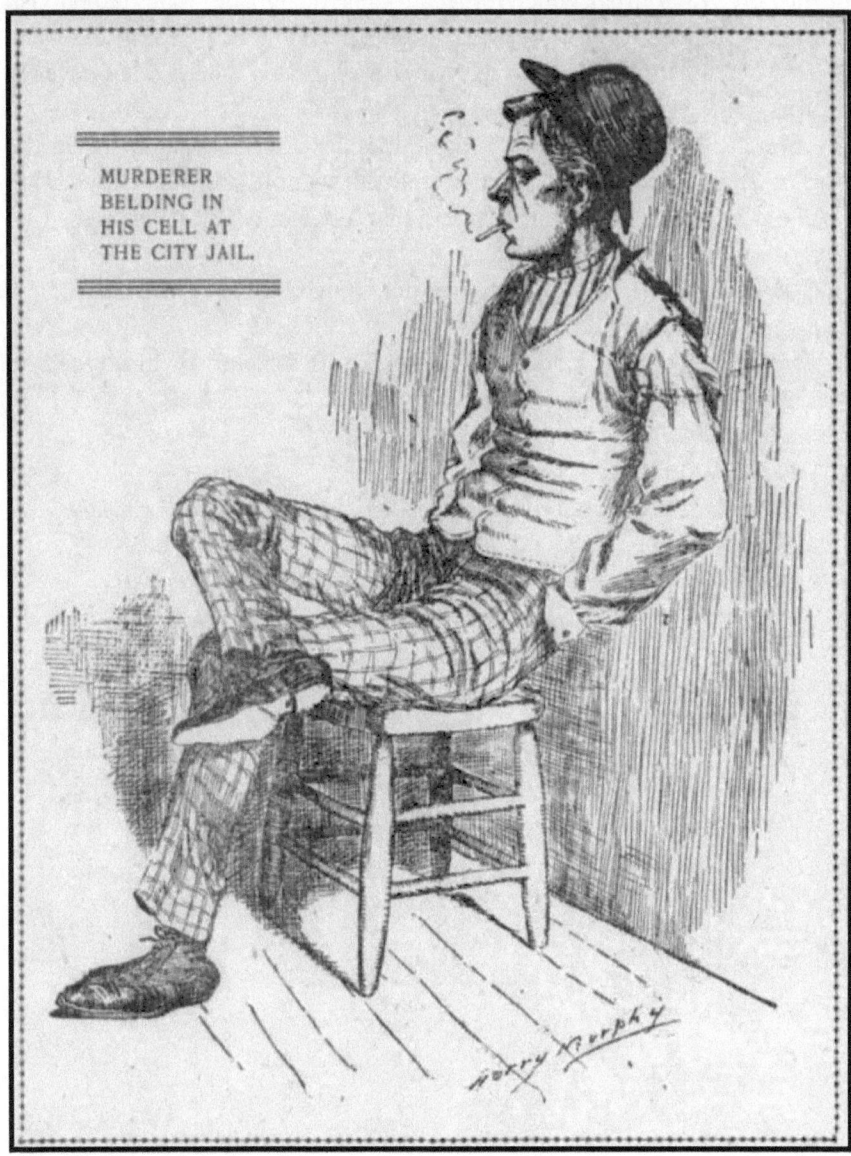

Alfred Belding as he appeared the day after he murdered his wife, mother-in-law, and their houseguest, sketched by Oregonian artist Harry Murphy for the Sunday, July 13, 1902, edition. (Image: UO Libraries)

them the blackjacks. They would then clobber their way to freedom, retrieve the guns, and start a glorious new life on the lam, like Butch Cassidy and the Sundance Kid or something.

But the cops found the note. So they made plans to be ready when Cora showed up the next time. But, unfortunately, the *Oregonian* burned them by publishing the details of the attempt before it was made (scooping the upstart Oregon Journal, which respected the embargo and waited to publish until the following day). Cora, who said no one had said anything about the plan to her, was mortified, and left for San Francisco the next day, never to return.

Finally, on March 27, 1903, the Supreme Court having affirmed the verdict, Alfred Lester Belding mounted the scaffold and was hanged. He declined to say anything, but left behind a letter in which he expressed no contrition for what he had done.

"Why should I not prefer to see her (Sylvia) in the grave than know that she was living in shame?" he wrote.

Little six-year-old Eddie apparently wasn't a factor for him when he made that choice.

Sources and Works Cited:
- Necktie Parties: Legal Executions in Oregon 1851-1905, *a book by Diane Goeres-Gardner published in 2005 by Caxton Press;*
- Portland Morning Oregonian *archives, July1902 through March 1903.*

ONE FOR THE LADIES, SORT OF.

In the "Unwritten Law" era, as we've seen in the previous chapters, the standard courtroom defense of murderers who wanted to claim its protection was "temporary insanity." The idea was, one tried to convince the jury that the killer was driven so completely out of his head by the prospect of some marauding Lothario coaxing his wife into infidelity, or seducing his sister or daughter, that he lost his grip on sanity and killed the interloper in a murderous rage.

For a few years, this worked more often than it didn't. But it never worked very well for women, and it surely didn't work at all in the late 1870s for Caroline Briggs — who, arguably, really *was* temporarily insane.

Here's the story:

Caroline Briggs was in her late 50s, and she and her husband George were basically the first family of Josephine County. They'd been among its earliest settlers, they were very prosperous, and they lived in a big stockaded log-cabin compound on the banks of Sucker Creek known locally as "Fort Briggs" (built, originally, to resist Indian attacks). They had two sons, four daughters, and by now several grandchildren as well.

Then in late June 1874, one of their daughters — 31-year-old Julia Briggs Floyd — died in childbirth while trying to deliver her third baby.

Caroline, the family matriarch, was crushed by this — and, by all accounts, unhinged.

Three days later, with quite possibly the worst timing in the history of the universe, one of her other daughters — 17-year-old Carrie, the baby of the family — came tearfully to her mother to tell her that she'd been seduced by the local schoolmaster, John Dalmater, who was now refusing to marry her.

Dalmater had been courting Carrie for some time, and Caroline and George had been very encouraging, believing that he would be a fine match for her. But, apparently Dalmater wasn't endowed with as high a moral character as they had thought.

This news — the imminent prospect of her youngest daughter having a baby out of wedlock — seems to have pushed Caroline over some sort of a threshold. Around 9:30 a.m. on June 30, she proclaimed her intention to go down to the little one-room schoolhouse and settle the matter on the spot. So she seized her walking cane and headed for the door. One of her sons, David, came with her — and brought along his father's Henry rifle, just in case.

The two of them found Dalmater in front of a classroom full of children and teenagers. They marched right in.

Some of the newspaper reports of this incident say Caroline started out by demanding that Dalmater agree on the spot to marry Carrie, and that his refusal prompted her assault. This would make sense — but historian Diane Goeres-Gardner, after reviewing the court transcripts, writes that the assault commenced almost immediately. "It's time this matter was settled!" Caroline screamed, and started hammering on him with her walking cane. "Shoot the son of a bitch!" she yelled to David.

Dalmater, no doubt knowing he could soak up a lot more punishment from a cane than he could from a Henry rifle, made a grab for the weapon and the two men wrestled over it while Caroline continued raining blows down on Dalmater's head.

The fight spilled out into the front of the schoolhouse. Finally Caroline got in a really solid hit, knocking Dalmater down, and David got control of the rifle. Dalmater tried to crawl away from David, trying to reach a tree that he hoped to hide from David behind. He made it most of the way to the tree before David got a clear shot, and then —

Caroline continued beating Dalmater after the fatal gunshot, and this may be what finally galvanized some of the neighbors and older students to seize her and pull her off him.

Dalmater wasn't dead, but he was mortally wounded. He lasted just a few hours, basically just long enough to write and sign a final sworn statement. In it, he swore he had not seduced Carrie Briggs.

But it hardly mattered. If Dalmater hadn't "ruined" Carrie, her mother certainly had, by proclaiming her seduction in front of an entire classroom full of witnesses; and, on top of that, shooting a man in the back as he crawls painfully away is extraordinarily dishonorable behavior. The Briggs family went, on the instant, from being the first family of Josephine County, to social pariahs.

Mother and son were thrown into the county jail and held without bail. It seems unlikely that they were denied bail because authorities thought them a flight risk — more likely, they were worried that someone might lynch them.

It took several months to empanel a grand jury and hear testimony from the 18 witnesses, but when the inquest was done, the grand jury voted to charge both of them with murder.

The Briggs family was shocked, but they should have expected this. Feeling against Caroline and David was running so high in the county that the prosecutors were forced to move the trial to Jackson County; every potential juror in the Kerbyville area, it seemed, was already convinced of their guilt.

Caroline's trial came first, in late June 1875. She had filed an affidavit that she was being treated for mental illness, apparently in support of a temporary-insanity plea; but when the verdict came in, it was Manslaughter, with a five-year prison sentence. So, it certainly could have been worse; but it wasn't the "not guilty by reason of temporary insanity" verdict that she'd hoped for.

Ironically, the "temporary insanity" play got quite a bit more traction at David Briggs' trial, held in November 1875. His defense team presented an expert witness, Rev. S. Skidmore of Ashland, who assured the jury that when David fired the fatal shot, he did so at the direct command of his mother, and in that moment he didn't know right from wrong. The reporter from the Oregon Sentinel thought it sounded like a game-changer, and would result in acquittal.

But, unfortunately for David, his case had been built around a claim of self-defense; David had already claimed that Dalmater had been drawing a pistol when he fired. It had to be one or the other — either he shot Dalmater because his mother said so, or he shot him because he was afraid the schoolteacher would draw on him.

The jury, in the end, opted for "none of the above." David drew the same verdict, and the same sentence, as his mother: Manslaughter, five years.

Apetition for a pardon for Caroline Briggs was drawn up right away; the local newspaper got hold of a copy, and published it. Most Southern Oregon residents were still pretty hostile to the idea.

But, a little over two years later, Gov. Stephen Chadwick did pardon her, and Caroline Briggs' three-year self-inflicted nightmare was finally over.

David was pardoned by Gov. Chadwick a little later, after serving roughly two and a half years. He stayed in Josephine County, where he became a miner. He married a local girl and they had three children — one of whom, working the family vocation, struck a huge vein of gold; the family promptly staked a string of mining claims that made them quite rich.

And Carrie Briggs married a Jackson County man the following year. They had five children together. But, whatever her mother thought or assumed on the fateful morning she took her cane to town, it appears Carrie was not pregnant with John Dalmater's child. So regardless of whether she and Dalmater had been intimate, the whole affair at the schoolhouse had been for nothing.

Sources and Works Cited:
- Murder, Morality and Madness: Women Criminals in Early Oregon, *a book by Diane L. Goeres-Gardner published in 2009 by Caxton Press;*
- Portland Morning Oregonian *archives, July 1874;*
- Salem Oregon Statesman *archives, September 1875.*

PART V:

SERIAL KILLERS AND DEADLY STRANGERS.

Statistically, "stranger danger" — well, isn't. The chances of any of us being murdered by a random person whom we have never met is vanishingly small.

But it does occasionally happen. And when it does, the randomness frightens us a little, and makes the story of the killing especially compelling. After all, dangers that we understand can be defended against; but homicidal strangers are like lightning strikes, and there's not much we can do to understand and guard against them ... other than locking our doors.

The *frisson* of fear we get from stories of serial killers is similar. A serial killer is a person who walks, talks, and acts like one of our friends and acquaintances — but secretly is no such thing. How can we protect ourselves from bloodthirsty strangers masquerading as our friends, just waiting for their chance to quench a bit of cold steel in our heart's best blood?

The best we can do is, again, lock our doors. And, of course, thank our lucky stars that we never ran into one of these Oregon characters:

THE ANGEL OF DEATH.

Thomas B. Sawyer, the lead teleplay writer for "Murder, She Wrote," says the writers for the classic CBS TV show used to affectionately refer to the lead character as "the Angel of Death."

Week after week, the kindly and inquisitive Jessica Fletcher (played, of course, by Angela Lansbury) just happened to be on hand when someone was murdered, and week after week she played a key and sometimes heroic role in the investigation. By the end of the series, she had just happened to be in the right place at the right time to help out with a whopping 264 episodes' worth of deadly skullduggery.

Central Oregon had its own version of the Angel of Death in the form of "Professor" Ray Van Buren Jackson. His record wasn't as good as Jessica's; he played a starring role in only three oddly-similar homicides, had bit parts in three more, and is suspected of involvement in several beyond those. His record is worse in another way, too: None of the murders of which he helped in the investigation were ever really solved.

Lake County historian and journalist Melany Tupper is the historian who identified this pattern during seven years of research through back issues of local newspapers and courthouse records, along with interviews with locals; the case is laid out in her book, *The Sandy Knoll Murder*.

In her research, Tupper found an astonishing array of dramatic and sometimes deadly events — run-ins with neighbors, disappearances of large sums of money, and of course high-profile unsolved murders — that swirled around Jackson's life, and which paint a pretty grim picture of the man himself. It's all circumstantial evidence, but there is an enormous amount of it.

Ray Jackson grew up in Sodaville, near Lebanon. He was left-handed, and his teachers were determined to "fix" this "defect" — which they did, although he had to be held back two years in school to do it. It turned out to be great training for a future forger, though. The ability that he was forced to cultivate, to write with either hand, brought with it an ability to imitate almost anyone's handwriting.

Jackson followed in the footsteps of his older brother by going to college and getting a teaching certificate. Everything seemed to be going well, until the summer of 1895 — when two things happened that, historian Tupper suggests, pushed him over the edge and into true psychosis.

First, his favorite uncle was run over by a railroad train before his eyes at the bottom of Singer Hill in Oregon City. It was a singularly grisly accident, and a tremendous trauma for young Ray Jackson. The train collided with wagon Jackson's uncle was driving, killing his horses and literally running over his head while Jackson watched.

Then when Jackson got home to Beaver Creek, where he was working as a teacher in the local school, he learned he was wanted by the law for having forged a couple vouchers. His career as a Clackamas County schoolteacher was over.

Jackson went on the lam for a year or so, during which he was able to continue teaching at Klamath Falls; but eventually he was caught, tried, convicted, and sent to the state penitentiary for a two-year stretch.

He was released in 1898, but a year later he was back in again, this time for a robbery committed in Baker County.

If you're keeping track, the places in which Ray Jackson had established his bad reputation now included the entire Willamette Valley, plus Jackson and Josephine counties in the south, and Baker County in the east. There wasn't much of Oregon left in which Jackson could get a fresh start. And people travel; if Jackson set up housekeeping in, say, Shaniko or Bend, sooner or later somebody would travel to town and recognize him.

But the remote stockland of Lake County was different. The nearest railroad was more than 100 rocky, bone-jarring wagon-road miles away, and Silver Lake and Lakeview were on the way to basically nowhere; you didn't come *through* town unless you were coming *to* town. So, hard characters like Jackson often came to Lake County to get away from the reputations they'd forged in gentler places.

Now, as he left the state pen for the last time, Jackson did exactly that.

He talked his way into a job teaching first through eighth grade at Silver Lake, moved into the school house, and started calling himself "Professor Jackson" — although he wasn't credentialed as a professor and had never taught above the eighth-grade level.

It's hard to imagine this happening today — a man who's spent three solid years in the slammer being put in charge of small children. But nobody seems to have asked any probing questions about the man's background, and perhaps Silver Lake's options were limited. Oregon teachers were very poorly paid in the early 1900s.

The prison mugshot of Ray V.B. Jackson, taken when Jackson was admitted to the Oregon State Penitentiary on forgery charges in 1896. (Photo: Central Oregon Books)

In any case, Jackson soon established a reputation as a strict disciplinarian. He kept a pair of buggy whips in the classroom, and used them — both the butts and the lashes — on older students who misbehaved. Accounts of his classroom management, and things he said to others in the community, suggest his goal in meting out corporal punishments may have been more than just discipline — that he may have actually been deriving pleasure from it — although it's impossible to say what was actually in his mind at the time. But he confided to a neighbor that he always took his single-action Colt revolver and baseball bat to class with him. And at least one of his students narrowly avoided serious injury, when Jackson hurled a heavy glass inkwell at his head.

Jackson's run as Silver Lake's schoolteacher was relatively short; he was there from 1902 to 1908. But it didn't end the way you might think it would have; he was promoted, not fired. In 1908 Jackson was elected superintendent of Lake County Schools, and moved to Lakeview.

A 10-mule freight team passing through downtown Lakeview in 1900. This is the town in which Ray Jackson served briefly as superintendent of the Lake County School District, eight years after this photo was made. (Photo: UO Libraries/ Wasco County Pioneer Assoc.)

It was in Lakeview that Jackson's career in education was definitively put to an end. Once he was in charge of the whole show, the temptation to make grabs from the till was apparently too much. Two years later, he was indicted for embezzling money from the district, and he resigned in 1911.

After that, Jackson was involved in a number of ventures involving cattle ranching, retail business and homesteading. He never went back to teaching school.

The most extraordinary part of Jackson's life, though, was his personal connection to at least nine suspicious homicides — three of which were declared suicides and six of which remain officially unsolved:

R.I.P.: J. Creed Conn, March 4, 1904.

John Creed Conn, a prominent Silver Lake merchant and owner of a mule-team freight line, disappeared on a frosty morning while going to fetch the mail for his store. Seven weeks later, after an extensive manhunt, his well-preserved body was found staged on a little hillock (the "sandy knoll") on a nearby cattle ranch — put there in an apparent attempt to suggest one of the ranch's cowboys had done it. Before planting the body, the killer beat the face to unrecognizability and shot it a second time using an old Colt .38 stolen from Conn's store.

The coroner's jury, apparently concerned to protect the cattle ranch from bad publicity, ruled it suicide — something very few people bought, given how difficult it is to shoot oneself twice with a single-action revolver and then beat one's own face to a bloody pulp. Other circumstances were also suspicious: Conn at the time of death was trying to figure out what had happened to the proceeds of a $3,000 loan missing from his bank account; this missing money was never found, and Conn's

John Creed Conn

brother had to pay the loan off with the proceeds of his liquidated estate.

Ray Van Buren Jackson ate breakfast with Conn on the morning of his murder and was the last person to have spoken with him. As an important witness to Conn's last activities, he provided key testimony to law enforcement on what he said and where he went after breakfast, and gave detailed information for newspaper stories.

Jackson also knew about the $3,000 loan which Conn had taken out. And Jackson was a convicted forger. Could he have forged a promissory note to steal the $3,000? Conn would have asked the bank to send him the note back, and upon receiving it he would have instantly seen what happened. Could Jackson have asked him to meet with him privately so he could give back the money, and then given him something else instead?

Well, we'll never know for sure. But it sure holds together as a story. And get this: Jackson bought about $3,000 worth of cattle right after Conn disappeared. This is what provided him the wherewithal to go into cattle ranching after he was fired from his job as Lake County Schools superintendent. He sure didn't finance that purchase on a schoolteacher's salary.

R.I.P.: Zelma "Ethel" Martin, April 1, 1904.

Just a few weeks after Creed Conn vanished, Ethel Martin, an 11-year-old schoolgirl, stayed late at the schoolhouse where Jackson was the teacher. A half-hour after arriving home that afternoon, she died of apparent poisoning. Her death was ruled accidental; there was some strychnine nearby, and it was believed she'd eaten some.

But strychnine is very bitter, and no 11-year-old would eat it on purpose; moreover, it kills in hours, not minutes. Tupper argues she more likely ate something laced with a more subtle poison such as arsenic at the schoolhouse, possibly after discovering something relating to Conn's body, which — if Jackson was the killer — would probably have been stored there.

The circumstances of Ethel's death are unclear. What's not unclear is that she consumed whatever poison killed her in Ray Van Buren Jackson's schoolhouse.

R.I.P.: Julius Wallende, Dec. 27, 1907.

Julius Wallende was a young homesteader, just getting started, new to Silver Lake. There is no clear connection to Jackson except for a plethora of spooky similarities to the Conn murder. Wallende was shot to death, then the killer warehoused the body for 11 weeks before beating the face to unrecognizability and planting the body in the creek near where Conn was found, artistically arranging it so it would freeze into the ice face-up. The killer then communicated prolifically to the press, writing an anonymous letter to the Portland *Oregonian* to help guide searchers to the body and, after a suspect was (wrongly) identified, another anonymous letter giving details of how to find him.

R.I.P.: Emma Dobkins, March 2, 1910.

Officially, Emma Dobkins died of "angina pectoris" in Lane County. However, Lake County residents said she committed suicide after a "tainted relationship" with Jackson, who was a great pal of her brother Frank. She may very well have died naturally in childbirth while trying to deliver a baby conceived with Jackson, but "angina pectoris" (chest pain) is a strange thing to list as a cause of death, especially for a woman under 30.

But well-meaning people tried to protect her reputation afterward by being vague on the documentation, so it's hard to know for sure how she died or what (if any) role Jackson might have played in her death.

R.I.P.: Harold Bradley, Dec. 29, 1925.

Bradley was a hired hand on Lincoln "Link" Hutton's large and successful ranch. He was shot twice with a .30-30 while going with Hutton to work on a car. Link Hutton's wife, Leona, testified that after the first shot she heard him yell, "Link, you've shot me." Jackson, a neighbor, testified in the subsequent murder trial that Link came to his place and confessed to him. (Link was acquitted, so apparently the jury didn't believe it. Which is understandable; Hutton was a respected Ben Cartwright type, and Jackson a squirrely ex-jailbird and convicted felon.)

This is largely speculation — but there is some evidence Jackson and Leona Hutton were having an affair at the time of the shooting. Could Jackson have planned to shoot Hutton and frame Bradley, then move in with the widow, trading his hardscrabble life as a small-time homestead farmer for a life of ease as the lord of the manor at a major ranching operation? Hutton and Bradley were built similarly and there wasn't much light; perhaps that bullet was meant for Hutton.

By the way, Bradley's wounds were potentially survivable, but he did not survive them. Perhaps this is explained by the fact that he was left alone with Jackson for an hour after the shooting.

R.I.P.: Ira Bradley, May 1, 1930.

Ira Bradley was Harold Bradley's father. He was found beaten to death with the butt of a revolver at his ranch, a mile and a half from the Harney County line. His face, too, was beaten to unrecognizability. The killer planted evidence at a neighbor's house, but the neighbor had an alibi — he was in town buying a new Ford when it happened.

Luckily, another neighbor was on hand. This neighbor helpfully called the Harney County authorities — forgetting, apparently, which county he was in. Harney County officers came, checked out the crime scene, loaded up the body and took it to Burns — then discovered it was Lake County's case. In the ensuing confusion much footprint evidence was lost, and the killer was never identified.

And yes . . . by now you've guessed exactly who that helpful neighbor was, haven't you?

R.I.P.: Harry "Roy" Wilson, Edward Nickols, and Dewey Morris, winter 1924.

These three men were spending the winter of 1923-1924 in a trapping cabin at Lava Lakes, taking care of a small fox farm in exchange for a cut of the proceeds when the furs were sold. One or more killers got the drop on them and killed all three, then chopped a hole in the ice that covered Big Lava Lake and slipped the bodies in.

A fugitive felon named Charles Hyde Kimzey was the prime suspect in the killings. But Kimzey was working with an accomplice, a glib-talking charismatic person who has never been identified. Based on similarities in the cases, historian Tupper is convinced that accomplice was Jackson — who was, in fact, known to be one of Kimzey's friends.

These murders — "The Trapper Murders" — are discussed in much more detail in the next chapter.

R.I.P.: "Professor" Ray Van Buren Jackson, Feb. 1, 1938.

Jackson was found dead in an upstairs room of his house, having apparently shot himself with a .30-30. Oddly enough, he chose to shoot himself in the chest, not the head, using a stove poker to actuate the trigger. He was 68 years old.

One particularly odd thing about Jackson's record of helpfulness is that this list covers a significant slice of all the murder and suspicious-death cases in Lake County from 1899 to 1930. There were others, but this list hits the high points and then some. Each time, there was some connection to Ray Van Buren Jackson — indeed, in in most of them, Jackson was a central player. What are the odds?

In her book, Tupper makes the case that Jackson was a sociopath and serial killer in an age that didn't really know what either of those things was. She's probably right; he displayed some of the characteristics we associate with sociopaths — glibness, absolute lack of social fear, impulse toward grandiosity, promiscuity (one of his nicknames was "Tomcat Jackson"), etc.

But you don't have to buy her argument about that to see that there was something funny, and deadly, about this particular man. He was an easy liar, a great actor, an accomplished forger and a serial embezzler — among other things. He was entrusted with the entire community's school children for a decade, and at least one of them died under suspicious circumstances right after coming home from school. And nearly every time there was a brutal suspicious homicide somewhere in Oregon's third-largest county, he just happened to be on hand, helping out, giving advice, talking excitedly to the cops and to the press.

The pattern is hard to miss, isn't it?

Sources and Works Cited:
- The Sandy Knoll Murder: Legacy of the Sheepshooters, *a book by Melany Tupper published in 2010 by Central Oregon Books;*
- Western Echoes: A Western Autobiography, *a book by Earl F. Moore published in 1981 by Tremaine Publishing.*

THE TRAPPER MURDERS.

As the first day of March 1924 arrived, L. Sarah Wilson's worry and alarm mounted. Something had happened. Something bad. Her son, 36-year-old Harry "Roy" Wilson, had promised he'd be back at her home in Bend sometime in February. Roy was a former U.S. Marine (8th regiment, 1917-1919), and his word was solid gold. If he didn't do what he said he was going to do, it was because he couldn't.

Roy's mother was convinced that he hadn't come home to Bend because he'd been murdered.

Roy was a logger who worked for Brooks-Scanlon Lumber Co. of Bend. Late the previous year, he and a co-worker, 23-year-old Dewey Morris, had agreed to spend the winter at a remote cabin by Big Lava Lake with another onetime co-worker, 53-year-old Edward Nickols. Nickols was spending the winter at the cabin tending to the cabin owner's small fur farm of silver foxes, in exchange for a piece of the action when the furs were sold.

The job promised to be a pleasant one. The foxes didn't require too much care; they had to be fed each day, of course, and their water kept topped up and unfrozen; but that was about it. Meanwhile, the three men were free to run traplines for the wild foxes, martens, and other valuable fur-bearing animals around the lake.

Nickols was particularly keen to have company for the winter, and especially the company of a trained warrior like Wilson, because there was some bad blood between him and a former partner, Lee Collins.

This man Collins was a somewhat slow-witted fellow from Idaho, who had the habit of talking rapidly through his teeth while affecting a toothy and insincere smile — like a fast-talking Jack Nicholson character. He had spent the previous winter at the cabin helping Nickols tend to the fox farm. At the end of their partnership, though, the fur markets were at a low point, and the fox farm's owner decided to wait to sell the furs until prices were better. Collins, who of course wanted his money immediately, interpreted this as an attempt by Nickols and the owner to cheat him out of his share; so, happening to know where Nickols had $500 stashed near the cabin, he stole it and disappeared.

When Nickols reported this crime, investigators told him that Collins wasn't the man's real name. He was, actually, Charles Hyde Kimzey, a convict who had recently escaped from the Idaho State Pen, where he had been serving a 14-year sentence for burglary.

With the help of the information Nickols gave police, Kimzey was tracked down and they very nearly caught him. But after he slipped out of their clutches, knowing who had ratted him out, Kimzey made it very clear that he would now be gunning for Edward Nickols at his very first opportunity.

And, of course, Kimzey would know exactly where to go to find Nickols, since the cabin and fox farm hadn't gone anywhere. Plus, if he waited to take his revenge until the dead of winter, he'd be able to also steal the fox pelts — valued at about $1,800 — plus whatever else Nickols might have found on his trapline that winter. Revenge for the ratting-out, plus a nice wad of cash — a tempting prospect for a felon on the run.

So, with this in mind, Nickols got his two friends to come out to the cabin with him, and they settled in for the winter.

On Jan. 15, 1924, Allen Willcoxen, a neighboring trapper and friend of both Nickols and "Collins," came by and spent the night in the cabin with the three men. He was the last person to have ever seen them alive ... other than their killers.

Time went by, and winter ripened into early spring. The last day of February came and went with no sign of Roy Wilson. Sarah Wilson would not be comforted. Other relatives assured her that the boys were probably just fine, maybe snowed in at one of the shelter shacks along their trapline, and it was no big deal ... but, no sale. Sarah Wilson was convinced that something awful had happened to her son and his friends.

SERIAL KILLERS *and* DEADLY STRANGERS.

Dewey Morris, Roy Wilson, and Ed Nickols with their cargo sled outside of the cabin by Little Lava Lake. This photo was probably taken when Morris and Wilson were dropped off at the cabin to spend the winter with Nickols. This was probably the sled that was used to transport their bodies to Lava Lake for disposal early the next year. (Image: Central Oregon Books)

Finally a couple of family members saddled up and made the trip out to Lava Lakes for a visit. They arrived on April 13.

What they found there certainly gave them reason to worry that Sarah might be right. The cabin had been unoccupied for some time; the wall calendar still had the January leaf showing. The last meal eaten in the place appeared to have been breakfast. No one had bothered to clean up or put away dishes; indeed, the whole cabin was in a very unkempt condition, which was not at all in character with how Nickols, Morris, and especially ex-Marine Wilson kept their things.

Well, all of that could have been explained away; conceivably, after the three men left for whatever reason, a traveler might have come by and, finding the cabin vacant, lived in it for a few days. But where the men might have gone was another tricky question. Their bedrolls, most of their heavy winter clothing, and all but two of their guns — a Colt .22 revolver and Wilson's war-souvenir Luger automatic — were still in the cabin. Where would the three of them have gone without heavy coats or firearms?

There was a meal out for the farm foxes, but the foxes were gone. Had they escaped, or had someone stolen them?

The visitors made the rounds of the boys' trapline. They found the frozen corpses of several martens and wild foxes in the traps. Yet there were no pelts in the cabin. Had they not been running their trapline, or had someone stolen all their pelts?

Answers were not slow in coming to light. On April 20, the visitors found a big spot of blood in the snow; it was sandwiched between a lower and upper layer of clean white stuff, as if it had been spilled and frozen several weeks or months earlier. There were also tracks, visible despite an inch or two of snow having fallen since they were made, of a heavily-laden sled having been pulled away across the snow in the direction of Big Lava Lake.

Following those tracks, the investigators found that they went out onto the frozen lake, and ended at a spot where someone had chopped a hole in the ice ... a hole just big enough to slip a body through. And caught in a crack in the ice near the edge was a medium-length strand of sandy-brown human hair.

Then someone found the missing foxes. They'd been killed, skinned, and hidden in the bushes.

There was no longer any room for doubt: The three trappers had clearly been murdered, and the motive was either robbery — or revenge.

A few days later, Portland furrier Carl Schumacher, having seen the coverage of the mystery in the Portland *Morning Oregonian*, contacted the police to report that two men had

A prison mugshot of murder suspect Charles Kimzey as he appeared in 1952 at age 67, while serving a life sentence for attempted murder in the Oregon State Penitentiary. Kimzey was paroled five years later. (Image: Central Oregon Books)

The searchers, having just retrieved the bodies of the three trappers from Lava Lake, prepare them for transportation to Bend, in April 1924. (Image: Deschutes Pioneers' Gazette)

brought four silver-fox pelts in to his shop on Jan. 22 — seven days after the three men had last been seen alive.

Schumacher remembered the situation well, because the pelts had been mishandled; one of the two trappers, who stayed and chatted with him for half an hour or so about various trapper-related things and seemed to be an old hand at the game, apparently didn't know how to properly stretch and cure a valuable pelt, and although the pelts weren't ruined, they had lost considerable value as a result.

By the time Schumacher contacted the cops, they were already looking into Charles Hyde Kimzey as a suspect. They showed Schumacher a photograph. Schumacher said he couldn't give a positive I.D., but the photo definitely looked like it could be one of the men — the taciturn one who carried the pelts in, not the gregarious fellow who'd chatted him up.

But Kimzey was still on the lam. There was still no sign of him when, a month or two later, the ice in the lake melted.

When it did, police got out on it in boats to look for the three corpses. They soon found them, tied lines around them, and towed them to the boat landing.

The bodies had most definitely been murdered. Nickols had been hit with a shotgun blast at close range, which had torn away part of his face and chest. Wilson had also been shotgunned, in the right shoulder, and subsequently shot with a pistol behind the ear. And someone had gone berserk with a blunt instrument on Morris's face.

Police already had a suspect in the killings, of course: Charles Kimzey. But they knew, from evidence at the scene, that the killer hadn't worked alone. That much was obvious just looking at the body of former U.S. Marine Roy Wilson. Wilson had been hit in the shoulder with a shotgun; then, later, someone had managed to get close enough to him to shoot him in the head with a pistol. It seemed pretty unlikely that anyone could have done that without help. Of all the various categories American citizens can be assigned to, if "wounded Marine" isn't the most dangerous, it's certainly at least in the top five.

Also, the Portland furrier who'd bought the fox furs stolen from the murdered trappers definitely remembered two men. One had been quiet and taciturn; the other, garrulous and friendly. The friendly one had chatted volubly about trapping, the wilderness, Bend, and various other things, clearly trying to charm the furrier. The other had looked a lot like Kimzey, but looking at the mugshot, the furrier couldn't be sure; the man he'd seen had dropped the furs and left, saying nothing and doing nothing to call attention to himself.

Had it been Kimzey? Maybe. Everyone involved with the case was sure it had been. But, without proof....

Kimzey was finally caught in Kalispell, Mont., in 1932, eight years after the murders, when one of his former jailers recognized him on the street. Immediately after his arrest, he raised eyebrows by saying, "They think I killed those trappers, but I didn't, I was in Colorado working on the Moffatt Tunnel at the time."

The alibi was a little shaky, and Kimzey was so ready with it that authorities were pretty sure he'd fabricated it after figuring out he'd need it. They figured they could break it if they dug into it deep enough; but they also figured it wasn't worth bothering with, because the evidence of Kimzey's guilt was all very circumstantial. They really didn't think they could nail him on it.

He knew it, too. So when they brought him in, he figured he'd come out of it all OK. He was probably a lot more worried they'd extradite him to Idaho, where he was still wanted for breaking out of prison.

But they knew something he didn't. A year or so before the Lava Lake murders, Kimzey had hired a car to drive him to Idaho. Halfway there, apparently while stopped in the middle of nowhere for a "call of Nature," Kimzey had clobbered the driver, W.O. Harrison, knocking him out. Then he'd bound him hand and foot with bailing wire and thrown him down a nearby abandoned well, obviously expecting him to die there; and drove on in the stolen car.

But Harrison did not die. He woke up, untangled his wrists from the wire, climbed out of the well, and found his way to a ranch — ironically, it was the Last Chance Ranch — to get help.

Lava Lake as it appears in the summertime, with South Sister, Broken Top, and Mount Bachelor in the background. (Image: Wikimedia/PeaceLoveScoobie)

Harrison was able to positively identify Kimzey as the man who had tried to kill him. And attempted murder was a pretty beefy charge. It wouldn't send Kimzey to the gallows, but it could put him away for life, and as far as Deschutes County Sheriff Claude McCauley was concerned, that was much better than nothing.

"Utah wanted Kimzey for murder" — another largely circumstantial case, involving another hired-car driver, in 1925 — "and Idaho wanted him back on an escape charge," McCauley recalled, nine years later, "but I decided he'd be safer in Oregon. We still had the attempted murder charge hanging over him, and I accordingly sent for W. O. Harrison."

McCauley doesn't recount the effect it had on Kimzey when Harrison's name was first mentioned and his would-be killer realized he'd survived to testify against him — but it was probably deeply satisfying to the outraged lawman.

Kimzey pleaded not guilty, of course. No one was in any mood to offer him any kind of plea deal.

"Harrison easily identified Kimzey as the man who had so nearly murdered him," the sheriff recalled. "The jury found Kimzey guilty as charged after three hours of deliberations. Two days later Circuit Judge T. E. Duffy sentenced Kimzey to life imprisonment in the Oregon State Penitentiary."

And so the Lava Lake triple homicide remains officially unsolved to this day, although almost everyone involved was sure the man who did it got put safely away. The judge was certainly sure of it; in the 1930s, life sentences were very seldom handed down for attempted murder. A decade or two later, Kimzey would use the disproportionateness of that sentence as his main argument for early release to the parole board. Eventually, in 1957, roughly 25 years into his sentence and now in his early 70s, Kimzey was paroled out of the joint. He promptly decamped for Idaho, where he lived out the rest of his life without, as far as I know, causing any further trouble.

The question remains, though ... who *was* Kimzey's accomplice? Who was the glib, smooth-talking man who chatted up the Portland furrier while negotiating the sale of the stolen (and mishandled) fox pelts? Who was the unknown "social engineer" who somehow lured Nickols, Morris, and Wilson out of their log cabin almost completely unarmed so that Kimzey could wreak his vengeance upon them? Remember, they knew who Kimzey was and they were expecting trouble from him. They were not expecting trouble from whoever knocked on their cabin door that fateful day, and, except for Wilson with his Luger and whoever was packing the .22, they left their weapons in the cabin when they followed him out ... which strongly argues that they didn't know trouble was afoot until they were standing in the open and lead was in the air.

Author Melany Tupper makes the case that the accomplice was none other than Ray Van Buren Jackson, Central Oregon's "angel of death" — and Jackson was one of Kimzey's known associates. Of course, Jackson was exactly the kind of glib, easy talker described by the furrier, and the kind of guy who could sell the three trappers a story that would lead them out of their safe, fortress-like log cabin to their deaths.

But, in the final analysis, nobody really knows. And it's extremely unlikely that anyone ever will.

Sources and Works Cited:
- *"Grisly 1924 Lava Lake murders still 'unsolved,'" an article by Jim Crowell published on May 31, 2012, in the* Deschutes Pioneers' Gazette;
- The Trapper Murders, *a book by Melany Tupper published in 2013 by Central Oregon Books;*

- *"The Lava Lake Murders mystery in Oregon still baffles people today,"* an article by Tyler Willford published Jan. 11, 2017, on *thatoregonlife.com;*
- Portland Morning Oregonian *archives, April and May 1924.*

THE MAN WITH THE HOOK.

As urban legends, go, it's one of the oldest and scariest:
A teenage couple drives to a secluded spot late at night and parks, planning to do some of the usual canoodling. But before they do, a news bulletin interrupts the music on the radio. A psychotic killer has escaped from the asylum, the DJ reports breathlessly. He's missing his left hand, and wears a steel hook on the stump of his arm as a prosthetic.

The boy wants to ignore the news and smooch some more, but the girl is too freaked out, so he reluctantly starts the car and drives her home. When they get there, she makes a frightening discovery: A steel prosthetic hook, hanging from the door handle on the passenger side.

A chilling and enduring story, and one that's still being told today. But it's just a story ... right?

Right. Because in late November 1960, in the northwest hills of Portland, when the man with the hook showed up, he got 'em. The two young lovers never made it home.

That, in any case, is the strong suspicion of Portland historian Phil Stanford, who delved into the notorious 1960 double murder of sweethearts Larry Peyton and Beverly Allan to write the definitive book on the case.

What Stanford found was that a particularly disturbing suspect who turned up early in the process was simply not taken seriously. And if he had been, there's a good chance that a dozen murders — including, some investigators think, maybe even the Zodiac killings in Southern California 40 years ago — would have never happened.

Here's the story (or, rather, a sketchy overview of the story — there is much more in Stanford's book):

The story starts out just like the Man with the Hook story: with Peyton and his girlfriend, Beverly Allan, cruising downtown Portland on a Saturday night in Larry's 1949 Ford two-door sedan, and ending up "parking" in a secluded place in Forest Park.

The next day a policeman, driving through Forest Park in search of stolen cars, came across Larry's Ford. The door was open, there was blood everywhere, and Larry was slumped in the driver's seat. He'd been stabbed 23 times with a four-inch-long knife.

As for Beverly Allan ... there was no sign of her.

No sign, that is, until more than a month later, when her badly mutilated body was found in a ditch, within sight of passing cars on Sunset Highway outside Portland.

Police detectives, already coming under considerable pressure to get things done, started immediately with a campaign that involved filtering through an unbelievable volume of low-quality leads. The Multnomah County Sheriff, who had ruined the crime scene by rummaging around in the car before the investigators got there, now tried to make up

Larry Peyton's car as it was found at the crime scene. (Image: Ptown Books)

Larry Peyton and Beverly Allan in 1959 or 1960. (Image: Ptown Books)

for it by dashing off letters to other law-enforcement agencies around the country asking about similar crimes. Eager convicts in prisons nationwide started talking their heads off, whether they knew anything about the case or not, in hopes of cutting a deal. And several mentally unbalanced people started pestering the cops with tip after red-hot tip.

One of the early leads the cops stumbled across was a prison-hardened tough guy with the odd and memorable name Edward W. Edwards. Edwards had been snooping around the crime scene the day after Peyton's body was discovered, and 10 days later he was caught setting off fire alarms as a prank. He had a minor unexplained bullet wound in his upper arm. Police revoked his parole, tossed him in the county lockup and made plans to interrogate him first thing Monday.

Meanwhile, the cops were looking into a couple of unruly teenage drinking parties that had been held near the crime scene that night. These parties were packed with troubled teens and young adults, male and female, some of whom knew and disliked Larry Peyton. Many of them had criminal records for minor robberies and burglaries. There were weapons — a couple knives, an automatic pistol found in a garbage can — and there were stories of fistfights and plenty of possible motives.

By the time Edwards was arrested, the cops were already working on several promising theories, and he was very much a back-burner kind of suspect. So when he escaped from the jail over the weekend and disappeared, they didn't much worry about it.

They certainly didn't ask themselves why a seasoned crook who knew very well how the system worked would want to avoid questioning badly enough to break out of jail and go fully on the lam over a minor misdemeanour charge.

Edwards moved east, and eventually was caught after an especially lucrative bank robbery that landed him on the FBI's Top 10 Most Wanted list for a short time. (Although he liked to claim he had an I.Q. in the high 130s, he wasn't able to figure out that paying cash for a new Cadillac and a truckload of new things for his apartment might attract some attention.) A hair sample was sent to Portland, and, after a comparison with a hair found on Beverly Allan turned out not to be a match, he was eliminated as a suspect.

Eventually, with the help of an astonishingly sketchy collection of "witnesses," the authorities charged three of the partygoers with two counts of murder. One was acquitted; the other two were convicted, and sentenced to life-plus-25. Within just a few years, both were paroled. Nobody believed they'd done it — not any more.

But if not them, who?

Early in 2009, the Wisconsin State Police dusted off a cold-case file from 1980. Someone had followed two young lovers as they walked home from a wedding reception, pounced on them, stabbed the man to death, and raped and strangled his fiancée. By the time the bodies were found by hunters, six months later, they were badly decomposed ... but not badly enough for the killer's DNA to be gone from the scene. Samples had been preserved in anticipation of a day when technology would advance enough to test them. That day had come.

The cops ran the test, and hey, jackpot! It came back a match to none other than Edward W. Edwards.

In July of 2009, the Wisconsin State Police arrested Edwards — who by then had aged into a 76-year-old blob of a man in a wheelchair on oxygen — and charged him with two counts of murder.

With Edwards' name in the news, authorities in other places started contacting Wisconsin. It seems he'd been at the scene of a number of other crimes that looked a lot like the Peyton-Allan murders. In some of those crimes, he'd even been a suspect.

Edwards was in Great Falls, Montana, in 1956, when a young couple was murdered. The 19-year-old male was found lying beside his car, hands tied, shot in the back of the head; his girlfriend was found six miles away, also shot through the head.

Then there was the death of two high-school kids in Akron, Ohio, who'd gone on a date in 1979 and never come back; they weren't found until six years later. They'd been shot and stabbed. Edwards was mentioned as a "person of interest."

And Edwards, in 2010, confessed that he was the guy who murdered two young lovers in Doylestown, Ohio, in 1977 — again, execution style, with a shotgun blast to the back of the neck.

It's also worth noting that he was around the San Francisco Bay area during the Zodiac Killer's reign of terror.

And, of course, he'd been nosing around the crime scene at the Peyton-Allan killing too.

That puts him at the scene of at least five double-murders involving young lovers, over a 25-year stretch. What are the odds?

The Man with the Hook died on April 7, 2011, just a few weeks into a life sentence in Wisconsin. He never did say whether he was the man who killed Larry Peyton and Beverly Allan, and Multnomah County decided not to reopen the investigation.

So we'll probably never really know.

Sources and Works Cited:
- The Peyton-Allan Files, *a book by Phil Stanford published in 2010 by Ptown Books;*
- *manwiththehook.com;*
- *murderpedia.org.*

THE DARK STRANGLER.

October 20, 1926, could easily have been the day Mrs. M.D. Lewis died — suddenly, silently and violently.

She was doing some work around a small house she had for sale in the Sellwood neighborhood of Portland when an old car pulled up in front of it and a small man with black hair and a dark complexion stepped out. Rude and brusque, he beetled into the house as if he owned it, muttering "House for sale" as he passed her.

Lewis, of course, found his manners completely offensive. Perhaps that was why she disliked him on the spot.

But there may have been something else, too, because when she heard him shouting down the stairs — "Come upstairs and see what's wrong with this door!" — something clearly told her not to go.

Instead, she called upstairs that he should not worry about it, and the door would be fixed. He did not reply.

Moments later, she heard him coming back downstairs, and he went into the basement. Then up the stairs came that abrasive voice again: "Come down here and see what's wrong with this furnace!"

The furnace? Lewis, now thoroughly alarmed, ran outside the house and, from outside, shouted to the man to come see the flowers she'd planted in the yard.

"To hell with your flowers!" the man shouted back, and hurried upstairs and left the house. A few moments later he was driving away — fast.

The next day, the worried father of 37-year-old widow Mabel Fluke was searching for any sign of her in the house she'd been showing for sale just a few blocks from Lewis's the day before. He didn't find her ... but the police did, two days later, in a dark corner of the attic.

She'd been strangled with a scarf.

Mabel Fluke was the second of three Portland women who fell victim that week to one of the first known serial killers in American history — a man who would come to be known in the newspapers as "The Dark Strangler." By the time her body was found, both the other two had been discovered: Beata Withers, 35, found at the bottom of a trunk full of clothes in the room-for-rent she was showing; and Virginia Grant, 59, found in a crumpled heap in the basement of a house she had for rent ... behind the furnace.

At first, police had thought Withers' death had been suicide, although it seemed a pretty weird way to go, smothering oneself at the bottom of a trunk of clothes. And Grant's death had looked like it could have been heart failure. But as for Fluke, that just wasn't possible, and besides, she'd been robbed of her jewelry.

Also, once they took the time to check, authorities quickly figured out that all the victims' bodies had been, in the euphemism of the day, "outraged" after death. This hadn't been obvious, because the killer had carefully re-dressed the corpses afterward.

By the time they figured all this out, the Dark Strangler was already a thousand miles away, at a boardinghouse with a room for rent in San Francisco, with his fingers around yet another feminine throat.

But Oregon had not seen the last of the Dark Strangler. By late November, he was back in Portland. Perhaps he was looking for another woman to murder when he came to see the room in Sophia Yates' lodging house on Third Avenue. For whatever reason — perhaps because there were two other women there as well, the lodgers in the other rooms — he rented the room instead of murdering the landlady.

Giving his name as Adrian Harris, the Dark Strangler spent Thanksgiving with Yates and her lodgers. They found him very nice — polite, soft-spoken, very intelligent, but a bit of a religious fanatic. When he learned the women didn't have enough money for a Thanksgiving dinner, he offered to spring for the whole spread if they would cook it for him.

"Adrian" also was generous in other ways. He gave both Yates and one of her lodgers, Emily Crawford, bits of expensive jewelry — jewelry that he had, of course, pulled from the fingers and ears of freshly slain murder victims a few weeks before.

Yates and Crawford didn't know that, of course. What they did know

The booking mugshots of Earle Nelson, a.k.a. The Dark Strangler, after his arrest in Winnipeg.
CREDIT: The Winnipeg Sun

was that Yates had gotten nicer gifts than Crawford, the discovery of which unfortunate fact now caused the two of them to exchange some sharp words.

"They must have gotten loud about it," writes historian J.D. Chandler in his book, *Murder and Mayhem in Portland, Oregon*; "because suddenly 'Harris' burst into the room. 'I'm going to beat it,' he said. 'You two will have the police up next.' He ran from the house and drove away, leaving two days' rent unused."

On the day after Thanksgiving, "Harris" checked into another boardinghouse. This time, he didn't stay long, or give anything away. And the next day, the body of the landlady, 48-year-old Blanche Myers, was found stuffed under the bed.

After that, Portland was on high alert; but, perhaps knowing the turf was burned there, the Dark Strangler never returned. Instead, he struck out on a sort of six-month-long blood-soaked road trip, leaving bodies behind him in Council Bluffs, Kansas City, Chicago, Philadelphia, Buffalo, and Detroit. Then, following a pair of murders in Winnipeg — including one of shocking brutality, perpetrated with a hammer — he was snagged by the Mounties while trying to make his way back to the U.S. border.

Left in his wake, the Dark Strangler left the murdered bodies of at least 21 women — probably more than 30 — and one 8-month-old baby.

The Dark Strangler's real name turned out to be Earle Leonard Nelson, and he'd had — as so many serial killers have — a rough childhood. His mother died of syphilis shortly after his birth, leaving him to be raised by a fanatically religious grandmother. He was expelled from elementary school at age 7 for violent behavior. By age 18 he was in San Quentin, serving time for a burglary charge.

After his release, he was in and out of mental hospitals over the following decade or so, until he embarked on the nationwide murder spree that brought him to Portland — and subsequently to Winnipeg.

It was in Winnipeg that Nelson's sordid life story turned its final page. Sentenced to hang for his crimes, he stood on the platform on Jan. 13, 1928, and said, "I declare my innocence before God and man. I forgive those who have injured me, and I ask pardon from those I have injured."

Unimpressed, the executioner pulled the lever and away Nelson went.

"The hangman's rope was a little too short," Chandler writes in his book, "and it took Nelson nearly 15 minutes to strangle to death. Some thought it was poetic justice for the 'Dark Strangler.'"

It is at least worth considering the possibility that this oversight in preparing Nelson's noose was not accidental.

Sources and Works Cited:
- Murder and Mayhem in Portland Oregon, *a book by J.D. Chandler published in 2013 by The History Press;*
- Portland Morning Oregonian *archives, October 1926, and December 1927.*

THE RAILROAD JOB.

On the bitter cold winter night of Jan. 22, 1943, a beautiful 21-year-old woman named Martha Brinson James was settling into her sleeping berth in a crowded Pullman coach, headed for San Francisco.

Young Mrs. James would not live to see the sun come up on Jan. 23. And the circumstances that led to her death are, 70 years later, still emerging from a cloud of mystery not unmixed with deliberate obfuscation — but one of the few things we do know, with near certainty, is that the man sent to the gas chamber for this crime was innocent of it.

Here's the story as it was told the next day in the Portland *Morning Oregonian*:

Martha Brinson James came of a blue-blooded Virginia family, her father a good friend and neighbor of the governor of that state. On the night of her death, she had been married for just four months, to a dashing young Navy pilot named Richard James. The two of them were traveling from Seattle to their new home in California, where Richard had been stationed as a reserve Naval aviator. Richard, a lowly Ensign (the lowest rank of commissioned Navy officer), was sent on a troop train; his wife followed a few hours behind on the Southern Pacific West Coast Limited.

The West Coast Limited was packed on that chilly day. It was still early in the Second World War, and the tide of war was only just starting to turn in favor of the U.S. Military personnel and their families were being shuttled all over the country, and trains, like all bits of home-front infrastructure, were being run as Spartanly as possible; traveling on them was not fun. They were crowded and cramped. In one car, a family of five was packed into two twin-bed-size berths. The windows were blacked out under wartime rules, making the train car into a coffin-like box hurtling through the night. Inside that box, people sweated, swore, emitted noxious gases, feuded, got carsick ... and, after midnight or so, tried desperately to sleep.

At about 4 a.m., the passengers on Car D were startled awake by a scream — a woman shouting, "I can't stand this any longer — oh my God, he's killing me!" They rushed to pull aside their curtains and saw the form of a woman who had obviously fallen out of her berth, lying on her back in the middle of the aisle. Standing over her was a uniformed Marine Corps private, apparently the first on the scene. He was covered in the blood that was still spurting from her throat, which had been savagely slashed.

The Marine, Pvt. Harold Wilson, said he'd been in the bunk just above hers when he heard her scream; he'd pulled aside the curtains in time to see her falling out of her berth, and to see a dark, heavy-set man running from the scene.

"He kind of turned a little sideways, so I could just get the side of his face," Wilson told investigators later. "It was pretty full. He had on a brown pin-point stripe suit. I think he was about 5 feet 10 inches, and he had short hair. The light was so dim I couldn't tell whether he was a light Negro or a dark white man."

Hastily pulling on his pants, Wilson said, he'd jumped down from his berth to see if she needed help, but had quickly realized she was beyond the reach of aid.

When the train arrived at Eugene, authorities went through it as carefully as they could. There was a trail of blood drops that led to the back end of the train, which suggested that perhaps the murderer had jumped off into the night; but then again, some or all of that trail was likely left by Wilson, the too-late would-be rescuer. Other than that, the evidence was scant. The victim's throat, early reports claimed, had been slashed with something dull or blunt; the weapon wasn't found.

At Eugene, Wilson was taken into custody as a material witness, along with an African-American dining-car waiter who matched the vague physical description of height, build and complexion he had given.

The Sunday Oregonian's coverage of Martha Brinson James' murder used this photograph, which was from her wedding four months before. (Image: Oregonian)

LOVE, SEX and MURDER in OLD OREGON

As you can imagine, the entire country found this story riveting. More than one historian has compared the whole thing to a story from one of the many tawdry "true detective" pulp-fiction magazines. It had all the elements ... all the elements but one, that is: A villain. For it soon appeared that the local law-enforcement authorities were stumped on this one.

Tracks were found in the snow near where the train had been when the murder took place, and even some blood. But that trail went cold when

A newspaper photograph of Robert E. Lee Folkes as he appeared the day he was extradited to Albany to stand trial for the murder of Martha Brinson James. (Image: California State Railroad Museum)

authorities found the tracks came from and returned to a local farm; the farmer said he'd suffered a nosebleed from the cold. Clearly whoever did the killing had remained on the train.

There was that dining-car waiter. But he was quickly eliminated as a suspect. He had been asleep in a berth at the other end of the train, and had several solid witnesses to back up his alibi.

Then there was Pvt. Wilson, of course, found standing over the body with blood all over his hands. But Wilson was a U.S. Marine, and one rather *expects* Marines to run to the rescue of women who cry out in the night. Nobody wanted *him* to turn out to be the guy who did it; it would be like learning that a firefighter was a secret serial killer. How would that look to the citizens of a country at war, its trains and subways packed with young men in uniform? How would home-front logistics be affected if women started looking at every young man in uniform as a potential predator? How would it reflect on the military; how would it affect home-front morale?

So the authorities were quite relieved when a third suspect was found: a cook by the name of Robert E. Lee Folkes.

The official story was that Folkes was fingered after Pvt. Wilson recalled seeing him in the kitchen as he raced through in pursuit of the brown-suited man, and noticed he was sweaty-looking. So the Los Angeles Police Department had brought him in for questioning. Folkes, the LAPD claimed, had maintained his innocence until confronted with assurance that two women who said he'd made aggressive passes at them earlier in the evening had positively identified him from his mugshot, at which dread news he "broke down" and confessed it all.

Wilson, who freely and frankly acknowledged how bad things looked for him, greeted the news that Folkes had confessed with an obvious sigh of relief. "Boy, am I glad to hear that," he said.

He wasn't the only one. Folkes was everything mainstream 1940s Americans might expect to see in a suspect, and then some: sophisticated and urban in that jazzy Harlem-Renaissance way, he appeared in court sporting a bright-blue "zoot suit." Moreover, he was Black — which in 1940s America made stories of his alleged wickedness a whole lot easier to sell than would have been the case had he been white. The Reconstruction-spawned myth of the lazy, lust-crazed, "uppity" Black man running about raping and murdering white maidens was still resonating in 1940s America — hence the detail from Folkes' "confession" about making aggressive passes at white women on the train.

For the law-enforcement authorities who wanted, more than anything, to get the situation resolved one way or the other, having Folkes as a suspect made their job much easier. A story could easily be crafted that would plug into that mythos, and 1940s Americans — especially rural ones, from a state with a tiny and marginalized Black population — would barely even glance at the evidence before eating it right up, no questions asked.

And that's exactly how it went at Folkes' murder trial, a sensational proceeding held in Albany at the Linn County Courthouse. It ended on April 22, 1943, when a jury of Albany-area housewives, millworkers, and farmers brought back the inevitable verdict against the strange, well-dressed Black man who stood facing them. It was "guilty."

The trial was so laden with stereotypes and literary tropes that the Hearst newspapers' Sunday magazine *American Weekly*, the following month, recapped the whole affair with a dramatic package headlined, "Actual Crime with All the Settings of Fiction." It laid out, in sensationalistic prose with lurid illustrations, the official storyline: Murderer Robert E. Lee Folkes, a cook in the train's dining car — having spent the evening shirking his job duties, drinking cheap liquor, and making boorish passes at random white maidens, and now afire with carnal lust — tiptoes into the Pullman coach, planning to rape the lovely young Martha James at knifepoint. When she awakens and screams, he cuts her throat to silence her, then leaps out of the berth and races back to the kitchen, where he stations himself over a cold stove and pretends he's been cooking eggs on it the whole time.

Meanwhile, a brave and noble U.S. Marine has heard the scream and is racing to her rescue — alas, too late to do anything but help penetrate the murderer's defenses, break his alibi and see that justice is served.

Left unmentioned in the *American Weekly* account were a couple other literary tropes that the trial fitted especially well. It was every bit as race-baitey as the 1915 movie "Birth of a Nation," depicting Black Man as a bestial creature with an uncontrolled lust, ever yearning to "defile" the daughters of middle-class white people. In other ways, it was almost a straight rip-off of the railroad-train variant of the classic "locked-room mystery," like "Murder on the Orient Express" by Agatha Christie.

These similarities to known narrative patterns, according to Western Oregon University professor Max G. Geier's book about the case, were not coincidental.

Also left out of the story are a wide range of inconvenient facts that make Folkes' guilt almost impossible to believe in — chief among which are the fingernail clipping samples that were taken and tested after the murder, and revealed traces of nothing but starch, grease, flour and baking soda — absolutely no blood.

Geier makes a powerful case that Robert Folkes was a scapegoat, a target of opportunity seized upon to solve a very specific set of problems faced by nearly everyone in a position of authority. To win a conviction against him, prosecutors tried, successfully, to distract from the lack of actual evidence by manipulating their story to make it as familiar as possible, and appealing to the prejudices that had made "Birth of a Nation" such a popular movie in those dark pre-war years of nationwide Jim Crow-ism.

In fairness to those jurors, this likely wouldn't have worked on its own. But in combination with a confession that had almost certainly had been either fabricated or beaten out of Folkes during a three-day interrogation session with Los Angeles Police Department officers at the city jail, it was more than enough.

One of the most striking things about this case, though, is how overwhelming was the evidence against that Marine who claimed to have come too late to Martha James' rescue — Pvt. Harold Wilson.

Pvt. Harold Wilson, it turned out, had been released from the brig the day he boarded the train in Washington; he'd been locked up there for an alleged sexual assault. His commanding officer was sending him to a combat unit, in the same way misbehaving German soldiers were sent to the Eastern Front. He might very well have been thinking this train trip would be his last few hours of freedom.

And the witnesses' accounts dovetail perfectly with an attempted sexual-assault-at-knifepoint gone wrong. Each remembers the words slightly differently, but most agree it started with a woman saying, "I can't stand this any longer!" followed by, "He's killing me!" and a horrible scream. Sleep-fogged passengers poked their heads out of the curtains to see Wilson already bending over the still-bleeding body. Then one of the passengers pulled the cord to summon the steward, and it was only after that bell rang that Wilson started shouting that murder had been done.

Wilson's story started out sketchy and changed almost every time he retold it. First he claimed to have run to the end of the train in pursuit of the killer and seen no one; then, when a trainman replied that he had to have seen at the very least a cook, a waiter and a steward, he changed his story to include all three of those characters. He miscounted the number of cars he ran through and then said maybe he hadn't made it to the back of the train after all (although one source says a blood trail was found leading to the end of the train). He claimed it took him nine steps to get to the end of the car in pursuit, when he was less than 6 feet from it. On the witness stand, he was unable even to identify his military unit. And one of the witnesses recalls him actually trying to plant a bloody towel in the bathroom between the murder scene and the cook's car.

But in court, the prosecution seemed to fight desperately to avoid even considering the possibility that Wilson had any role in the murder other than that of too-late would-be-rescuer. The railroad ordered its employees not to cooperate with Folkes' defense attorney. And the prosecution even constructed, in an Albany railroad yard, a life-size diorama of the murder train — except it had been modified so that the cook's car, in which Folkes was working, was one car away from the murder car instead of five or six.

But why? Why would all the authority figures, from the railroad's house detective all the way up to Oregon Gov. Earl Snell and maybe even higher, have acted in this way, to hang a man they should have at least suspected was innocent of the crime?

We can't really know the answer to that question. But if you consider the consequences that might have resulted from Wilson being publicly accused of this crime, it begins to make a lot more sense — especially in the context of an America in its darkest wartime hour.

Let's start with the Southern Pacific Railroad. Geier, in his book, makes an excellent case for the railroad having had a strong incentive to pin this killing on Folkes. To the railroad, Folkes was a somewhat dangerous man — an intelligent, articulate, well connected Black man who also happened to be a prominent member of a union that the railroad really wanted to break. Sending him up the river in the face of plenty of evidence of his innocence would send a powerful message to members of that union that it could not protect them.

The various law-enforcement organizations charged with investigating this crime also shared a strong incentive to pin it on Folkes rather than trying to indict Wilson for it. The reason was simple: to save face. There's no ambiguity here: They all bungled it badly. First, they didn't secure the crime scene; the train stopped at several stations, with people freely allowed on and off, before law enforcement people met up with it at Eugene to start the investigation.

And when the agencies finally did get involved, they did it like a pack of paparazzi at the Oscars. There was the Lane County Sheriff's Office, the Eugene Police Department, the Oregon State Police, the railroad's own in-house detective bureau, and, once they got to the scene, the Linn County Sheriff's Office. Federal investigators from the U.S. Navy and FBI soon weighed in. Witnesses were interviewed and re-interviewed, all in a big room so that they could hear each other; naturally, their stories started to influence one another. Evidence was mishandled, stepped in, tracked around, and then cleaned up. Then, to top it all off, the railroad company parked the "murder car" on a spur line right next to the biggest U.S.O. facility in the

SERIAL KILLERS *and* DEADLY STRANGERS.

Robert E. Lee Folkes consults with his defense attorney, Leroy Lomax, left, as his friend and adviser William Pollard, right, looks on. (Image: Oregon Journal)

region for a week, where it (and any lingering uncompromised evidence) received hundreds of visits from curious soldiers and sailors.

A day or two after the crime took place, the story was in the headlines nationwide, and federal law-enforcement officials were making some very uncomplimentary remarks about evidence-handling and crime-investigating skills out in Oregon. A nationwide public-relations disaster was in the offing, and the only possible hope for heading it off was a quick and decisive conviction.

That much we know, as a matter of public record. But there are good reasons to believe that's not all. Here's the speculative scenario:

Oregon authorities can see it's important to find somebody to pin this on, and fast, so that they can get back to not being a national laughingstock. But the most likely suspect, Wilson, has had a week in which to get his story straight, and because he's white and a military man, any jury will choke on the "reasonable doubt" introduced by their failure to secure the crime scene. Prosecuting him will only result in a high-profile acquittal that will showcase every detail of their incompetence and make them look even dumber. What's needed is a fall guy to pin it on. And nobody's more vulnerable to that sort of judicial lynching, in 1943 America, than one of the train's African-American crew members. A provincial jury made up of white people whose familiarity with Black people consists entirely of racist pulp-mag stories about savage Black rapists attacking pure white maidens will be far more likely to convict such a man in the absence of any real evidence of guilt. And such a fall-guy just happens to be handy, so with a little help from the LAPD's jailhouse interrogation squad, they fabricate what they need, handcraft a pulp-magazine-style account of the crime, and get busy selling it to the jury.

So, is this what happened? We can't really know for sure. But it seems very likely. The motive was certainly there.

But the agency with the most compelling motivation to crucify Folkes was the U.S. War Department. Here's why:

Imagine, for a moment, that you are an 18-year-old single woman, and it's early 1943 — close to the darkest hour of the war. You're doing your best to be brave, and everyone must make sacrifices, so you're riding trains unchaperoned and walking to your home-front manufacturing job in the dark by yourself. But it's OK, because you feel safe with all the uniformed soldiers and sailors around. Strong and brave and confident, they represent security to you, and you feel sure that if you should ever need anything, you could ask one of them to help you out.

Then suddenly you hear about a story from the West Coast: A U.S. Marine has been accused of having raped and murdered a pretty girl just like you, in a Pullman sleeper car just like the ones you're riding in regularly, all by yourself, on long war-related trips. Suddenly you're looking at those soldiers and sailors in a completely different way — as potential threats rather than as sources of comfort. And every other pretty woman in the country is doing the same. They're avoiding rail travel. When forced to take an overnight train, they're arriving at their destinations exhausted and unrested. Worse yet, other low-quality men in uniform are starting to jump on this criminal bandwagon. There's another assault, and another. Soon women are refusing to travel alone on rail cars and wondering if they're safe on the streets. Morale, at this most key point in the war effort, collapses.

And it all could have been avoided if . . . if the crime had been committed not by a uniformed soldier, but by, say, an African-American railroad cook. Then it would be more of a random sort of threat; a Black train cook climbing into a Pullman berth with a passenger would be so unusual that people would view it as a freak incident rather than a new threat to guard against.

Looked at this way, railroading Folkes was almost a patriotic duty, and his subsequent execution wasn't much different from a death on a battlefield. It may even have saved lives.

But the price of that non-outcome was a grave injustice, an innocent man killed and a guilty one not only set free, but released from the duty assignment that would likely have cost him his life. And in fact, out of all the military personnel in that "murder car" on the night Martha James was killed, the only one who survived the war was Pvt. Harold Wilson.

Sources and Works Cited:
- The Color of Night, *a book by Max G. Geier published in 2015 by Oregon State University Press;*
- "Murder on No. 15 . . . .," *an article by Neil Barker published in the September 2011 issue of* Oregon Historical Quarterly;
- Portland Morning Oregonian *archives, January 1943.*

PART VI:

VIGILANTE MURDER.

Oregon, in the 1800s, was a long way from everywhere. Until the arrival of transcontinental telegraph lines made it possible for Pinkerton detectives to communicate with the head office, it was a capital place to go if you were running from the law; even if you were a fugitive from justice, with a little luck and a lot of brass you'd do fine. You could even rise through the ranks of society to become one of the state's most honored citizens, as John M. Hipple (who served in the United States Senate under his criminal alias, John H. Mitchell) did.

It was also a great place for folks who just wanted to be left alone.

That combination of attributes naturally attracted more than a few Old West-type bad guys to the state. And when those fellows did what Old West-type bad guys are wont to do — cheat, steal, claim-jump, swindle, and rustle — the good people of their communities needed to do something to protect their rough-hewn new society from trouble.

What they were supposed to do, of course, was look to the law. But that wasn't always possible. In parts of the state that were three days' journey from the county seat, calling the sheriff usually wasn't a viable option.

So these frontier types, accustomed to solving their own problems, were usually ready, willing, and able to posse up and supply their own law enforcement.

There were, obviously, a few drawbacks to this approach ... these, for instance.

THE MASKED ASSASSINS.

In the old Linkville Cemetery in Klamath Falls, if you should find yourself wandering through reading headstones, you just might stumble across one near the east entrance that features the most startling epitaph you're ever likely to read:

"LEE and JOE, Children of H.C. & M.T. LAWS," it reads, "murdered by masked assassins. June 24, 1882; Aged 19 Years; Aged 15 Years."

The gravestone is a relic of a grim and dark time in Oregon, and the Western range country in general — a time of rustlers and vigilantes, of six-gun justice and lynch mobs. It all took place so long ago that documentation is often scant, and what remains is usually slanted in favor of the side of the argument that won (or survived).

This cryptic gravestone is the only physical evidence remaining of a short but hot family feud that left four dead and several more wounded — a sort of condensed frontier-Oregon version of the Hatfield-McCoy wars.

It started with a man named Henry C. Laws, who, in the late 1870s, was the leader of an outfit called The Bonanza Regulators — a gang, essentially, based out of the town of Bonanza and dedicated to keeping newcomers and outsiders from grazing their livestock on the federally owned rangeland in western Lake and eastern Klamath counties, which the Regulators wanted to use exclusively for their own herds.

But it wasn't outsiders that Laws was destined to have trouble with; it was other locals — specifically, William Calavan (sometimes spelled Callaghan) and his sons. Calavan, one day, found what he thought were his own cattle in Laws' herd, and moved to take possession on the spot. Laws reacted by grabbing a club and letting Calavan have it, causing a lasting injury (although of what type I haven't been able to learn).

After that, tensions between the two families grew steadily worse until finally, one day in late winter of 1882, Laws, driving a herd of cattle up a path in the snow, met Calavan's two sons, Frank and Jimmie, on horseback. The two lads refused to move off the path to let the cattle through. Words were exchanged, then angry shouts, and, finally, hot lead.

It's not clear who started the shooting. Both sides, of course, blamed each other. But when the gunsmoke had cleared, Henry Laws had been shot in the calf, Jimmy's horse had been shot out from under him, and 15-year-old Frank Calavan had taken a bullet somewhere important. He made it home on his horse, where he died shortly after his brother arrived on foot.

Laws was arrested, of course, and taken to Alturas, Calif., for possible prosecution. But from the very start, there was a good deal of confusion as to who had jurisdiction; the crime had happened almost right smack on the state line between Oregon and California, and of course neither state was eager to go to the trouble and expense of doing another state's legal duty. California, having been handed the opportunity to make the first ruling, predictably decided it had happened in Oregon, and sent the case packing northward.

A month later, in March, a preliminary hearing was scheduled in the town of Linkville — which today is known as Klamath Falls — to sort through this and other questions. Linkville having no dedicated Hall of Justice back in 1882, the hearing was to be held in a hotel — referred to in various sources as the Linkville Hotel, the Greenman Hotel and the Lakeside Inn.

Whatever the hotel's name was, it soon proved its inadequacy as a holding facility for accused murderers. That night, a gang of about 18 masked men slipped into the lobby with cocked shotguns in their hands.

Rumors of the gang's plans had preceded them, though, and the sheriff had put out the call for locals to defend Laws from the lynchers; the hotel was full of armed defenders. When the masked men stepped into the lobby with drawn guns, they got the drop on everyone in the room; but the presence of so many men with guns in the lobby seems to have unnerved the lynching party considerably.

"Where is Laws? Someone show us Laws," barked the leader of the gang, according to the recollections of Linkville resident Rufus Moore, one of the defenders, 40 years later. Turning to a young boy, he repeated his

VIGILANTE MURDER.

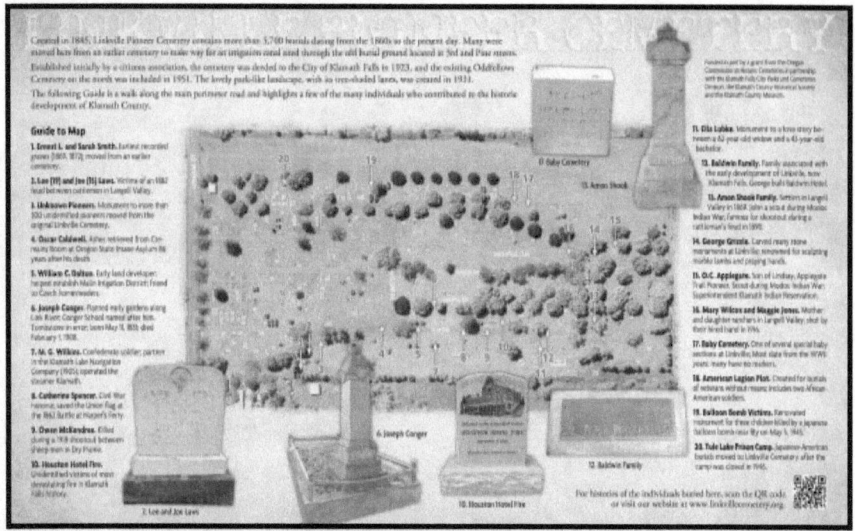

This map accompanies a walking tour of the Linkville Pioneer Cemetery; it includes the location of the Laws gravestone, as well as several others that mark the final resting places of victims of the 1880s range wars. (Image: Klamath County Historical Society)

demand: "Take this candle and show us to Laws." But the boy stood petrified with fear, apparently unable to move.

So the leader took the candle in one hand and his gun in the other and started up the stairs. And that's when someone opened fire on him from the top of the stairs, obviously aiming at the candle.

"The leader backed away from the doorway and said, 'Stand your ground, boys,'" Moore recalled. "But his men all stampeded and several shots rang out in the room. The concussion extinguished all the lights. I heard a man cry, 'Oh!' followed by a sound like running water. It was blood, we later learned."

It was indeed blood. The gunshots had been accidental discharges; when the panicked lynch-mob members had broken and run, many of them had forgotten that they had cocked blasters dangling from their trigger fingers. Several of them actually dropped their weapons in their panic, and the impact when it hit the floor set off at least one shotgun — it was found on the floor with one barrel fired and the other at full cock. And apparently its full load of shot had, by sheer bad luck, hit Deputy Sheriff J.F. Lewis in the leg. The close-range blast had torn away Lewis's femoral artery. In seconds his body had drained itself of blood and left him dead on the floor.

Now in full panic-stricken retreat, the would-be lynch mob members were racing for their horses, their shotguns lying forgotten on the floor of the hotel behind them or dangling forgotten (but still cocked) from their hands. Several more accidental discharges resulted, including one that

The entrance to the Linkville Pioneer Cemetery, a photograph taken for the cemetery's application to the National Register of Historic Places. (Image: NRHP)

removed a hat and a shock of red hair from one of the mob members and another that slightly wounded the local justice of the peace, William A. Wright. But no one ever figured out who any of the masked men were.

The next day the hearing was held, as scheduled. But because young Frank Calavan had been shot in a gunfight, it wasn't high on the court's priority list; in that violent age, dropping someone in a gun duel barely even counted as a killing, and it was only because of the victim's young age that it was being investigated at all. Predictably, it was decided that the case was really California's after all, and California having already decided that it was Oregon's, that was effectively an end to the case.

Only, of course, it wasn't really the end.

The real end would come three months later. Henry Laws' two sons were out in a pasture near their cabin, butchering a steer. They had a quarter of beef hanging on a tree near a wagon to haul it, and both of them were standing in the wagon cutting up the meat when the rimrock above and behind them started crackling with rifle fire.

Lee Laws went down like a stone, shot through the heart. Joe Laws, the younger brother, took cover behind the wagon; atop the rimrock he could see the horsemen, masks over their faces, Winchesters at their shoulders. "You would shoot a boy, you cowards!" he screamed at them.

VIGILANTE MURDER.

Bullets were flying all around him, breaking spokes off the wagon wheels and kicking up puffs of dirt by his feet. Then one of them shattered his leg.

After that, the masked riders rode away. A third boy, also named Henry Laws (probably a third brother, although that isn't clear) hurried out of the cabin and brought the badly crippled Joe in to do what he could.

Joe, as you will have guessed from the message on his gravestone, subsequently died of his injuries. Their father, Henry C. Laws, heard about the murders during a trip to Ashland for supplies, when he stopped at a settlement along the way. He sent word for his family to join him there, and they shook the dust of their old homestead from their feet — never returning again.

As for the Calavans, they apparently left the area as well; nothing further is heard about them.

But someone must have remained behind who cared about the Laws boys enough to carve that dramatic epitaph on their shared headstone.

Sources and Works Cited:
- Klamath Falls Evening Herald *archives, July 1923 and January 1941;*
- Klamath Falls Herald and News *archives, May 2012;*
- *National Register of Historic Places application for Linkview Pioneer Cemetery;*
- *Personal correspondence with author/historian Kerby Jackson.*

THE PRINEVILLE VIGILANTES.

It was the Ides of March — March 15, 1882. A.H. Crooks and Stephen Jory were blazing the boundary lines of some land — cutting big marks in trees to mark what they claimed was the property line — near the ranch of a man named Lucius Langdon, near Prineville.

The two of them broke for lunch, and when they returned, Langdon was waiting for them — with a shotgun.

A few noisy, smoky seconds later, Crooks and Jory were dead. And their killing marked the start of a two-year period of rule by masked gunmen and lynch mobs in the Prineville area that sounds, today, like the plot of a Louis L'Amour novel — the story of the Crook County Vigilantes.

"When a band of men went outside the law ... to revenge the killings, they also hanged an innocent man, and started a rule by gun and rope that is one of the blackest chapters in Oregon's history," local rancher and future sheriff James Blakely told a *Morning Oregonian* reporter, many years later.

Blakely himself was no unbiased observer. He would, two years later, be the leader of the community group opposing the Vigilantes. Blakely's anti-Vigilante group called itself the Moonshiners, because they kept watch when the moon was out, looking for masked Vigilante riders. (Remember, this was decades before Prohibition, when the name "moonshiner" would come to mean something entirely different.)

Blakely's chief opponent was a frontier character named Colonel William

"Bud" Thompson, a hard-fisted rancher, gunfighter and newspaperman. Although Colonel Thompson denied involvement with the Vigilantes, he wrote an eloquent defense of their methods in his book, published 30 years later, along with a noticeably Vigilante-friendly version of the whole story.

It is chiefly from the reminiscences of these two men — Blakely and Thompson — that we have the story of the Vigilante era. And their stories, as you can imagine, diverge wildly in places.

According to Blakely's account, he (Blakely) was in town with Langdon's hired hand, W.H. Harrison, when he heard the news that Crooks and Jory had been gunned down. Both men hurried to join a posse that was coming together to go out to Langdon's ranch and bring him in. Another posse went to Langdon's brother's place, in case he'd gone there, but the killer was found at his own ranch.

Colonel Thompson's account is a bit different. In it, he says Harrison wasn't with the posse; instead, he was with Langdon at the brother's place, and Harrison and Langdon fled when they heard the posse approach. Thompson also claims that they found 10 men who were completely unknown to them in the house with Langdon's brother.

It's this detail that most convinces me that Thompson's is an unreliable account, for in it these 10 armed men are not arrested and nothing is ever heard from them again, as if they were minor characters in a Western pulp-magazine story. It's almost certain that he made this up in order to claim the Langdons were the leaders of a gang of outlaws, a gang conveniently made up entirely of strangers from out of town, and to justify the what was about to happen to Harrison, the hired hand — more on that in a minute.

In any case, the posse brought Langdon home under arrest, with Harrison riding with them as a posse member. Langdon was entrusted to Deputy Sheriff John Luckey, and everyone went to bed.

Very early the next morning, though, as Deputy Luckey was sitting by the stove, the Vigilantes made their first move.

"The door was suddenly opened and I was caught and thrown backward on the floor and firmly held, while my eyes were blinded and immediately a pistol was fired rapidly 5 or 6 times. I heard someone groan about the time the firing ceased," Deputy Luckey wrote in a subsequent report to his boss. "I went to Langdon and found him dead. I looked around and a masked man stood at each door, warning by ominous signs for no one to undertake to leave the room."

The Vigilantes then grabbed Harrison — it's not clear whether he was in the room with Langdon when the masked riders burst in, or whether he came later, attracted by the activity. Langdon's attackers put a rope around his neck and used a horse to drag him through the streets of Prineville to the bridge, where they strung his by-now-lifeless body from a banister.

This killing marked the beginning of the Vigilantes' reign of their own special kind of law and order in Prineville country — enforced by masked riders with drawn guns and ready ropes.

"The 'Vigilantes' who banded together that night to shoot Langdon and lynch the innocent Harrison stuck together for two years, getting bolder and bolder," Blakely told the *Oregonian*.

The November 1950 issue of Masked Rider Western, a pulp-fiction magazine, features cover art that, by sheer happenstance, is remarkably close to what actually happened to W.H. Harrison at the hands of the masked Vigilantes who lynched him.

The group took to sending death threats, with skull-and-crossbones emblems, to various people around town — some of whom, certainly, were rustlers and criminals, but others of whom were simply fellow ranchers opposed to their methods.

Colonel Thompson claims the escalation in Vigilante activity was in response to an increase in criminal activity, apparently by the unknown gang of 10 outlaws first encountered in Langdon's brother's house.

Public opinion appears to have been on the Vigilantes' side at first, which gives some credence to Colonel Thompson's claim that the group formed out of frustration with ineffective local law enforcement. But it didn't stay on their side for long. In fact, it seems to have turned on them later that year, in December, when the Vigilantes lynched a horse jockey named Charles

Luster. The Vigilantes claimed Luster had been about to steal some horses, but most folks in town happened to know that Luster had just refused to throw a horse race at the behest of some prominent Vigilantes who'd bet against him; the sudden declaration that Luster was a horse thief seemed disturbingly convenient.

Moreover, in the process of getting even with Luster, the Vigilantes also killed another young man, a friend of Luster's who was with him that night; the two of them ended up hanging from a juniper tree together with the rancher they'd been having dinner with, and the rancher they'd been working for was shot through a window at a Prineville saloon the same night. Colonel Thompson later tried to claim the four of them had been part of a gang that had ridden through Prineville earlier in the day shooting into the air and threatening to burn the town down, but his is the only account that mentions anything of this kind; again, it seems likely that he was just making up a story to justify the Vigilantes.

In any event, after this incident, the residents of Prineville started to definitively turn against the Vigilantes.

But even after the Charles Luster incident, the Vigilantes had some community support. Before they'd formed, law enforcement in the Prineville area had been very light, and by several accounts worse than useless. The Vigilantes may have been scary, but they did bring something approximating law and order to the area — at least, at first.

And that's probably why, when the governor created Crook County in January 1883, the county officers and court officials he appointed were nearly all drawn from the ranks of the Vigilantes. (According to state law, when a new county was formed, the officials would all be appointed by the governor, and then run for their offices in the next election year — which in this case was 1884.)

The Vigilantes' popularity didn't last long. It's hard to see how it possibly could have. They were a gang of masked riders on "borrowed" horses dispensing summary justice by stealth and by night, and keeping the town in line by delivering death threats signed with a skull and crossbones. Nothing scary there, right?

But even the slowest Prineville residents eventually got the message loud and clear: The Vigilantes weren't the solution; they were the problem. They were accountable to nobody, and they were out of control.

Oddly enough, this was a problem for the Vigilantes too. The Vigilantes always claimed their goal was to be part of a solution to the frontier lawlessness of the early '80s, and for most of them, there's no reason to doubt their sincerity. But now they were getting blamed for every bit of lawlessness that happened in Crook County, including several murders that may have been completely unrelated to their gang's activities.

One of these was a rancher who was found shot in the head, around the same time another rancher vanished without a trace. Both ranchers had made critical comments about the Vigilantes in public, so most residents assumed these were revenge killings. But nobody really knew.

The other problem the Vigilantes had was a predictable one. Because they operated anonymously, every time an individual member of their gang did something bad, the stink rubbed off on the whole bunch of them. This was a particular problem, because Vigilante honcho Bud Thompson was such a loose cannon.

A few months after the election, there was an argument between two young men in a Prineville saloon. One of them, 17-year-old "Mossy" Barnes, pulled a gun on the other, who was unarmed, and shot him in the chest. Before he died, the victim told Jim Blakely he'd recognized the gun Mossy had used to shoot him as belonging to Bud Thompson.

Thompson denied this, but didn't do himself any favors when, several months later, he gunned down the murdered man's brother in another saloon. Blakely, who claims he was there, says Thompson walked up behind him and shot him in the back of the neck, execution-style. Thompson, in his memoirs, says he shot the man in an Old West-style gunfight after the victim tried to draw on him.

Crook County officials investigated, but the grand jury declined to indict; Blakely blames this on the presence of so many Vigilantes in county office. The widow sued in civil court and won a $3,600 judgment, though.

After this incident, two things happened: First, Blakely got together with two other Prineville residents — John Combs and Sam Smith — to form the nucleus of an anti-Vigilante "gang" called the Citizens Protective Union, which became better known as the "Moonshiners."

The Moonshiners made a point of never wearing masks or operating in secret. They called themselves "Moonshiners" because they stood watch on moonlit nights, making sure there were no masked riders galloping around delivering letters or bullets.

The second thing that happened was, Thompson left town; perhaps he saw the writing on the wall. He moved to Alturas, Calif., where he ran the town newspaper and got involved in another round of vigilante activity that resulted in several lynchings there.

Back in Prineville, though, things were reaching the boiling point. The stockmen's association that the Vigilantes all belonged to had a meeting and, essentially, marked out Blakely as their next hit. They also boasted that it was time for them to have it out with the Moonshiners and break their gang up for good.

By this time, though, membership in the Moonshiners had swelled to about 75 heavily-armed citizens — probably four times as many as there were Vigilantes. These now all assembled, at Blakely's request, to make a show of force — the goal being to get the Vigilantes to either stand up, or stand down.

Down the main street in Prineville they rode to the saloon where the Vigilantes were drinking, and arranged themselves on the street outside.

"The gang members were looking out the windows of Til Glaze's saloon," Blakely told *the Oregonian*. "I was fighting mad, and so were the rest of us. We were ready to fight it out right there. 'If you think you can stop us, come on out and try it!' I hollered at the gang."

Outside the saloon, thumbs toyed with the hammers of Colts and Winchesters and horses paced nervously. Inside, all was silent. Nobody moved.

Finally the Moonshiners dispersed, going back to their shops and ranches and workbenches. They'd made their point.

Humiliated and chastened, the Vigilantes never rode again after that. And a few months later, when Crook County held its first election, all the Vigilante officials were kicked out of office, and Blakely was voted in as sheriff.

Sources and Works Cited:
- "When the Juniper Trees Bore Fruit," an article by Herbert Lundy published in the March 26, 1939, issue of the Portland Morning Oregonian;
- *East of the Cascades*, a book by Phil Brogan published in 1977 by Binford & Mort;
- *Reminiscences of a Pioneer*, a book by Col. William "Bud" Thompson published in 1912 by The Plaindealer.

WHO GOT SHORTY?

The disappearance of sheep rancher Shorty Davis has got to be Central Oregon's oldest cold case... there are older unsolved crimes, but it's hard to think of an older one that people are still thinking about. It's been almost 120 years since the affable, odd-looking pioneer vanished, and locals are still spinning theories about what might have happened.

The most popular theory, then and now, is that he was a victim of the last round of the Oregon range wars — the Crook County Sheepshooters outbreak of 1896-1906.

Another good possibility, supported by local resident Dorothy Lawson McCall — former governor Tom McCall's mother, by the way — is that he was murdered by one of his neighbors, an ill-tempered cattleman who later proved the low quality of his character by perpetrating a murder-suicide on his wife after some financial setbacks.

Whatever happened, it seems to have left no trace of the stockman. He took with him only his horse, his saddle, and (some sources say) a gun. He left behind 800 acres of good ranch land, roughly 3,000 head of sheep, about 60 cattle, 14,000 pounds of wool in the barn ready to be shipped to market — and lots of very puzzled friends. A $1,000 reward was promptly offered for anyone who could find him or his body. No one ever claimed it.

LOVE, SEX *and* MURDER *in* OLD OREGON

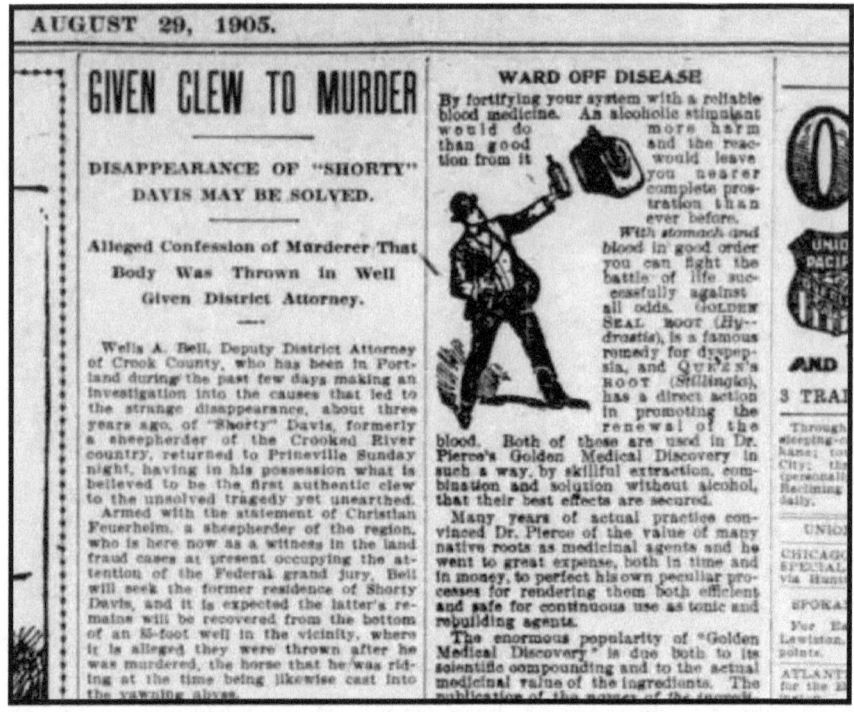

Leonidas "Shorty Davis" Douris's disappearance was covered extensively in newspapers, although no photograph of him was apparently available. This headline appeared in the Portland Morning Oregonian after a man claimed he'd been dumped into an old dry well. It turned out not to be true. (Image: UO Libraries)

Shorty Davis first came to Crook County when it was still part of Wasco County, in 1881 — the year before the formation and reign of terror of Colonel William "Bud" Thompson and his Prineville Vigilantes.

It's a fairly reliable maxim that all men nicknamed "Shorty" are either very short or very tall; and in Shorty's case, it was the former. He was a powerful, barrel-chested man, with very long arms and an unusually large head, but with very short legs; it was as if he were a dwarf from the waist down and a giant from the waist up. He was a dark man, olive-skinned and with black hair. And there seems to have been something about him that inspired friendship and trust.

Upon arrival as a penniless laborer in his mid-20s, he immediately started working for local sheep outfits, taking his pay in sheep at the end of every season and acquiring land every chance he got. By 1895 he had a substantial acreage — three quarter-sections plus a ranch with a house and barn on it. He also had a big flock of sheep.

But 1896 was the year a group of cattle ranchers got together to do

VIGILANTE MURDER.

something about the "sheep problem." The increasing popularity of sheep ranching in central Oregon was putting pressure on the publicly-owned rangeland. Legally anyone was allowed to graze anything on that land at any time; but the cattlemen felt that since they had been there first — well, actually, they *personally* hadn't, but there had been cows on the range before there had been sheep — they should be entitled to first rights on it.

They decided that when they found a flock of sheep grazing on public land that they had "claimed" for their gang, they would sneak up on the sheepherder, tie him up, and massacre the sheep. They took their style and tactics from Thompson and the Vigilantes, wearing masks and riding by night and sending anonymous sinister threatening messages to anyone who opposed them; in fact, historian David Braly reports that a number of them had been members of the Vigilantes, 15 years before.

And so, slowly at first but with increasing boldness over the following decade or so, they started doing this. By the time a long-suffering and exasperated federal government ended the squabble by establishing a grazing-permit system, tens of thousands of sheep had met an untimely end at their hands.

Shorty, of course, had a lot of sheep, and ran them on lands that cattlemen were pleased to think of as their own turf. So, tensions rose as the 1890s ripened into the dawning of the new century.

Then one mid-August day in 1900, Shorty's neighbors heard a big commotion at his ranch: all the animals were bawling and bleating. They were, it turned out, hungry. Shorty had apparently left without feeding them.

Or maybe he didn't leave. In any case, he was never seen again.

Shorty was declared dead less than a month later — which seems unusually hasty, even by the standards of a century ago, but Shorty had a lot of valuable property and most likely some of the would-be bidders were well connected; they would have wanted to hurry things up before any relatives could find out the estate was up for grabs. If so, this tactic worked. Shorty's relatives wouldn't learn of his disappearance until several years after it happened. Meanwhile, a desultory run of advertisements in nearby newspapers didn't turn up any heirs, so his stock and land were auctioned off — and the bidders got the land and stock for about 15 cents on the dollar of its actual value.

Meanwhile, the Sheepshooters were getting increasingly bold. In 1903 alone, they killed over 10,000 sheep. Community opinion was starting to turn against them, as it had with the Vigilantes two decades before, and for similar reasons; they were powerful, scary, anonymous, and accountable only to themselves. Plus, they hated sheepmen. It was only natural that suspicion would fall on them for Shorty's disappearance.

In 1905, a witness in a land-fraud trial in Portland claimed Shorty had been murdered and dumped into an old dry well on his property. The well was excavated; it contained no trace of Shorty. Apparently the witness had made up the story just on the off-chance that the murderer had disposed of the body that way, so that he could snag the $1,000 reward.

In 1909, a spring flood exposed some bones in a creekbed near Prineville, and on the basis of that evidence Charles Colby, the neighboring cattle rancher who had feuded with Shorty, was arrested. He was released for lack of evidence — although Dorothy Lawson McCall remained personally convinced of his guilt. The bones apparently were not Shorty's.

By that time, though, Shorty's relatives had been found.

His real name, it turned out, was Leonidas Douris; he was a Greek by birth. He had changed his name to conceal himself from other Greeks, including his relatives, who had an awkward habit of putting the bite on him for loans and then never paying them back. Shorty was a nice guy — apparently too nice for his own good — and therefore easy to take advantage of. It had become a big enough problem that he literally went on the lam from his friends and family to short-circuit it.

Shorty's brothers came to town to wrap up all his affairs and to collect and distribute what was left of his estate. But still there was no trace of Shorty himself.

Over the following years, Shorty Davis became something like a municipal obsession in Prineville, and remained so for decades afterward.

The family that bought his old farmhouse got used to knocks on the door from fresh-faced Shorty hunters wanting to poke around the property. Rumors directed others to a particular rock at the mouth of Sanford Creek. In the early 1950s, a skeleton was unearthed during construction of a new bridge, and the first words on everyone's lips were, "We found Shorty!"

But they hadn't. It was someone else.

Most recently, in March 2008, Shorty's grand-niece, Anastasia Douris, came to the U.S. to learn more about him. The family back in Greece had heard that he'd been murdered by cowboys, who had taken over his ranch. She found that, far from being a forgotten victim of Old West violence, her relative was Prineville's municipal mystery — still.

So, what really happened to Shorty Davis? It seems unlikely that, if he died of natural causes, no body would have been found. During the years when a $1,000 reward was being offered, people were crawling all over the landscape looking for clues. If he'd drowned in a river, his horse would have been found; if the horse had slipped off a trail and over a cliff, someone would have found the bodies or bones.

So it's most likely someone hid him deliberately, presumably after murdering him. And if that's the case, unless his murderer was incompetent, we'll almost certainly never know.

Sources and Works Cited:
- *"Synopsis of story of Leonidas Douris aka Shorty Davis," an article by Anastasia Douris published on the Douris family Website at dourisfamily.org;*
- *"What Happened to Shorty Davis?" an article by Katie Wennerstrom published in the Summer 2008 issue of* Prineville Territory *magazine;*
- *"Where's Shorty?" an article by David Braly in* Little Known Tales from Oregon History *(Geoff Hill, Ed.), a book published in 1991 by Sun Publishing.*

KILLING BERRY WAY.

One summer day, nearly 160 years ago, Deputy Frank McDaniels arrived back home in Canyon City after a long and grueling manhunt.

McDaniels was exhausted. But he'd got his man. He had murder suspect Berry Way in custody, and now all that was needed was to bring him to The Dalles for trial.

A large group of local Canyon City miners had a different idea, though. Instead of going to all that trouble, with the possibility of Way getting let off by some bleeding-heart big-city judge, why not take care of justice right now, right here in Canyon City, DIY-style?

By the time McDaniels was settled in with his prisoner in one of Canyon City's saloons, they'd already formed a committee, with a chairman and a secretary. They met in another saloon — apparently a very large one, because there were 460 of them — to get things organized.

Initially, their plan was simply to get hold of Berry Way and fructify the nearest juniper tree with him in classic vigilante style — no muss, no fuss. But Ike Hare gave an impassioned speech, urging the committee to, as it were, be a kinder, gentler lynch mob — and give the accused a full trial before hanging him. That way, it would be legit. Unlike, you know, those other mob killings that sometimes happened in the frontier West.

"Yes, gentlemen," he concluded to approving cheers in what must have looked disturbingly like a scene from the movie *Paint Your Wagon*. "We will give him a fair and impartial trial. We know him to be guilty, and we will hang him anyhow."

The matter was put to a vote, and the committee members voted overwhelmingly to give Berry Way that "full, fair trial" before stretching his neck. That settled, they hustled out the door of the saloon and across the street to the other saloon, in which Berry Way was being kept, guarded by Deputy McDaniels.

They told McDaniels what they wanted. Nothing doing, he told them.

"I can't release him," he said. "I took an oath to protect and to see that the law is sustained. Everyone go home now and let the law do its job."

The Canyon City citizens did not want to hear this. But Deputy McDaniels was a highly respected lawman, and his word carried a lot of weight. Grumbling, the crowd dispersed, and perhaps McDaniels thought that was an end to the matter.

If so, he thought wrong. A few hours later, when he stepped out of the saloon, a group of men who had been waiting for him pounced on him. They hauled him away and confined him, probably in some sort of makeshift jailhouse. Then they hustled back to the saloon and collected the now-unguarded Berry Way.

Way was wearing an Oregon boot and probably shackled to the bar as well. They shattered his shackles and, at gunpoint, marched him down the street to John Fenessey's house.

Upon arrival, the committee set up a complete "miners' court" according to their best recollections of how a court of law was supposed to work. One of their number was declared sheriff; twelve more were empaneled as a jury. One was appointed prosecutor, and another got to play the role of Berry Way's defense attorney. Of course, none of them had any training or credentials. The closest to legitimacy this kangaroo conglomeration got was the judge, who was John Strowbridge, the local justice of the peace.

With all the "officials" in place and looking more or less like a real court proceeding, the trial got under way.

Berry Way was probably guilty of the crime he was charged with, although of course we can never really know, and he maintained his innocence to the end. A couple months before, he had left with mule skinner Frank Gallagher on a pack train trip from Canyon City to The Dalles. The pack train had never arrived, and on May 1, some travelers had found Gallagher's body near Cherry Creek — shot in the head, and robbed of everything, including his entire pack train and $80,000 in gold. And a little later, Berry Way was seen with some of the stolen goods.

When Deputy McDaniels had learned of this, he'd set out with a posse,

VIGILANTE MURDER.

Howard A. Black, curator at Grant County Museum in Canyon City, Oregon, holds the skull of Berry Way and a "California collar," or noose, of the type Way was hanged with, in this 1963 photograph. (Image: Ben Maxwell/ Salem Public Library)

caught up with Way, and arrested him. But then, late one night while the posse members slept, Way had slipped out of his bonds and escaped. The severely embarrassed McDaniels had actually put up $250 out of his own pocket as a reward for his recapture.

Eight days later, Way had turned up in the town of Auburn, and McDaniels had gone out, picked up his trail, tracked him down, and re-arrested him. And it had been on his return with his prisoner to Canyon City that the vigilance committee had formed, and taken matters out of his hands.

Now, in "court," this whole story was presented to the "jury." The "prosecutor" and "defense attorney" questioned and cross-examined witnesses just like on *Perry Mason*, and finally the "jury" retired to a separate room just like real juries do at real trials, and half an hour later they emerged to deliver their inevitable "guilty" verdict. The whole thing would have made for a pretty good Vaudeville comedy show, if not for the deadly gleam in everyone's eye and the very real hangman's noose waiting inevitably for the defendant like the curse of Damocles at the end of it.

Berry Way was sentenced to be hanged, of course; but the committee, keen to differentiate itself from those barbaric lynch mobs that just murder people willy-nilly, voted to break with lynch-mob tradition by scheduling the "execution" for 2 p.m. the next day rather than just stringing him right up.

And so the next day — June 4, 1863 — Berry Way stood on the makeshift scaffold, looking out over a crowd of about a thousand gawking faces. Invited to give his last words, he calmly told the crowd that he was innocent of the crime of killing Gallagher. He went to his death maintaining his innocence, despite full knowledge that he'd be hanged either way, and regardless of the protestations of clergymen who reminded him that he'd be damned to Hell if he died with a lie on his lips.

All of which may have led some in the crowd to wonder if they really had made a mistake ... and maybe, just maybe, to regret not having let him go to The Dalles for a real trial rather than settling for a locally produced Vaudeville show.

Today, Berry Way's skull is on display at the Grant County Museum in Canyon City.

Sources and Works Cited:

- Necktie Parties: Legal Executions in Oregon 1851-1905, *a book by Diane Goeres-Gardner published in 2005 by Caxton Press;*
- *"Gold and the Gallows," an article by Angel Carpenter published in the Sept. 25, 2012, issue of the* Blue Mountain Eagle.

PART VII:

JUST PLAIN MURDER.

Murder doesn't always come in neat categories. Sometimes it's just murder — in hot blood or cold, for gain or for glory or for no apparent reason at all.

A frontier state like old Oregon was bound to attract some folks who would be, shall we say, at risk for turning violent. And, of course, it did. Here are a few of their stories:

THE FIRST MURDERER.

It's hard to tell, just from reading between the lines of the court documents; but it's probably a safe guess that Nimrod O'Kelly's neighbors did not like him.

It was the spring of 1852, and the Oregon Trail emigrations had just gotten started a few years earlier. O'Kelly had been one of the very first; he'd come out on the Overland Trail in 1845, then traveled south in the Willamette Valley until he came across a nice 640-acre parcel that he could claim under the applicable laws — 320 acres for himself, and 320 acres for his wife.

Trouble was, he had come out by himself, and he hadn't anticipated the opportunity. His attempts to send a letter back East to his wife asking her to come out and join him did not meet with success until several years later, and when she finally did get it, she couldn't just drop everything and hop on the next wagon train.

So as the years rolled by, other settlers came and set up claims nearby, and several of them were very skeptical about his marital status.

This was a thing that single men did somewhat regularly in those days — claimed a double portion, and then went looking for a woman, any woman really, that they could marry in order to keep it — before a neighbor got wise and filed a competing claim. O'Kelly, though, wasn't looking for a wife; he claimed he already had one.

One of O'Kelly's neighbors, Jeremiah Mahoney, was confident enough that O'Kelly was cheating the system that he filed a competing claim on

Mrs. O'Kelly's 320 acres, and started living on and working the land in the manner prescribed by the Donation Land Act.

Of course, this didn't exactly win him a prominent place on O'Kelly's Christmas card list. Hostility between the two Irishmen grew very quickly. It's also a distinct possibility, given later developments, that O'Kelly was Irish Catholic and Mahoney was Irish Protestant — and if so, that would mean they would have had a baked-in reason to hate each other even without the land fight.

The situation continued for several months, with O'Kelly and Mahoney exchanging git-off-my-lands in lieu of hellos every time they met. Which of the two was the more aggressive in pursuing his claim, we don't know; but we do know that O'Kelly took to carrying his shotgun everywhere he went.

Finally, on May 21, 1852, the feud escalated to physical violence, and O'Kelly shot Mahoney dead.

That evening, Mahoney's wife, worried because he hadn't yet come home, went to some of her neighbors and asked them to help search for him. O'Kelly, of course, was the primary suspect. But the neighbors couldn't find him; he was on his way to Marysville (today's Corvallis) to turn himself in and make a statement about what had happened.

According to the statement, Mahoney had belligerently approached O'Kelly, demanded to know why he always carried a gun, announced his plan to take the gun away and beat him over the head with it, and then made a grab for it. O'Kelly claimed he didn't even remember cocking the gun and never actually meant to shoot; but the thing went off in his hands as the two men struggled over it.

But, of course, O'Kelly could say anything he wanted at that point, right?

A warrant for murder was issued that very day, and a special court session convened about a month later — for the first murder trial ever held in the Oregon Territory.

The prosecution alleged that Nimrod O'Kelly was a land pirate who had fraudulently claimed extra land, and that he had murdered Jeremiah Mahoney to prevent losing it, and to intimidate his other neighbors so that none would challenge him.

There was no evidence one way or the other, but the jury unanimously found him guilty and sentenced him to be hanged.

The hanging was scheduled four weeks after the trial, so O'Kelly's attorney raced to appeal to the state Supreme Court. He cited nine critical errors in the prosecution. Most of these were procedural — inadequate notice, the wrong verbiage used in the charge documents — but several of

A letter sent by Nimrod O'Kelly to Oregon Territory Representative Joseph Lane in 1851, detailing the trouble he'd had in getting his family to join him on his land claim in Benton County. (Image: Oregon Historical Society)

them were whoppers. For instance, the county commissioners didn't select the jurors as they were supposed to do — which suggests the jury may have been empaneled informally and deliberately packed with hostile neighbors. Hostile neighbors would have been easy to come by, as O'Kelly was Catholic and most of the immediate area was settled by hardcore anti-Catholic Protestants.

Plus, the entire community seems to have been already convinced of his guilt. Mahoney was an Irishman, but he was apparently very popular in the Marysville area (hence the speculation that he was an Irish Protestant); O'Kelly had to be sent to a neighboring county to await trial, for fear of a lynch mob being formed and storming the Benton County Jail.

Also, the court did not require the grand jurors to be sworn, nor did it examine them as to qualifications — again, raising the specter of jury-picking.

Finally, the verdict wasn't rendered in open court, nor in the presence of the defendant. Apparently the jury just sent word to the judge that the guy was guilty, and went home.

So the case went to the Supreme Court on appeal — and the Supremes handed down an absolutely astonishing verdict on the case:

They acknowledged the errors, but affirmed the verdict anyway. They explained that, given that the O'Kelly was obviously guilty, because his was the territory's first murder case, letting him off on even a very serious technicality would be poisoning the well of justice at its very source.

"Time was when the unfortunate accused was dragged to trial without counsel, or a fair chance for self-defense," Chief Justice George H. Williams wrote, by way of explanation. "Then other rules prevailed, and courts tried to make technicalities the means of justice; but, when a prisoner comes before our courts with more privileges and presumptions in his favor than he otherwise could have, these olden rules cease with the reasons on which they rested, and criminals cannot be allowed to take refuge from the judgments of our liberal laws in the cobwebs of an antiquated practice."

Perhaps hoping the territorial governor would take the hint and remove this somewhat thorny problem from his plate, Williams added that executive clemency was the only appropriate way to address procedural errors in a case where a defendant's guilt was stark and obvious, adding, "If judicial compassion now bends the laws to suit a seemingly hard case, a door may be opened through which the midnight assassin and mercenary murderer may escape from the punishment due to their crimes."

By the time the Supreme Court had gotten around to hearing the case, it was 1854 — two years after the murder conviction. During this time, passionate pleas had flown thick and fast from all over the state into the territorial governor's office, arguing both for and against a pardon for O'Kelly.

And now we come to a point in this story where sources conflict.

In his 1935 article, McNary writes that the governor did not intervene, despite the pleas. So, the local court scheduled June 9, 1854, for the hanging. But the hanging never took place, because the Cavalry came to the rescue — almost literally.

It seems that O'Kelly's allegedly-imaginary wife, Sarah O'Kelly, left Missouri on the Oregon Trail in the spring of 1854 to join her husband, along with their several children. Word reached them en route that O'Kelly was about to be hanged for murder. So their oldest son took a horse and raced ahead of the wagon train.

He beat the clock, appearing at the Benton County sheriff's office and introducing himself to Sheriff T.J. Right, and letting the lawman know the rest of the family was on the way.

This, of course, changed everything. O'Kelly went from a pirate trying to unlawfully seize another man's land by force of arms, to a legitimate landowner defending himself and his property from — well, a pirate. It also was, in that age, far less of a big deal to hang a single man than it was to deprive an innocent wife and children of their family breadwinner.

Sheriff Right opened the cell door and set O'Kelly free — although he had no authority to do any such thing, he was confident that the law would catch up and everything would be all right.

This was certainly irregular, and that irregularity is something to consider, because historian Ronald Lansing (writing in 2005) gives a completely different account.

According to Lansing, the governor's office actually intervened three times in the case, each time under a different governor: first to delay the hanging while the Supreme Court considered the appeal; again, after the Supreme Court's sentence, in response to Justice George Williams' hint, when he commuted the sentence to two years in prison; and a third time, in March 1856, when he was actually pardoned.

In any case, eventually the O'Kellys did get their full section of land — but it didn't happen until 1881. By the time it did, Nimrod O'Kelly had died of old age; but he probably would have been content to know his wife and children at least had a home.

Sources and Works Cited:
- *"Oregon's First Reported Murder Case," an article by Lawrence A. McNary published in the December 1935 issue of* Oregon Historical Quarterly;
- *"Nimrod O'Kelly," an article by Ronald B. Lansing published in* The Oregon Encyclopedia *(oregonencyclopedia.org) on Sept. 19, 2019.*

THE DEAD MAN'S REVENGE.

The sun had just gone down on a warm early-summer night, and the twilight was in the final stages of fading away when Union Pacific Railroad special agents Buck Phillips and H.G. Schneider stepped into the railroad yard to make the rounds.

There had been some issues in the railyard. A gang of thieves had been systematically pillaging the railroad. Their M.O. was a simple one, and evidently pretty effective: they'd sneak aboard an outbound boxcar full of cigarettes and, while the train was en route, start chucking boxes of smokes out the door; other members of the gang would come along afterward and retrieve them. They were clearly doing this at night, because the following day railroad agents would usually find a case or two that they'd missed. And this had been going on for three months.

So Phillips and Schneider weren't just making the rounds the night of June 14, 1921. They were looking for somebody, and they had to have been a little nervous about what might happen when they found him.

The two of them walked along the train, one on each side, flashlights in hands, revolver holsters unsnapped and ready to draw.

Phillips saw a dim outline bundled up on a flatcar loaded with machinery: a man, riding the rails. Technically, this was illegal, and the two agents — "bulls" — were supposed to kick him off. But as a practical matter, Phillips and Schneider didn't much care about rail riders, as long as they weren't causing any trouble.

Boxcar bandit suspects Dan Casey and John Burns. Casey was hanged for murder; Burns was extradited to Ohio to serve a lengthy sentence for armed robbery.

"Where are you going?" Phillips asked him.

"Headin' for Baker, chief," the bindlestiff said, adding that he was going to Eastern Oregon for the hay harvest.

Phillips nodded and moved on. This would turn out to be a mistake. If he'd paused a moment and asked another question or two, the traveler might have told him that a couple rough-looking customers had passed by him just before the two bulls arrived, moving in the same direction up the train.

The agents moved on, methodically working their way up the side of the train. A few cars later, Phillips saw what he was looking for: an open boxcar door.

In 1921, on the Union Pacific line to Troutdale, boxcars did not roll around with their doors open. They were full of freight, and they were sealed shut. If that boxcar door was open, it was because somebody had opened it.

Phillips pulled his revolver out and brought his flashlight up. "Come on out of there," he barked.

There was silence for a moment. Then the inside of the boxcar lit up with four bright fiery flashes as the sound of pistol shots split the night.

Three .38-caliber bullets lanced into Phillips — one in the upper arm, one in his thigh and a third in the lower chest. He crumpled to the ground. Then two men jumped out of the boxcar and ran.

Schneider scrambled under the boxcar and, once on the other side, got up and emptied his .38 Special at the fleeing shadowy forms. Phillips managed to get three shots of his own off before losing consciousness.

He never regained it. Two hours later, in the hospital, he died.

The next morning, Portland Police Detective John Goltz was on the scene, and police and railroad agents searched the area carefully. They didn't find much — but they soon realized one of the bulls' pistol shots had hit one of the bad guys. There was a substantial blood trail leading away from the train.

Over the next few days, Goltz worked on the case. His investigation led through several dead ends, but the publicity the case had generated was helping quite a bit. One key breakthrough happened when a truck driver reported that he'd been hired to move some large, mysterious boxes, fairly frequently, from the Davis Hotel, located at 123½ Russell Street in Albina, to a nearby grocery store. It seemed kind of weird to be moving freight through a hotel like that.

Then an anonymous tipster called and suggested Goltz might want to talk to a man named Dan Casey, who might be staying at — you guessed it — the Davis Hotel.

When police arrived at the hotel, the owner, John Burns, was friendly and helpful — and loud. "DAN CASEY?" he boomed. "AIN'T NOBODY HERE BY THAT NAME. I HAVEN'T SEEN HIM SINCE LAST WEDNESDAY."

Then a woman walked out of one of the rooms. Goltz asked her, straight out: "Where's Casey?"

"I haven't seen Dan for a week," the woman replied.

Meanwhile, Mr. Burns was slowly unlocking doors in the hallway, making sure the locks made plenty of rattling noises. "I TOLD YOU CASEY WASN'T HERE," he bellowed cheerfully. "BUT SEEING AS HOW YOU ARE BULLS, I SUPPOSE I'LL HAVE TO SHOW YOU AROUND."

In the first room, the detectives found a black doctor's bag full of bandages, and in the second room, a basket full of bloody gauze. There was also a loaded .38 Special with dried blood all over it, and a box of blasting caps. The trail seemed to be hotting right up.

And yet, half an hour or so later, Goltz and his men were getting ready to leave. They hadn't found their man.

Like the cocky suspect on an old episode of Columbo, Burns now started laughing at them. "You see, copper," he jeered, "I wasn't lying to you. Casey ain't here."

Then Goltz realized there was one more room they hadn't searched — the one the woman had emerged from earlier.

When they walked into it and started searching, one of the detectives gave a sudden yell.

"Look out!" he cried out. "There's somebody under that bed!"

At the same time, a long arm snaked out from under the bed and dove under the pillow, then emerged gripping a revolver.

"Drop that gun!" shouted Goltz, getting his own out and pointing it at the figure under the bed.

It was indeed Dan Casey, and he was promptly arrested and given medical treatment for not one but two gunshot wounds — both from the same bullet, which had gone through his forearm and lodged in his chest. Clearly it was one of Phillips' dying shots, fired at him as he was exiting the boxcar, since all six of Schneider's shots had been from behind.

Ballistics test done on the bloody revolver proved it had been the one used to kill Phillips, and the Baker-bound bindlestiff identified Casey out of a line-up. A jury soon made it official, and sentenced him to hang.

Two years later, at the Oregon State Penitentiary, it was done.

Sources and Works Cited:
- *"The Boxcar Murder: A Northwest Mystery," an article by Stewart Holbrook published in the Feb. 23, 1936, issue of the* Portland Morning Oregonian;
- Portland Morning Oregonian *archives, June and September 1921.*

THE BOOTLEGGER.

It was well after 8 p.m. on the night of April 16, 1922, around 82nd and Division in Portland, and Albert Bowker was getting nervous.

His 49-year-old brother, Frank, had left downtown Portland at 7 p.m. in a touring car with a slim, charismatic 24-year-old man named Russell Hecker. Hecker had a contact, known to him only as "Bob," who had dozens and dozens of cases of Johnny Walker Black Label for sale at $85 a pop. So Frank had scrounged up all the money he had, borrowed another $600 from his housekeeper, tucked his .38 Special into his pocket, and gone with Hecker to go get it from the backcountry barn where it was all stashed.

They'd all planned to meet up an hour later, after Bob had his money and Frank had his whisky, at 82nd and Division. But now, as the night dragged on past 9 p.m., Albert was starting to worry that things might have gone sour.

They had.

The next morning, about the same time Albert Bowker was finally realizing he would have to go to the police, Hecker's brother's business partner was probably thinking the same thing. Hecker had borrowed the car from him the night before for a quick run out to the outskirts of East Portland, and had never returned.

But at 9 a.m., young Russell himself poked his head in in the door, looking freshly scrubbed if not very well rested, apologizing for keeping the car late. The car, he said, was parked a couple blocks away, near Second and Pine.

Relieved, the car's owner sent one of his salesmen to retrieve the car and take it to a tire shop. Upon arrival, the salesman couldn't help noticing the seat cushions looked a little funny, as if they'd been replaced with brand-new ones. The rubber floor mats looked new, too, and that was particularly noticeable because the rest of the car was — well, drenched with blood. The interior, the running boards, even the undercarriage.

Hecker was soon in custody, and the police had many pointed questions to pose to him; but he'd spent the morning getting advice from his father and his attorney, and both had told him to clam up, so he did.

However, Police Chief Leon Jenkins did manage to learn, from Hecker's father, the location of the body. Hecker had dumped the body, wrapped in a hop sack and weighted with rocks, over the rail of the bridge across the Calapooia River at the end of Queen Avenue, in Albany.

The investigation revealed the apparent rendezvous point for the whisky buy: a lonely stretch of road between Gladstone and Oregon City. Witnesses said a touring car had come there around 7:30 and parked just off the highway, tucked back into some trees. Some time thereafter, neighbors heard a shot. The blood trail started a few hundred feet south, apparently dripping from the chassis of the car.

Farther south, the attendant at a service station in St. Paul remembered the car coming in for gasoline. The attendant had seen blood between the driver's fingers when he removed his gas cap, and he was shaking so badly he'd dropped the cap. It had rolled under the car, and when the attendant ducked down to retrieve it, he'd noticed more blood dripping off the running boards. Perhaps understandably, the attendant hadn't asked any questions — or dared to peek into the floorboards of the back seat where the lumpy, crimson-stained hop sack lay — but he remembered the visitor well.

At the Albany Hotel, they remembered him, too, but by the time he was signing the guest register there, the body was gone and he'd cleaned the blood off his hands. He checked in around 2 a.m., took a bath, wrote a letter to his father, bought some cigarettes, and left for Portland before dawn the next day.

In court, Hecker finally told his full story: On the drive to Baker's Bridge, he claimed, Frank Bowker had been awful company, waving his .38 around and talking like a big-shot gangster. On the way, he'd suggested they simply play the liquor buy like a stick-up — rob "Bob,"

JUST PLAIN MURDER.

News coverage in the April 18, 1922, issue of the Portland Morning Oregonian included this photo spread, showing (clockwise from top) the murder car; Detective Mallett of the Portland Police Bureau with murder suspect Russell Hecker; and victim Frank Bowker. (Image: UO Libraries)

keep the money and the booze too. "It means $1,200 or $1,400 to you," he added, "and he can't do anything with this gun in his face." But Hecker said he told him no, a deal was a deal.

Then, Hecker claimed, when they arrived at the rendezvous point and he tried to signal "Bob" with the car's spotlight, Bowker had freaked. "Are you double-crossing me?" he yelled, and out came the .38 again, and from three feet away, in the dark closed interior of a touring car on a chilly April night, Bowker fired, sending a bullet whistling past Hecker's ear and off into the night. Hecker, luckily, had borrowed a .45 automatic from his former employer, so he whipped that out now and returned fire. One shot, to the head. And then there was blood everywhere.

Hecker had brought a hop sack to put the cases of liquor in. Now he stuffed the body into it and laid it somewhere out of sight, probably on the floorboards of the car. He was, of course, freaking out; he couldn't go back to Portland, possibly ever; Bowker's brother would be gunning for him now. So he drove south, making for his home town of Albany.

"I needed gasoline," he told the jury, later on, at his subsequent trial. "I thought I could get it some place where they wouldn't know me. I saw a filling station at what they call Horseshoe Park (St. Paul). I drove in and got the gas and tried to act natural so they wouldn't suspicion me. The man didn't say anything ... he just looked hard at me."

He then drove, in confusion and dismay and panic, around Albany until he came upon the old bridge over the Calapooia, where he stopped and got the hop sack — still dripping blood — and heaved it over the rail. Then he cleaned himself up as best he could in the field, checked into the hotel to clean himself up more thoroughly, and drove back to Portland. Somewhere along the way he stopped to clean up the car some, too.

It was a pretty good story. But there were several reasons why it was hard to buy. First, as the prosecutor was not slow to point out, the only witness to Frank Bowker's boorish behavior and plans to rob "Bob" was the man who had killed him. Also, Hecker had gone through Bowker's pockets after killing him. Why would he do that, unless intending to rob him of the liquor-buying money?

But most damningly, there was no evidence that more than one shot had been fired. Witnesses near the bridge testified to only having heard one. So, what about that .38 shot, with which Bowker allegedly tried to kill Hecker, making it self-defense? With his eyes full of the muzzle flash of that .38 going off in his face, how likely was it that Hecker would be able to see (and shoot) Bowker's head? And how did Hecker account for the shot having entered the *back* of Bowker's head rather than the front?

On the other hand, had Hecker set out to murder Bowker, he would hardly have used a borrowed car and gun, or driven half the night with a body in the car to within blocks of his parents' house only to stay in a hotel — would he?

Maybe not. But when sent into its chambers to ponder these things on July 1, the jury took only an hour or so to come to a decision: Guilty of first-degree murder.

Four days later, he was sentenced to be hanged. It never happened, though. A combination of good timing, excellent counsel, and the

JUST PLAIN MURDER.

intervention of a naïve newly-elected governor resulted in Hecker's sentence being commuted. Fifteen years after his death sentence was handed down, he was a free man.

Sources and Works Cited:
- Murder in Linn County, Oregon: The True Story of the Legendary Plainview Killings, *a book by Cory Frye published in 2016 by The History Press;*
- Portland Morning Oregonian *archives, April 1922.*

THE PLAINVIEW KILLINGS.

On a broad flat stretch of the Willamette Valley floor, just across the freeway from the town of Shedd, lies a little cluster of buildings and a Mennonite church — all that remains of the little town of Plainview, Oregon.

This tiny, bucolic hamlet was, 95 years ago, the scene of a pair of murders that are still talked about in west Linn County today, the result of a Prohibition liquor raid gone horribly wrong. They've become known as the Plainview Killings.

It all started out as a minor liquor raid on a rural farm, very similar to a thousand other Prohibition-enforcement operations in rural Oregon in the 1920s. What made this one different, other than the final outcome, was the fact that the preacher from a local temperance church came along.

No one really knows why Sheriff Charles Kendall brought a preacher with him that day. But it's possible, maybe even likely, that doing so cost him his life, as well as the minister's.

The farmer's name was Dave West, and he was one of those prickly, individualistic mountain-man types, originally from rural Indiana. West had lived on a 40-acre farm near the tiny hamlet of Plainview for 11 years. He was in his late 60s, but still just as prickly as ever — and just as good a shot, too: his skills as a sharpshooter were locally famous.

Until that day in 1922, West's nearest brush with the local criminal-justice system had been a prosecution for poaching. In general, he minded his own business and expected others to mind theirs, occasionally enforcing this preference with a pair of callused, farm-hardened fists.

But part of the "own business" Dave West minded had always been a small still, located in the woodshed. There he produced small quantities of high-test grain alcohol, which he used for drinking and for making a home-remedy liniment for rheumatism. Of course, after "bone-dry" Prohibition passed in Oregon in 1915, he'd only admit to using his moonshine for the liniment; but nobody was really fooled.

Still, even after it was patently illegal, Dave West continued to run his still, more or less openly. His position was that since he was just making enough for his own personal use, and it never left his property, it was none of anybody's business what he did in his own barn.

And Sheriff Kendall seemed to have agreed with that sentiment at first. Certainly he must have known about the little still for months, maybe even years, before he ever did anything about it.

But on the afternoon of June 21, 1922, Kendall was on his way to the West farm to, finally, enforce the law. And he'd brought the pastor of the First Christian Church, Rev. Roy Healy.

Why he did that is still unclear today. The Albany Democrat-Herald later said Healy was doing research for a book he was writing on liquor-law enforcement. Another theory was that the sheriff had only launched the raid, with some reluctance, in response to a complaint lodged by the Reverend, and that the Reverend had then insisted on accompanying him to make sure it got done and that Sheriff Kendall wasn't tempted to look the other way, or pretend West wasn't home, or let him off with a stern warning rather than making an example of him for the guidance of the righteous.

Either way, it seems pretty clear that Dave West took it badly. He seems to have assumed that Healy was there to gloat over his downfall. And for a man of West's temperament, that sort of thing was simply not to be borne.

According to the recollections of West's wife, Ellen, Kendall and Healy arrived at about 3 p.m. West was outside working, and his nephew's family was also there to help with haying season.

Sheriff Kendall asked Ellen West if there might be any alcohol on the premises, and she went and fetched a bottle of the family-recipe rheumatism liniment. No no, he replied; he was looking for drinking-liquor.

At that point, Dave West entered the house, and the conversation started to become heated. West, thinking Kendall and Healy were interrogating his wife, started out upset and only got more so. Accounts of the conversation

JUST PLAIN MURDER.

Ward's Butte as seen from the main intersection in Plainview, looking southward on Manning Road. Dave West's farm was near the foot of the butte. (Image: F.J.D. John)

that followed vary, with some sources saying the sheriff delivered a stern lecture and others claiming he apologetically told West he'd have to be booked on charges in Albany and offered to bring him back home afterward. Then the sheriff and the minister stepped outside and made their way to the woodshed, to dismantle the still.

They left behind an increasingly agitated Dave West. West grew angrier and angrier until, with a shout of, "I can't stand it!," he grabbed his Remington .32 rifle and, over Ellen's objections, stormed out of the house.

Outside, he saw the two men emerging from the shed. Kendall was carrying two bottles of moonshine, which he set down by the gate. West shouldered his rifle — and shot him through the heart.

The Reverend Healy ran for the road, screaming for someone to call the police. From his place of concealment, West watched him and, when the coast was clear, shot him too.

After that, West sent for his nephew, who was away at a neighbor's house; when he arrived, he was sent forth to bring the coroner and tell what had happened. After that, the Wests tried to have a normal evening, knowing very well that it would be their last. And finally, around 6 p.m., Ellen West left the house to stay with her son — and Dave West took up his rifle and went back to the barn one last time.

Meanwhile, back in Albany a great excitement was brewing. The district attorney was deputizing a posse of eager local residents to go out and bring West in. Someone had slipped the word to the press, and reporters had motored in from Portland, Eugene and everywhere in between. By 10:30 p.m., a large group of armed men was cautiously closing in around the property.

The house was soon searched, and proved empty and quiet as a tomb; but nobody seems to have expected West to make his final stand there. The barn, near the still: that's where they would find him.

Cautiously they approached. Finally one of them, a 19-year-old named Alton Williams, slipped up to the door and entered. Walking cautiously through the place, rifle up and ready, he suddenly tripped over something on the floor and went sprawling — and saw that what he'd tripped over had been a corpse, still clutching the rifle that had killed him — the third and final victim, if that's the right word, of the day's violence.

It was Dave West.

Sources and Works Cited:
- Murder in Linn County, Oregon: The True Story of the Legendary Plainview Killings, *a book by Cory Frye published in 2016 by The History Press.*

THE PREPAID SHANGHAIING.

Most of the time, the shanghaiing of sailors in old Astoria and Portland was a spur-of-the-moment kind of thing. The keepers of sailors' boardinghouses only resorted to it when a ship captain needed a crew for an imminent departure, and there weren't enough legitimate sailors staying in the boardinghouse who could be forced to ship out to fill the order.

But there was at least one sailor who arrived in Portland with his shanghaiing already planned, premeditated and paid-for. And it probably would have worked just fine if his would-be shanghaier hadn't killed him in the attempt.

Frederick Kalashua was a big burly Finn, and no ordinary sailor. He was a ship's carpenter, and apparently a pretty good one; so he was far more valuable to the captain of the ship he arrived on, the 190-foot British barque *Candidate*, than the average sailor would have been.

When Kalashua arrived in Portland in late June of 1886, he was angry with the captain of the *Candidate*, and didn't much care who knew about it. The skipper, he said, had fed him very poorly and forced him to share a cabin with a Black man. Although the captain had promised to move the roommate to other quarters and to improve the food, it seemed Kalashua was enough of a racist that having been forced to share his quarters with a

Black man had been an unforgivable insult. He arrived in Portland ready to quit, and when he checked into Jim Turk's sailor's boardinghouse he immediately put his name down on the list of sailors seeking other berths.

He also asked one of the boardinghouse runners, Pat O'Brien, to go to the *Candidate* and get his box of carpentry tools, which were his own personal property and valued at about $250 (about $7,000 in modern money). O'Brien tried, but the captain refused to let him take the tools. He — the captain — had no intention of letting his carpenter leave his employ, and had made arrangements that he was confident would ensure that Kalashua was safely back on board when the *Candidate* moved on.

Those arrangements essentially amounted to a prepaid shanghaiing. The captain had deposited $60 with the British consulate, to be handed over to boarding master Turk after the *Candidate* cleared port with carpenter Kalashua safely on board. Turk, of course, knew this, and was making plans to earn the cash.

Unfortunately for everyone involved, he was depending on a big dumb thug named Daniel Moran to implement those plans.

On July 8, Moran went out drinking with Kalashua. As Moran knew, and maybe Kalashua did too, the *Candidate* was scheduled to depart at the next high tide — 3 a.m. the following morning. Moran was working to soften the big Scandinavian up a bit.

Over the course of the day, Moran would later testify, the two of them wandered the waterfront, soaking up drinks — "thirty or forty" apiece, if we can believe that. As they were making the rounds, Jim Turk asked Moran what he was doing.

"I am going to fix this fellow off," Moran replied, according to Turk's testimony, and resumed bar-hopping.

Near supper time, Moran decided it was time to do the deed. So he chirped, "Let's take another drink!" and led Kalashua and several others to a nearby saloon owned by James Kelly. Unbeknownst to all, he had made arrangements with Kelly to slip Kalashua a Mickey. It was about to be night-night time for the big squarehead, who would be waking up the next morning aboard the ship he so wanted to leave with the captain he so hated — or so Moran thought.

But Kalashua was feeling sick from all the booze. He staggered to the edge of the sidewalk, vomited in the gutter, and then followed Moran into Kelly's saloon, where he declined to take a drink, asking instead for a glass of "soda water" (meaning a bicarbonate of soda, to soothe his upset stomach).

This probably was the moment things went off the rails. Moran and Kelly had made arrangements to drug Kalashua, and those arrangements

JUST PLAIN MURDER.

Ships in the Portland Harbor, sometime in the late 1890s. (Image: OSU Libraries)

almost certainly involved a shot of whisky laced with a carefully measured amount of opium (in the form of laudanum, probably). But Kalashua wasn't drinking it. So instead, Kelly had to sneak and dump some opium in the bicarbonate of soda, estimating the dosage on the fly. He then added some sugar, stirred it, handed it to Kalashua, and told him to "drink it up quick."

Kalashua did. Then he returned to the boardinghouse, stretched out on the sofa, and did not move until the death throes came.

He died a few hours later, and by that time there were three physicians on the scene, all of whom agreed he'd clearly died of an opium overdose.

Now, incidents like this weren't as common in 1880s Portland as popular legends would have us think; but they weren't exactly unheard-of either. It's debatable whether the death of some luckless hobo or laid-off logger in a shanghaiing overdose would have received much if any attention in the newspapers. But the involvement of the British consulate, and the status of the victim as a skilled marine craftsman, combined to give this story some legs. The ensuing trial was covered fairly extensively in the Morning Oregonian, although never on the front page.

Authorities soon had both Moran and Kelly in custody. Moran, who had a great deal of trouble keeping his hands to himself, made things easier for the cops by getting himself arrested for picking a fistfight with Pat

O'Brien shortly after the doping; so he was already in the slammer when the rap came down. This gave him a leg up on what turned into a race with Kelly as each jockeyed to be the first to flip, turn state's evidence, and squeal on the other. By the time Kelly was in custody and offering to do so, it was too late, and he was on the outside looking in.

And so, in early November, saloonkeeper James Kelly found himself in court answering a charge that was probably going to send him straight to the gallows: First-degree murder. Although the death had been an accident, because it had happened as a result of Kelly committing a felony (kidnapping) the statute called it Murder One.

Things were looking extremely bleak for Kelly as the evidence was presented. It was pretty clear that he had, at Moran's request, spiked Kalashua's Alka-Seltzer with a fatal overdose of opium. Moran, in the full confession he'd offered in exchange for leniency, had already testified that Kelly had leaned over to him after the doping and whispered, "I think I have given him too much, but never mind, the son-of-a-bitch can stand it."

Then came the moment when Moran was called to the witness stand, and the bailiff went to fetch him.

A few minutes later, the bailiff returned — alone. He'd found Moran's cell empty. As he'd learned, the jailer had left Moran in the hall while he went to look for another witness, who — although he also was supposed to have been locked up in a cell — had stepped out for a couple of cocktails before breakfast and not returned. So, while the jailer was out hunting for him, Moran had simply strolled out the front door.

Everyone was furious with the jailer after this, and the newspaper reporters dropped broad hints that it had been a conspiracy and the jailer was in on it. But there was not much to be done at that point. The judge ruled Moran's confession inadmissible, and a few days later — Moran still being on the lam — the jury ruled Kelly "not guilty."

Moran managed to stay lost for almost two whole weeks. He moved to Wallula, where he was doing a pretty good job of keeping a low profile until the temptation to get into another knock-down-drag-out bar fight became too strong for his feeble intellect to resist; at which point he was forced to leave town ahead of an angry mob. The sheriff's detective who was out looking for Moran soon heard about it, and picked up his trail there, finally catching him in Spokane Falls. And so, a week or two later, Moran found himself in court, facing the same charge Kelly had just been acquitted of: Murder One.

Following a short but eventful trial, Moran was convicted of first-degree murder.

The *Morning Oregonian* was very happy about this.

"Moran may now take what comfort he can out of the fact that he has succeeded in saving his accomplice's neck at the expense of his own," editor Harvey Scott wrote in a very crisp editorial after the verdict. "This verdict was much needed. It will put a check upon the practice long prevalent here of 'doping' sailors, so as to facilitate the industry of crimping, kidnapping or otherwise decoying or conveying them on shipboard, so as to get their advance wages. More men than Kelly and Moran have been in this nefarious business at our Northwestern ports for years, and it is high time that some one or more of the scoundrels hanged for it."

And hanged for it Moran certainly would have been, but for one little detail: Portland Police Chief Samuel Parrish testified that after Moran was arrested, he'd been locked away in a dark cell in solitary for three days and his repeated requests to talk to his lawyer had been ignored. The chief, who had been on the job less than two years and had no previous law enforcement experience before taking the job, testified that no one had actually *told* him to deny the request for a lawyer, but he'd heard district attorneys grumble about suspects getting to talk to lawyers and thought this was what was expected of him.

All in all, late 1886 was not the Portland law enforcement community's most shining moment.

Not too surprisingly, the case was overturned the minute an appeals judge learned about this.

Moran was eventually convicted of manslaughter, and sent back to the pen to start a 15-year stretch for the job.

Jim Turk, the owner of the shanghaiing shop, on whose behalf all this dirty work was being done and who would have reaped the $60 reward if it had been done properly, was never charged, or even seriously questioned — despite having essentially confessed to having known about Moran's plan to shanghai Kalashua for him.

Apparently everybody knew it wouldn't do any good. In the Portland waterfront of 1886, the fix was always in.

Sources and Works Cited:
- The Oregon Shanghaiers, *a book by Barney Blalock, published in 2014 by The History Press;*
- Portland Morning Oregonian *archives, July–December 1886.*

THE CHAMPAGNE RIOT.

It was Christmas Day in 1866. Officially, the Civil War had been over for a year and a half. Unofficially, though, not everybody agreed that its outcome settled things . . . especially in Douglas County, Oregon.

At the time, Douglas County was like a microcosm of the United States. There was a Republican majority in the more populous and powerful northern part of the state, which had voted itself into full control of county government, much to the fury of the resentful, disenfranchised Dixie-friendly majority in the south of the state. And like Washington, D.C., between the warring North and South, the county seat at Roseburg was located almost directly between the two regions.

Approval or disapproval of the outcome of the war, and the subsequent reconstruction program in the South, split the Roseburg community right down the middle, with Southern Democrats bitterly resentful and Republicans (and pro-Union Democrats) gloatingly triumphant.

Douglas County wouldn't really be at peace until the following year, with the outcome of an event that's been described — only partly in jest — as the last battle of the Civil War. It's known today as the "Champagne Riot," although it was more a brawl than a riot, and there was almost certainly no champagne involved. Whiskey, though — likely there was plenty of that.

The Champagne Riot started out as a Christmas party — or, rather, two Christmas parties. Feelings were so sore in the Roseburg area that the two sides each threw their own. The pro-Southern citizens threw their "Christmas ball" at Goode's Mill, near Roseburg city limits; the Unionists had theirs at the home of Joseph Champagne, in the tiny now-long-gone hamlet of French Settlement, six miles west of town.

Everything was fine and jolly and festive until about 3 a.m., when the pro-Southern party wound its way to a close, and the dancers and revelers started heading home to bed. But a small group of them, young hot-blooded men from old Southern families, decided the night was still young enough for some more action. They further decided that the place to go for that action was Joseph Champagne's place, where the damn Yankee sympathizers were celebrating their recent victory.

Armed to the teeth and well fortified with holiday spirits, these young troublemakers set out on horseback for French Settlement, four miles away.

The primary purpose of the visit was for one of the five, Solomon Culver, to settle a score with one of the Unionists, George Bennett. Culver's cousin, John Fitzhugh, came along, and three of Culver's friends — Abe Crow, Bob Forbes and John Hannon — rounded out the little war party.

Fitzhugh was a particularly interesting character. Reportedly a distant relative of Robert E. Lee, he was a prominent Democratic leader in Roseburg and the founder and former publisher of Roseburg's first newspaper — the *Roseburg Express*, which he launched in 1860, just before the Civil War broke out. It didn't last long; after the shooting started, federal authorities went looking for "copperhead" newspapers and shutting them down, and the *Express* — along with the *Albany Democrat, Corvallis Union, Table Rock* (Jacksonville) *Sentinel, Eugene Herald* and *Portland Daily News* — was suppressed.

What the erstwhile journalist did after that, for the duration of the war, isn't clear. Most likely he went east to fight. But there's one thing we know he didn't do, and that's give up on his pro-Southern beliefs.

Fitzhugh and his four comrades arrived at the rival gang's party around 4 a.m. Upon their arrival, they got busy making trouble right away. Culver found Bennett, whipped out his Dragoon revolver and pistol-whipped him across the face with it, breaking his nose.

Then the party's host, Frank Barringer, hurried to the scene, apparently to try to defuse the situation, and — presumably after a heated exchange of words, although the newspapers don't say — Fitzhugh pulled a derringer and shot him through the heart. Barringer slipped to the floor and died without speaking another word.

JUST PLAIN MURDER.

The Douglas County Courthouse as it appeared during the murder trial of the instigators of the "Champagne Riot" of 1866. Built in the early 1850s at a cost of $200, the old courthouse was replaced with a more impressive-looking edifice in 1868, and the old courthouse became what it had always resembled: a store. (Image: Oregon Historical Society)

Then fists, knives and pistols started flashing and flying as the fighting became general. The fiddle player, Ash Clayton, set down his instrument, grabbed a knife and used it to let some air out of Solomon Colver's left lung. Abe Crow took offense to this and, pulling his revolver, shot Clayton twice with it (once in the leg, and once across the scalp) and then slashed him across the head with his knife. Fitzhugh, now armed only with the empty derringer, rushed another partygoer named Tom Thompson — which turned out to be a huge mistake, because Thompson clearly knew his way around a six-shooter better than anyone else in the room.

Two gunshots later, Fitzhugh was done for the night — not dead, but badly wounded. Forbes and Hannon, seeing this, attacked Thompson and were also shot down — both hit in the stomach. Crow, suddenly realizing he was the only survivor of the little war party, gave full rein to the better part of valor and took himself off into the night at top speed.

Over the next week or two, much to the surprise of nearly everyone, nearly all the injured parties rallied and recovered. Only Bob Forbes, whose spine had been broken by Thompson's revolver ball, and Barringer, shot through the heart by Fitzhugh, died.

Fitzhugh was soon arrested, and put on trial for murder along with Hannan; Crow, who had made a dreadful mess of fiddle player Clayton, couldn't be found. It's not clear why Culver wasn't charged, but chances are good his sucking chest wound was still too serious for him to make a court appearance.

The "riot," which got extensive newspaper coverage all over Oregon, had brought the lingering resentments in Douglas County to a head, and hundreds of people took an avid interest in the trial. For most of them, it was more than a drunken act of petty criminality; it was a proxy fight between the forces of the North and the South.

When it was all over, the jury found both men guilty. But the judge sentenced them to very light sentences: five years for Fitzhugh, and one for Hannan.

The champions of Unionists and Southern Democrats alike decried the verdict in editorial pages and coffee houses — the one side complaining about the light sentences, the other about the guilty verdict. But after it was all over, and nobody's "team" had "won," Douglas County residents were finally able to settle down and live with one another — if not at peace, then at least not actively at war.

Sources and Works Cited:
- "Dixie of the Pacific Northwest," an article by Jeff LaLande published in the Spring 1999 issue of Oregon Historical Quarterly;
- Portland Morning Oregonian archives, January 1867.

THE JACKSON COUNTY REBELLION.

To call Llewellyn F. Banks a swindler was overselling things a bit; he seems to have really believed in what he was doing.

To call him a would-be fascist was simply wrong. Sure, he wanted to seize power, but he had no interest in starting a nationalist collectivist autocracy.

Still, after May 21, 1933, you could at least call him a convicted murderer.

The story of Llewellyn Banks' time in Jackson County is one of the weirder tales to come out of Southern Oregon. It started benignly enough, with his arrival as a wealthy newcomer to the prosperous regional cosmopolis of Medford. But by the time it ended amid murder and chaos, it had nearly all of Jackson County in an almost revolutionary uproar — a mostly forgotten episode that became known as the "Jackson County Rebellion."

Llewellyn Banks was an Ohioan by birth, but he'd made his fortune in citrus orchards in Riverside, in southern California. He was an articulate, charismatic entrepreneur who seemed to lead a charmed life, always leaping from risky move to risky move, somehow landing butter-side-up every time.

But he also had a mammoth ego bolstered with an unshakable faith in his own abilities, and that led — as it so often does with people like that — to a kind of endemic paranoia. When something bad happens to most of us, we put it down to either bad luck or a mistake on our part. But for a man like Banks, bad luck didn't exist, and mistakes were something other people made. That left the action of unseen enemies as the only acceptable possibility when things went badly for him.

Even during the good times, that paranoia occasionally led to trouble. In the mid-1920s, it led to a bitter feud with the Riverside growers' cooperative that prompted him to sell his orchards, leave Southern California and move his operations to Medford.

During the bad times, in his new Southern Oregon home, it was about to lead to considerably worse things than that.

Banks arrived in Medford driving a flashy, ostentatious Cadillac touring car with his wife, Edith, and their daughter, Ruth, around 1925. The little family settled into a beautiful Tudor-style home in the swankiest part of town.

Banks soon found a kindred spirit in a local real-estate developer named Earl Fehl, who owned and edited a local weekly newspaper, the *Pacific Record-Herald*. Fehl was also a perennial candidate for political office. Throughout the 1920s Fehl had run for mayor of Medford at every opportunity and, when he lost, blamed the local political establishment, which he called "The Gang." The fix was in, he constantly railed (in voice and in print), and the wealthy carpet-bagging swells from back east were running Jackson County for themselves.

In this view, Fehl found himself speaking for a vast majority of the people who dwelled outside of Medford, in the hills and woodlands, working mining claims or farming small patches far from town. Most of these people had lived in Jackson County all their lives, and they remembered what the place had been like before the rich families from back East had moved into the area and taken over, about 20 years before. They remembered, and they resented the social demotion and loss of local influence that had followed. And they also resented, bitterly, the ever-rising property taxes, county fees and especially the vigorous Prohibition enforcement that they were getting from their new self-appointed leaders in Medford.

And things were only getting worse. As the years rolled by, the "roaring twenties" were particularly good to Medford's social elite as the worldwide market for luxury goods such as the region's famous Winter Pears grew and strengthened; but the benefits largely passed the backcountry folks by. Their resentment simmered on quietly, ignored by the ruling elites ... for the time being.

Fehl was soon joined by Banks in pandering to this audience. Banks' efforts to get himself accepted into elite Jackson County society had not worked out, and he was already clashing with other growers who wanted to

JUST PLAIN MURDER.

A hand-tinted image of downtown Medford as it appeared in the late 1920s, when the Jackson County Rebellion was first beginning to brew. (Image: Postcard)

form a marketing cooperative like the one he'd feuded with in Riverside. Soon Banks and Fehl were allies and friends.

And then they also became colleagues. In the fall of 1929, Banks got the opportunity to buy one of Medford's two daily newspapers, and he jumped at the chance.

Now, at last, Fehl and Banks were in perfect position, ready to launch the media propaganda campaign that would, they hoped, propel them to political power by giving the disenfranchised country folk of Jackson County a ticket to vote for.

Fehl and Banks got started immediately with a campaign of savage, divisive editorial rabble-rousing aimed at energizing the rural Jackson County residents whom they had identified as their base constituency. They planned to keep it up for a couple years, whipping the rural residents' frustrations into active hostility against the incumbent elites, and then offer themselves and a slate of their friends as a political ticket.

There was a major complication coming around the next corner, though, for both these would-be insurgency leaders. Just a few weeks after Llewellyn Banks embarked on his new career as a newspaper editor and publisher, the bottom fell out of the stock market on the other side of the continent — and the country began a slow, terrifying plunge into the worst economic depression in its history. It would, over the next couple years, hit Jackson County with crushing force. And unlike the prosperity of the "roaring twenties," its effects would be felt by everyone. By 1932, the rural residents of Jackson

County were not merely angry — they were, increasingly, desperate. And they responded to the two publishers' campaign more wholeheartedly than the plotters had ever dreamed.

Llewellyn Banks and Earl Fehl were, in effect, sowing the wind. Within a couple years, both men would reap the ensuing whirlwind, and it would put both of them in prison along with several of their friends — and, directly or indirectly, it would put four other Jackson County residents in the ground.

The year of 1932 was probably the worst non-war year of the twentieth century, and it hit the Rogue River Valley as hard as it hit anyplace. That year was the psychological nadir of the Great Depression — a year of bank closures, suicides, hunger and civil unrest. Across most of the nation, as historian Jeff LaLande points out, the national mood was mostly one of bewilderment rather than anger ... but most of the nation didn't have two local newspapers doing their level best to crystallize that bewilderment into bitter hatred against local political leaders.

Jackson County did. And Jackson County entered 1932 on the brink of open hostilities. Some residents had even taken to carrying pistols on their hips, and armed guards and state police officers with submachine guns were not an uncommon sight on Medford streets.

Moreover, the owners of the two newspapers that were doing all the rabble-rousing — Llewellyn Banks of the *Daily News* and Earl Fehl of the *Pacific Record Herald* — were increasingly in desperate financial straits personally as the effects of the Depression worsened. Llewellyn Banks, who had leveraged himself extensively to finance the purchase of the *Daily News*, was in particularly bad shape. He was behind on payments to the former owners of his newspaper, and faced foreclosure on his orchards. He also was being sued by half a dozen different parties at the same time — creditors, union representatives and people he'd libeled in his newspaper.

The only hope for both of them seemed to be a total takeover of the Jackson County political and judicial machinery. That would enable them to stall their creditors and frustrate their litigants, while possibly also giving them suitably prestigious positions to transition into after the foreclosures and judgements finally did run their inevitable course.

Fortunately, Banks and Fehl had been gearing up for just such a takeover for years.

They'd refocused their editorial and organizational fire on local politics after a moderately disastrous attempt by Banks to unseat U.S. Sen. Charles McNary in 1930. The most memorable incident in that race had been when Banks tried to start a fistfight with a constituent who twitted him about the

JUST PLAIN MURDER.

The Jackson County Courthouse as it appeared in the 1930s, when Llewellyn Banks was holding massive political rallies on its lawn. (Image: Postcard)

California license tags on his Cadillac. He'd lost that race in a landslide, and decided that his time would be better spent trying to build a local power base rather than bothering with state office.

So after that, his column in the *Daily News* talked much less of statewide issues, and far more about "The Gang" — the elected officials in charge of Jackson County. And Earl Fehl — whose latest run for mayor had come tantalizingly close to success — backed him up with gusto in the *Record Herald*.

Now, after two years of steadily beating the drum for electoral war upon "The Gang," Banks and Fehl were ready to make their play.

It started with an attempt to recall a Circuit Court judge who was scheduled to preside over one of the lawsuits in which Banks was a defendant. Banks crystalized the recall movement into a political organization, dubbed it the "Good Government Congress," and started charging its members monthly dues. In spite of this expense, or perhaps partly because of it, it grew into an ominously large force of often heavily armed Jackson County citizens — mostly rural residents, working stiffs and the newly unemployed. Members would gather by the hundreds (and, occasionally, thousands) on the courthouse lawn to hear their leader speak, flanked by members of his own militia — the "Green Springs Mountain Boys."

Then came the election, and the Good Government Congress's candidates won some of the key positions in the county. In particular, Earl Fehl himself, having at last given up on tilting at the Mayoral windmill, was elected county judge, and Good Government Congress crony Gordon

Schermerhorn squeaked by on a razor-thin majority to become the new county sheriff.

It would have been a complete takeover had it not been for M.O. Wilkins' loss in the race to unseat district attorney George Codding. That loss hurt, since the D.A. had a lot of influence over the issues Banks and Fehl cared most about: their legal troubles. Already Fehl had lost his printing plant in a libel judgment, and Banks' creditors were trying to foreclose on his newspaper.

No matter. The two self-styled political bosses quickly set about consolidating their victory, whipping their Good Government Congress members into ever more dangerous frenzies with exhortations on the courthouse steps and in the pages of their newspapers. The rival daily newspaper, the Medford *Mail Tribune*, which was getting threatening letters every day, hired armed guards to protect itself from the angry crowds. Llewellyn Banks deployed paramilitary detachments of the Green Springs Mountain Boys, duly deputized by the friendly new sheriff, to guard his own newspaper's office and printing plant — although that was not for protection against political enemies so much as to prevent it from being seized by his creditors.

Meanwhile, ex-sheriff Ralph Jennings remained suspicious that the election that had kicked him out of office had been fraudulent. He'd lost by just over 100 votes — well within the range at which a recount is appropriate — but his efforts to arrange for one were being stymied by the new county judge, Earl Fehl. So he went over Fehl's head and appealed directly to the state of Oregon, which ordered the recount done.

This was a problem, because the election HAD been rigged — or, at least, an attempt had been made to ensure a positive outcome by strategically rejecting some ballots from the Eagle Point area on paper-thin pretexts. If those ballots were recounted, given how slim the margins had been, Sheriff Schermerhorn would almost certainly be declared the loser, and the Good Government Congress would lose the power to deputize members of the Green Springs Mountain Boys to provide muscle. Something had to be done.

And so, on February 20, 1933, something was done. It was done under cover of a massive Good Government Congress rally — at least 1,000 people, probably many more, assembled at the county courthouse for a particularly noisy demonstration.

"Do we want a recount? NO!" the multitude roared, and somewhere on a side street nearby someone revved a flathed Ford V-8 engine to cover up the sound of breaking glass ....

JUST PLAIN MURDER.

The front porch and entry door of the Llewellyn Banks residence, where Constable Prescott was murdered. (Image: Southern Oregon Historical Society)

Meanwhile, feeling the hot breath of the lien enforcers and bankruptcy trustees on their backs, Banks and Fehl were pressing forward with their "reforms" as fast as they could. The results of the election had been decidedly mixed, but both men knew it was their one shot, and they had to play it for all they were worth. They promptly and triumphantly proclaimed that the people had delivered a mighty mandate to oust Jackson County's political establishment — "The Gang" — and replace it with their organization, working on behalf of "the people."

A portrait of Llewellyn A. Banks as he appeared in the mid-1920s. (Image: Oregon Historical Quarterly)

It was a point that they'd been working up to for two solid years of nonstop propaganda in their two newspapers. And the two of them probably believed they had indeed won a mighty mandate. The trouble was, there seems to have been no doubt in anyone's mind but that a recount would reverse the election result. And a recount now seemed inevitable, now that Jackson County's once-and-future sheriff had blown the whistle and gotten the state involved.

To avoid that, Sheriff Schermerhorn actually went on the lam so that Jennings couldn't serve papers on him. But this, of course, was at best a temporary expedient. One could not do one's job as sheriff of Southern Oregon's most populous county from an outlaw hideout somewhere in the Siskiyous. What was needed was some direct action.

So on Feb. 20, the very night the judge ruled that a recount must proceed, while a mammoth crowd of Good Government Congress true believers rallied and chanted in front of the Jackson County Courthouse, a small crew of Good Government Congress operatives broke out a side window. They slipped inside, collected as many ballots as they could haul, and hustled them away — beyond the reach of recount.

The next day, when the election staff came downstairs to start on the recount, the burglary was discovered. Earl Fehl tried to blame ex-sheriff Jennings, and barely-elected sheriff Schermerhorn pledged a full investigation; but nobody was fooled.

The Oregon State Police certainly weren't. Officers were on the scene almost immediately, politely informing Sheriff Schermerhorn that their office would be conducting that "full investigation" and his assistance would not be required.

As it turned out, getting to the bottom of the burglary wasn't hard; the burglars hadn't done a very good job of covering their tracks. The case broke wide open when investigators found the charred remnants of a bunch of the ballots in the courthouse furnace.

Working from the tiny list of people who had access to the courthouse furnace, the state cops quickly zeroed in on a Good Government Congress member who worked at the courthouse. They picked him up, "took him downtown," and spent a long time discussing the subject with him. By the time they were done, they had a new list of people to arrest — a list that included Sheriff Schermerhorn, as well as Judge Fehl, the county jailer, and even the mayor of the town of Rogue River.

Sheriff Schermerhorn, it turned out, had stood watch and signaled the burglars with a flashlight when the coast was clear; one of his deputies had led the burglary team. Judge Fehl hadn't participated in the burglary, but was thought to have masterminded it.

Now things started to move fairly quickly. The Good Government Congress having resorted to extra-legal measures, its leaders were vulnerable to charges of criminal syndicalism, which drastically increased the seriousness of the charges they were likely to face. This fact, in turn, gave investigators much greater leverage when negotiating with participants in the conspiracy. And much as Llewellyn Banks might

Medford Police Constable George Prescott, who was murdered with a .30-06 rifle while trying to arrest Llewellyn Banks. (Image: Oregon Historical Quarterly)

have hoped for loyalty from his trusty Green Springs Mountain minions, none of them were going to take a felony rap and serve two dozen years of hard time to protect him.

And so the investigation quickly led, through a series of inquiries of the "what did the president know and when did he know it" type, straight to the ornate mansion of Llewellyn Banks.

Llewellyn Banks had made it clear that he would not go quietly. At the last Good Government Congress rally, held just after the burglary, he stood upon the courthouse steps shaking his fist at the building and shouting, "Unless justice is restored, I will lead the field in revolution against you people — now, make the most of it!"

But after that, he'd gone home and packed his stuff. Banks knew he was next. His creditors had finally managed to slip past his goon squads and padlock his newspaper, so he no longer had that outlet. His orchard lands were either going or gone. And his collaborators in the Good Government Congress were turning out to have very big mouths.

One of his supporters had a rustic log cabin on a mining claim deep in the forest. It would be a perfect place for Banks to hide out for a few months until all the gunsmoke and horsefeathers settled out of the air.

Banks had just packed his valise and had his hunting rifle, a .30-06, loaded and sitting on the table by the door. All that was left was to pick it up, walk to the car, and leave town.

Then there came a knock on the front door. It was Medford Police Constable George Prescott and Oregon State Police Sgt. James O'Brien. And they were there with a warrant for Banks' arrest.

Llewellyn Banks' wife, Edith, opened the door just enough to throw some papers out at the officers — papers intended to challenge the officers' right to make the arrest. Prescott stuck his foot in the door before she could close it. And then Banks came up behind Edith with his .30-06 — and put a round into Prescott's chest.

Prescott, shot through the heart, died almost immediately. O'Brien, of course, retreated at top speed and called for backup. Soon dozens of cops swarmed the house; but a siege was avoided when Banks voluntarily surrendered into custody.

Banks seemed utterly unrepentant, and claimed to be confident that he'd be vindicated when the investigation was done — that he had been fully justified in "defending his home" from the marauding constable with his deadly door-stopping foot.

The force of some 30 state police officers who'd come to town to investigate the ballot burglary now decided enough was enough, and spread out through the streets of Medford with shotguns and tear gas rounding up Good Government Congress members.

Later investigation turned up evidence that Banks and his aides had actually made plans to kidnap the district attorney — the one official they hadn't been able to defeat at the ballot box with any amount of cheating — and warehouse him at a remote cabin in the hills, where he could be kept out of action as long as necessary or even quietly killed if it came to that. They also had a contingency plan for launching an actual armed guerilla insurrection from the hills of Southern Oregon. How much of this was serious and how much was fantasy isn't known; but it's worth remembering that in 1932, many people felt they were living in the economic End Times, and fascism, which was not yet discredited as a political philosophy, had positioned itself as a way forward out of the Depression.

Llewellyn Banks was convicted of second-degree (unpremeditated) murder at the ensuing trial, and sentenced to life in prison. For the rest of his life, his family tried diligently and sometimes shamelessly to arrange for him to be pardoned. One state prison official was fired for allegedly accepting a bribe to advocate for him. But all the various governors approached by the family and its agents recognized a political suicide rap when they saw one, and declined to help. Banks died in prison in 1945.

Earl Fehl drew a four-year sentence for his part in the ballot theft, and sorta-ex-sheriff Gordon Schermerhorn got three. Most other defendants were found guilty and were sentenced to various shorter terms.

At the end of the whole debacle, the Medford *Mail Tribune* — the larger of Medford's two daily newspapers, which had, under the leadership of owner Robert Ruhl, kept a remarkably cool and level head throughout the crisis — received the Pulitzer Prize for meritorious public service in 1933. It was the first Pulitzer Prize won by an Oregon newspaper, and the *Mail Tribune* remains the smallest Oregon newspaper to have won one.

Sources and Works Cited:
- *"The Jackson County Rebellion," an article by Jeff LaLande in the December 1994 issue of* Oregon Historical Quarterly;
- *"Llewellyn and Edith Banks Trial, 1933," an un-by-lined article published at law.jrank.org.*

THE INTERNATIONAL MURDERER O' MYSTERY.

On the evening of December 1, 1878, all four prisoners in the Wasco County Jail, in the back of the county courthouse, were out of their cells and relaxing in the common area near a glowing woodstove. One, a horse thief named Tharp, was sitting by the stove with a Chinese man (whose name is not given in the newspaper account); James Cook, a great burly man with an English accent, was pacing up and down, dragging his heavy shackle (probably an "Oregon boot"), apparently lost in thought; and George Craig, a slender tow-headed young man of 22, was sitting on a bench contemplating his fall from grace.

He had indeed fallen a long way. Craig was in jail, and on his way to the state prison, for a crime three months before, when he and Cook had robbed Baldwin's Saloon in The Dalles. Craig's involvement in this crime had shocked the little community; he was the son of the late Polhemus Craig, M.D., a highly respected physician and druggist. The son hadn't risen to the heights of his father, though, and had taken a job as a flatboat operator on the river, then fallen in with a bad and dissolute crowd — a crowd that included James Cook.

After the robbery, Craig had fled to Portland, and it had taken a month or two for authorities to catch up with him. When they had, he'd quickly confessed — and implicated Cook.

The news had traveled faster than the law, and by the time Deputy Marshall Haine was knocking on Cook's door, he'd already heard they were looking for him. His Native American wife (or girlfriend; the newspapers don't say) had told the sheriff he'd gone to Boise. Haine had thanked her kindly and then asked what was in the giant crate sitting in a corner of the room.

"*Cultus ictas*," she replied — which is Chinook for "Bad things," or "garbage." This seeming suspiciously vague, Haine pulled his six-shooter and covered the box with it while directing the other deputy to tip it over.

"The box was upset and Cook stepped out, coolly remarking, 'Well, you 'ave got me coppered,'" the *Morning Oregonian's* The Dalles correspondent wrote.

Cook's coolness didn't last, though. When he learned that Craig had ratted him out, it turned to hot fury. At his trial, he firmly denied any involvement; and when he was convicted, it was almost solely on Craig's testimony.

But that was all over now. Craig and Cook both were on their way to the state pen to serve seven-year stretches. And Cook had finally gotten over his anger against Craig.

Or so it seemed ... until suddenly Cook, walking past Craig while pacing the jailhouse, suddenly pounced.

There was a terrible cry — a scream of "Oh God, take him off!" — and then came a horrible gurgle and a splashing sound.

Sheriff James B. Crossen hurried into the room from the front office, where he'd been working on some paperwork. By the time he got through the door, it was all over. Cook, with a straight razor he'd somehow gotten hold of, had seized his former partner by the hair and sliced his throat open to the spine.

Crossen pulled his pistol out, put it against Cook's head, and demanded to know where the razor had come from. Cook refused.

"Go ahead and shoot," he said. "I'd rather hang or have you shoot me than spend seven years in the penitentiary."

(No one ever did figure out where Cook got that razor from; but his Native American wife had been in to see him the day before, and it seemed most likely that she'd slipped it to him then.)

Just a few minutes later, Craig's aged mother arrived, intending to spend the night there in the jail with her son before his departure the following morning on the boat for Salem.

"Her cries would have melted the heart of any man not steeped to the very lips in crime," the *Oregonian's* correspondent wrote — almost certainly referring to Cook and his cocky heartlessness in the aftermath of the killing.

JUST PLAIN MURDER.

The historic First Wasco County Courthouse, built in 1859, as it appears today. The courthouse was the scene of both of James Cook's trials as well as the murder of George Craig. The courtroom was on the second floor, accessed by the outside stairway; the bottom floor consisted of the sheriff's office in the front, and the county jail in the windowless back of the building. The courthouse originally stood where City Hall is today, but has since been moved to 410 West 2nd Place. (Image: Ian Poellet)

The gruesome nature of this murder made a great impression on the public, and the newspapers got right on the story, trying to learn as much as they could about this cold-blooded razor killer. Who was he? What kind of life would lead to such an end?

James Cook was ready for them — with an amazing collection of hand-crafted whoppers.

"My earliest recollections of life are of being among the Indians — the Sioux," he told an *Oregonian* reporter in a jailhouse interview a few weeks later, lounging insouciantly on his bunk in the prison cell. "I never could find out who my parents were but I am under the impression that they were captured and murdered by the Indians while traveling ... I remained with the Indians for 16 years, and during that time was twice engaged in war against the whites.

"While with the Indians an Englishman, a Dr. Roach, who was hunting on the plains, came into our camp ... I was selected to guide the intruder out of our hunting grounds. The doctor took a fancy to me, and I concluded

The original Wasco County Courthouse as it appeared before 1884, when the current courthouse was built. This view shows the sheriff's office on the lower floor; behind was the jail with no windows on the Third street side. The narrow door to the right leads to the outside stairway whereby the courtroom on the second floor was reached. The one-story building farther to the right was the County Clerk's office. (Image: UO Libraries)

to accept his offer to accompany him in his travels as a body-servant and leave the Indians.

"After journeying about six months in the United States we left for India, where for 20 months we remained tiger hunting in the jungles ... Tired of India, we left for Africa ... We spent portions of the time in Abyssinia, the country surrounding the Red Sea, after which we crossed the great desert; thence to Alexandria, and after a short stay in Egypt we sailed for England. Remaining at the doctor's home for a short time, we left for Australia where I left the service of the doctor and started off on my own hook for America.

"I reached San Francisco all right, and after remaining there some little while I followed the crowd then rushing to Nevada ... then traveled through the state continuing my journey through Colorado and finally brought up in Texas where I was engaged as a stock driver. To this capacity I went to Arizona, and in 1865 found myself in Montana, from which place I returned to San Francisco.

"One morning I found myself on board the ship *Yenisei*. How I came there I could not comprehend at first, but shortly realized that I'd been shanghaied.

JUST PLAIN MURDER.

"We were bound for China, but never reached our destination. The ship ran on a reef, and myself and four others were the only ones that escaped to the mainland after being in an open boat for nine days without food and water. After our rescue we tooted it through South Anam, and then on to Canton. We were then went to Hong Kong, from which place I returned to San Francisco. I came to Oregon about 16 months ago, and have lived in and about The Dalles during the time."

Well, all righty then.

"Such is the history of his life that Cook gives," the *Oregonian* writer dryly concludes. But, he adds, "there was not one of those present who listened to the recital that believed it."

And yet this mouthful of malarkey is all there is about James Cook's past ... except for one thing: a newspaper report from the Oregon City Enterprise a little over a year before the killing: "James Cook, for trying to aid prisoners to make their escape from the penitentiary, goes back to that institution for a period of five years for his trouble, by order of Judge Boise."

This may refer to a different man, also named James Cook. And it doesn't explain how Cook got out of the penitentiary just a year or so into a five-year stretch. But, given the conditions in the state prison in the 1870s, it might explain his decision to avoid a prison sentence by escalating the charges to Murder One with a bit of revenge, and getting hanged instead.

On the morning of Feb. 7, 1879, James Cook went through the floor of the gallows with his lips still shut tight. He'd eaten a hearty breakfast that morning, visited briefly and unproductively with a Catholic priest, and declined to say anything further when invited by the sheriff to do so. Seventeen minutes later, he was dead.

We still have no idea even what his real name was.

Sources and Works Cited:
- Necktie Parties: Legal Executions in Oregon 1851-1905, *a book by Diane L. Goeres-Gardner published in 2005 by Caxton Press;*
- Pendleton East Oregonian *archives, December 1878 and February 1879;*
- Oregon City Enterprise *archives, October 1877)*

THE SUSPICIOUS GUNFIGHT.

In the 1890s, 47-year-old Kelsay Porter lived alone on a remote farm in the foothills of the Wallowas, in a tiny Union County community called Pine Valley. He was a shy, timid bachelor who had moved to this remote place for privacy, sometime in the 1880s. And for many years, he got his privacy, and lived harmoniously with the few neighbors.

But then the Mache family moved in next door.

Ben and Mary Mache, with their 17-year-old son Ben Jr., had blown into Pine Valley a few months before, and already they had a reputation in the community as "hard characters." This was especially the case with the younger Ben, who carried a six-shooter and used it far more than was considered appropriate. He didn't use it to shoot to kill — but he'd been known to send bullets zipping past people's ears to make his point. At Christmastime in 1895 he had just been released from the state prison, where he'd served a stretch for rustling cattle.

For Porter the problem was, the most convenient road to the Mache farm was a shortcut across Porter's land, which came within just a few feet of his barn.

Porter's initial request that the Maches use a different route was ignored. So he built a fence across it. The Maches tore the fence down. Porter went to the justice of the peace to complain; the justice told him to just ignore them, because there was nothing the law could do about it.

But word of Porter's complaint reached the Maches, and infuriated them. The elder Ben Mache threatened to kill Porter. Porter responded by having a judge put him in bond.

Young Ben Jr. was not under bond, though, and therefore could do as he wished without worrying about losing his bond money. So he decided to get even, and he and a friend rode out to Porter's farm with their six-shooters drawn. They found Porter working in his field, and opened fire — sending bullets zipping by his ears and into the ground near his feet. Terrified, Porter ran and hid in his house; thereupon, Ben and his friend leisurely stole some horse tack from his barn and went on their way.

It was after this incident that Kelsay Porter borrowed a Winchester rifle. He figured if the law wouldn't do anything, he'd better be ready to do something himself.

Then came New Year's Day in 1896.

The events of that day are still in some dispute. There are two versions: the one Kelsay Porter gave when he turned himself in later that day; and the one the Union County coroner and sheriff developed after looking over the scene. They may have had personal reasons to reach the conclusions they did — the facts of the case are still in dispute.

Here's Porter's version of the story:

On that day, the Maches were driving a sleigh pulled by two horses, returning home to their farm; Ben Jr. rode behind them. Porter was on the roof of his house, clearing off snow. As the sleigh passed his barn, Porter shouted at the Maches to stay off his land.

"You lie!" retorted the elder Mache. "This is a public highway. If you fence it up again, we'll kill you!"

Ben Jr. apparently thought this was his cue to go into action, and he once again filled the air around Porter's ears with buzzing lead. Porter jumped from the roof and again ran into his house — but this time, he didn't stay in it. He came out with the Winchester ready to go, and he appears to have gone clear berserk.

Ben Jr., sitting high on his horse, was the first to go down under a hail of Winchester lead, but Porter didn't stop there. The team bolted with the sleigh; Porter followed after, still firing. A stray bullet killed Mary Mache. Another hit one of the horses and it fell dead, pitching Ben Sr.'s body over into the creek.

Porter continued shooting into the now-dead bodies of his neighbors until all of his bullets were gone — there were 18 bullet wounds found in the Maches, plus the one that hit the horse.

So, that was Kelsay Porter's story: Basically, that he was attacked on his own land by armed assailants and he defended himself with the rifle.

JUST PLAIN MURDER.

But after traveling out to the farm from Union City, coroner E.R. Lang and sheriff's deputy J.H. McLachlin decided there was something fishy about it. Dr. Lang figured out that Ben Sr. had actually been killed not by gunfire, but by being clobbered with something — a rifle butt, most likely, he thought. So Porter had chased Ben Sr. down, and beat him to death? And then stood over his obviously dead victims thumbing cartridges into the side of the empty Winchester for as long as it took to do that, and then squared off and blasted away some more at the corpses. Why? Because he was still blind with battle fury? Or to stage the scene so it looked more like a gunfight?

Also, the deputy found, looking on that roof, that much of the snow on it was packed down, and it looked an awful lot like someone had been lurking there waiting for the sleigh to come along. From up on that roof, Porter would have been able to see, and shoot, a good long distance.

The Portland Morning Oregonian's staff artist published this sketch of convicted murderer Kelsay Porter shortly before his execution. (Image: Oregonian)

Had Porter actually waited there, shot the boy from ambush before he could reach pistol range, then chased after the parents as they tried to race away on the sleigh, picking Mary off and then shooting a horse to stop their flight? Had he then run up to the wreckage, clubbed Joseph to death with his now-empty rifle, reloaded, and pumped eight more rounds into the dead body so that it would look like it had been a fair fight?

What he saw at the scene convinced the deputy that this was the real story: cold-blooded assassination.

And, well, maybe it was; but the evidence still seems very circumstantial, and much of it makes no sense. If he had his choice of targets to pick off from his safe point of ambush, why would Porter have shot Mary Mache and not Ben Sr.? And it's hard to picture how after springing his ambush at rifle-shooting distance, safely out of reach of Ben Jr.'s pistol shots, Porter would have been able to get close enough to an uninjured Ben Sr. to club him to death.

It's also puzzling how much was made of the tramped-down snow on Porter's roof. Given that his life had been threatened, Porter could have been expected to be watching for the Mache clan's comings and goings, and the roof would have been the best place to do it; it does seem a bit of a leap from "watching for the Maches" to "watching for the Maches in order to murder them."

In the end, though, the jury in distant Union City bought the "assassination" story, and sentenced Kelsay Porter to hang for murdering the family. But many of the neighbors in Pine Valley were unconvinced, and outraged. Local historian Carmelita Holland remembers speaking with many people who were alive during the trial, and all of them characterized it as a railroad job. And maybe it was — it was certainly unusual, in 1890s Eastern Oregon, for a landowner defending his property from armed intruders to be even prosecuted for murder afterward, let alone convicted.

As the day of the execution drew near, Porter remained true to his shy, quiet nature. He gave no interviews and declined to say anything to the crowd of gawkers that stared up at him as he stood on the gallows on Friday, Nov. 9, 1897; he went to his death silent as a sphinx. But he wrote a short letter, just before his execution, and handed it to a Presbyterian minister to be released after his death.

"This is my last request on Earth," he wrote. "The real cause of my trouble is the way children are raised to live too easy, regardless of the law of justice and right. Parents, please raise your children with a principle that will defend their character."

Sources and Works Cited:

- *Stories, Legends, and Some Oregon History, a book by Carmelita Holland published in 1996 by the Pendleton Record-Courier;*
- Necktie Parties: Legal Executions in Oregon 1851-1905, *a book by Diane L. Goeres-Gardner published in 2005 by Caxton Press;*
- Archives of *Portland Morning Oregonian, Athena Press, The Dalles Times-Mountaineer and* Eugene City Guard, *January 1896;*
- An Illustrated History of Union and Wallowa Counties, *an anonymously authored book published in 1902 by Western Historical Publishing Co.*

THE WANDERERS.

In Charles Maturin's classic 1820 Gothic horror novel *Melmoth the Wanderer*, a sinister scholar named Melmoth, having sold his soul to the devil in return for an extra 150 years of life and suffering from the worst kind of buyer's remorse, wanders the Earth in search of someone who will, essentially, take over payments for him. If he can find someone to buy out his contract, he can die in peace and go to heaven — or, at least, not automatically be sent to hell.

In the summer of 1898, two young Oregon men found themselves in a similar situation. They had murdered a wealthy rancher on a trip across the Cascades, then belatedly realized how bad it would look to show up at the end of the trip without him. So they wandered around Lane County with increasing desperation looking for someone to lie under oath for them by swearing they had seen the three of them arriving in the valley together.

It didn't work — for them or for Melmoth.

The story started in March 1898, when 22-year-old Courtland Green moved to Condon to work. He had a friend there, another 22-year-old named Clarence Branton. Both Green and Branton had sweethearts in the McKenzie River valley, but weren't in a financial position to get married. Both were on the lookout for ways to make lots of money really fast. And Branton had a plan to do just that.

Branton's plan involved a local rancher named John Linn, who was

Claude Branton on the gallows, about to be hanged for the murder of John Linn, on May 12, 1899. (Image: Oregon Historical Society)

rumored to carry a purse with $1,000 in gold (worth $30,000 in 2018 currency) as walking-around money. Branton had sweet-talked Linn into partnering up with him on some horses. Soon it would be time to bring those horses over the pass to the McKenzie River valley to market. It was easy: they'd murder Linn in the most remote part of the trip. Between the $1,000 and the proceeds of the sale of the horses, they'd both have all the money they needed to set up housekeeping, and be right there in the McKenzie valley ready to pop The Question. One wonders if they made plans to be best man in one another's weddings.

That night they made camp around 9 p.m. at a place called Isham's Corral, one or two dozen miles west of the pass, near Alder Springs. Linn had spread his bedroll near the fire and was peacefully sleeping; it was now or never. Branton had brought along a cheap five-shot Iver Johnson American Bulldog revolver — probably a .32, although the newspaper accounts don't specify — and he now got that out and, after a whispered conference with Green (who apparently was getting cold feet) walked over to Linn with it and shot him several times.

Of course, the first thing the two of them wanted to do was find the $1,000 Linn reportedly carried. In that, they got a disappointing shock: all they found in his purse was $65 and an I.O.U. for $800. Linn had lent almost all his walking-around money to a friend before leaving on the trip.

But the short summer night was no longer young, and they had a body to get rid of before dawn. Branton and Green gathered wood and expanded the campfire into a massive funeral pyre. They tended it all night, trying to completely destroy Linn's corpse, which they chopped up with an ax to encourage better burning; and the next morning it was still smoking prodigiously, drawing a good deal of attention from nervous residents miles away, who feared it was a forest fire breaking out.

Leaving the bloody ax there beside the still-burning fire, the two of them then drove the horses down toward the valley, where they hoped to sell them. Along the way they met several people, who commented on the smoke and wondered if they knew about it. It was finally beginning to dawn on them that, when Linn's disappearance was remarked, they would be the prime suspects, having been seen leaving Condon with him and arriving in the McKenzie valley without him.

What to do?

The two of them decided what they needed was to find some rustic sucker willing to perjure himself by swearing that he had seen the three of them together, bringing the horses down.

And so commenced Branton and Green's Melmoth-like wanderings through the McKenzie Valley, horses in tow, looking for friends old and

An artist's sketch of the fence around the county jail, and the gallows which was built next to it, published the day of the execution in the Eugene Guard. (Image: Eugene Guard)

The above is the scene of the location of the killing of JOHN A. LINN by CLAUDE BRANTON and COURTLAND GREEN. It is at Isham's corral, a "dry" one, near the summit of the Cascade mountains, about one-half mile west of Alder Springs, and about 14½ miles east of McKenzie Bridge, and about 69½ miles east of Eugene. (Green is serving a life sentence in the penitentiary, having turned state's evidence. The mark O is where the fire consumed Linn's body, while the other mark denotes where Linn was sleeping when shot. The two trees were burned a height of 30 or 40 feet; the bloody ax was still lying on the ground when the view was taken.

A photograph of the crime scene published in the Eugene Guard on the day of the execution. (Image: Eugene Guard)

new who would be willing to perjure themselves in exchange for the pick of the herd.

Branton even made a fake beard so that he could pretend to be Linn at one spot. This didn't work, though, because the rancher he was trying to fool recognized his voice.

The two of them tried several times to sell the horses, too, but no one would take them because Linn wasn't there to sign the bill of sale.

Eventually it dawned on Branton that they were basically doomed, and his best shot was to cut and run. So the partners split up. Branton ended up in Kansas with the $65; Green, however, stayed in Eugene.

It may have been their plan all along for Green to finger Branton if the heat came on, and Branton to be gone on the lam. In any case, that's how it went down. Green, whose psychological state had deteriorated badly and whose alcohol consumption rate had skyrocketed, finally couldn't stand it any more and confessed to a friend, Lane County Sheriff's Deputy

JUST PLAIN MURDER.

John Day. Day took his friend directly to the district attorney, and the jig was officially up.

Meanwhile, Branton had underestimated the difficulty of life on the lam, and was suffering from homesickness. So a month or two later, he decided he might as well travel back to Oregon. Perhaps the fact that he and Green had spent weeks wandering around bugging people to perjure themselves about having seen a missing man without anyone apparently getting wise had led him to an underestimation of the intelligence of his fellow man. In any case, when he arrived back in Eugene he was nabbed on the spot.

Green, brought to trial, shocked the court by pleading guilty despite the strong probability that it meant the gallows. He lucked out, though: the charge, when it was made, was second-degree murder, meaning a life sentence rather than death. He served 10 years of that sentence in the Oregon State Penitentiary before being conditionally pardoned by the governor.

But Branton — with the help of Green's testimony — knew very well he couldn't even hope for a break like that. And sure enough, when the verdict came in, it was "guilty of first-degree murder," and the sentence was hanging.

Branton was kept in the county jail until the sentence could be carried out, and it was immediately clear he was a desperate man. When he was brought back to his cell, the instant the handcuffs were off him he leaped on Deputy Day, grabbing for his revolver. The two of them fought over the gun for a second or two; then the sheriff arrived and grabbed Branton by the throat, choking him until he let go.

Later Branton made a fake gun, carved out of pieces of food, and tried to bluff his way out of the joint by pointing it at Sheriff Withers. Withers, having good reason to know Branton wasn't armed, said, "Oh, come off it," and Branton passed it off as a joke.

Finally, on May 12, 1899, Claude Branton's sentence was carried out. His wanderings were finally over; but, unlike Melmoth, he wasn't expecting damnation to follow. He'd been baptized in prison, and spent the morning of his execution in Bible study.

Sources and Works Cited:
- Necktie Parties: Legal Executions in Oregon 1851-1905, *a book by Diane L. Goeres-Gardner published in 2005 by Caxton Press;*
- *"Claude Branton Hanging, 1899," an article by Allen Cain published in 2006 by the Oregon Historical Society on oregonhistoryproject.org;*
- Eugene City Guard *archives, July–November 1898.*

PART VIII:

JUST PLAIN SEX.

Sex, back in the years before the First World War, basically took three forms: The boring, socially sanctioned kind, between people married to one another; the non-boring, non-socially sanctioned kind between people married to third parties (or not at all); and the kind that was handled by professionals.

That much hasn't really changed, of course. What has changed is the legal status of the second and third kinds of sex: they've switched places. Around 1880, you could be sent to prison for adultery; but prostitution was perfectly legal in most of the state. Today, in all of the state and most of the rest of the country, it's the other way around.

Legal or not, though, prostitutes have always had to be creative in their interactions with society in general, and the law in particular. Their profession's running battles with cops, "social hygienists," and church congregations have, over the years, reliably provided some of the more interesting — not to mention racy — stories out of old Oregon history.

Here are a few of them.

THE FLOATING BORDELLO.

For owners of brothels, gambling houses and other "colorful" businesses, it's a legendary trick: When the police and city government start trying to run you out of town, you go — into an old steamboat anchored in the harbor.

The folks who wrote about history in the 1800s didn't talk a lot about things like this, so we can't know for sure. Plus, many of the folks who wrote history *after* the 1800s did an awful lot of wishful speculating and creative imagining. But as far as I know, the first successful Floating Palace of Sin ever to grace the western half of the North American continent was a two-story tavern-brothel parked smack in the middle of the Willamette River in downtown Portland in the 1880s, operated by an enterprising maritime madam named Nancy Boggs.

Now, before we dive into this story, there's something you should know about it. The story of Nancy Boggs and her "hospitality barge" is a somewhat slippery one. Most versions of this story can be tracked back to Edward "Spider" Johnson, an old waterfront tough guy and ex-shanghai-boarding-house runner, who shared this and many other nuggets of old waterfront lore with writer Stewart Holbrook over drinks in the early 1930s for a series Holbrook was writing in the Portland *Morning Oregonian*. Many serious Portland historians have dismissed this entire story as a hoax, something wholly made up by Johnson to get Holbrook to keep buying him drinks. This is possible ... but, in my view, unlikely. In 1931, the 1880s were still a

The docks at Albina as they appared in 1888, in a lithograph published in The West Shore magazine that year.

part of living memory for many older Portlanders, and a suggestion in the newspaper that a floating bordello was anchored near the Stark Street Ferry in 1882 would, if a lie, have elicited at least one or two letters to the editor from 75-year-old residents setting the paper straight. However, it is a good possibility that some aspects of the story have been distorted over years of telling and retelling. In fact, it's a lead-pipe cinch they have.

Like chocolate and peanut butter, history and folklore are "two great tastes that taste great together." But they have to be honestly labeled. In the case of this story, the chocolate and the peanut butter have been blended together so thoroughly that it's often impossible to tell where one starts and the other stops. So, keep that in mind as you read on.

Back in the early 1880s, what we know as Portland today was three cities: Portland, East Portland and Albina. There were three city governments and three police forces. There were three sets of liquor laws, too. This was understandable; the river cut right down between Portland and East Portland, and there weren't yet any bridges, just a ferryboat at the foot of Stark Street.

The opportunities the river created were obvious to local entrepreneuse and "riverboat" operator Nancy Boggs. First, she could move her

40-by-80-foot vessel up and down the river to respond to local market demand all along the river, from Oregon City to Linnton if she so desired. Secondly, when anchored between the two Portlands as she usually was, her employees could service both cities; boatmen in small skiffs, like Charon at the River Styx, were stationed on either side, and customers would simply hop in and be ferried to Nancy's little 3,200-square-foot island of iniquity.

And thirdly, Nancy paid no taxes to either city.

In the rough and gamey frontier towns of 1880s Portland and East Portland, it was this last item that bothered the City Halls — not morals, but money. Both towns, at the time, were fairly friendly to prostitution; land-based brothels were operating highly successfully on both sides of the river. In fact, the city's first police chief was part owner of the Oro Fino — a saloon and variety theater that, some historians believe, dabbled discreetly in the trade as well.

But these brothels paid liquor taxes. Nancy's did not.

Most of the time, Nancy's palace was anchored close to the Stark Street Ferry, which was at that time the only way to get across the river. This, naturally, was great advertising; but it also did a fantastic job of constantly reminding city officials on both sides of the river of her scofflaw status.

Several times, police from one side of the river or another tried to raid her boat. Nancy, tipped off by one satisfied customer or another, would simply hoist anchor and have her bordello towed close to the shore of the city that was not conducting the raid. The towns were bitter rivals, and their police forces did not cooperate with each other, so this strategy was effective for some time. (It's also extremely likely that at least some of the line cops on both sides of the river were sympathetic to her cause. More on that in a moment.)

Finally, in 1882, the two towns made common cause and attacked from both sides at once in what was probably Oregon's first-ever coordinated inter-agency prostitution sting.

Nancy had apparently anticipated something like this; or, perhaps she had been tipped off in advance. She had armed herself with a hose rigged to the boat's heating plant, blasting scalding steam — which, with screams of battle rage that could be clearly heard by watching City Hall V.I.P.s on both sides of the river, she turned on the approaching flatfoots. The steam, of course, made a tremendous hissing and impressive clouds as it blasted out into the chilly spring air, so it looked, from ashore, like a spectacular battle.

Faced with such determined and dangerous-looking opposition, of course, the cops conducted a strategic retreat. Stewart Holbrook writes that

Ships in the Portland harbor, shown in a lantern-slide image from the late 1880s or possibly early 1890s. (Image: OSU Archives)

some of them had steam burns that required ointment, but this seems super unlikely given how quickly steam cools down when it's blasted out into the damp coolness of a Willamette Valley spring day to mix with the 40-degree air.

It's certainly hard to avoid the impression that this battle was intended to look a lot fiercer than it actually was. Mayors and competitors-who-were-also-the-police-chief (on the west side at least) might have wanted Nancy shut down, but she clearly had some good friends among the regular beat cops — on both sides of the river.

Nancy was, of course, in the business of putting on shows; and on the river that day, she and the cops seem to have put on a doozie.

But that night, under cover of darkness, someone — nobody knows who — took a sharp knife and a rowboat, and paddled stealthily out to Nancy's anchored vessel. Once there, this unknown person cut Nancy's anchor line and set her bordello drifting down the river, headed for the Pacific Ocean.

And it was moving at a rather alarming pace. Despite its modern reputation as a rather staid and slow waterway, the lower Willamette moves right along when the water is high — as it was at this particular time.

As almost any Victorian-era woman would, Nancy first went for help to the one man still on board, a customer who had hit the jug especially hard and was sleeping it off. This fellow was every bit as helpful as you would expect a man like that to be. So Nancy let him sleep and, with a few words of reassurance to her girls, got in one of the rowboats and started pulling for the east side of the river.

She landed in Albina and immediately found the skipper of a sternwheeler. After she explained to him that a barge full of girls and whisky was in distress and needed help, the captain rousted his crew, fired the boilers and headed downriver to the rescue.

At dawn the next morning, Nancy's "hospitality" barge was back at anchor. One source says it was right back where it was the night before, in a little thumb-in-the-eye to whoever had tried to get rid of it; several other sources say it ended up anchored a few miles down the river, near Linnton. Quite what arrangement Nancy and her girls made with the captain and crew of the sternwheeler to thank them for their gallant midnight rescue is, happily, lost to posterity.

This battle might have been won, but Nancy must have known the war had just started and would likely not end well for her. Shortly after this incident, she brought her operation ashore, setting up housekeeping at a new joint on Pine Street near Third. Here, she paid her liquor taxes and had, as far as I've been able to learn, no further problems.

Sources and Works Cited:
- *Wildmen, Wobblies and Whistle Punks, a book by Stewart Holbrook published in 1992 by Oregon State University Press;*
- *"The Red-Lights of Portland," an article by Corri Jimenez in the Winter 1997 issue of The ASHP Journal.*

THE VICE CRUSADE.

One November evening in 1885, Portland residents walking past a row of tiny houses at Third and Yamhill heard screams coming from one of them.

Bursting in, they found the mutilated and lifeless remains of a 33-year-old French beauty known as Emma Merlotin. Someone had killed her brutally with a hatchet and then slipped away into the night.

Emma, whose real name was Anna DeCoz, was a well-known "nymph du pave," as the Portland *Evening Telegram* phrased it — basically, a courtesan. Her clientele included some of the city's most prominent bigwigs, and it was widely rumored at the time that her death had come at the hands of one of them — although 11 years later, a Canadian drifter confessed to the crime. It's also possible that her real killer was Richard Marple, the unpleasant fellow hanged for murdering his mother's lover with an ax in Lafayette in 1887 while helping her rob him. If you're reading this book from cover to cover, you'll remember him from earlier.

Until this time, most Portland citizens hadn't given much thought to the city's prostitutes. Everyone knew they were there, of course, and their trade had been illegal since the early 1870s — outlawed, the rumor was, at the behest of a city councilor who had picked up a social disease from a bordello girl.

But in the wake of the Merlotin case, suddenly the plight of the poor "fallen woman" and her "life of shame" was a topic that was coming up in street conversations and Sunday sermons.

It was all just talk until the early 1890s, nearly a full decade after Emma's death, when a pastor named Charles Locke came to Portland from Pittsburgh. Locke maintained that if Portland wanted the ladies of the evening to give up their profession, they had to be offered some kind of alternative. They couldn't be simply run out of town. He urged Portland to build a "home for wayward girls and fallen women," a place of refuge for prostitutes who wanted out and for teen girls at risk of being tempted into the business.

This idea met with immediate approval, and Portland's church folks got busy immediately. By 1895, the project was well under way. With adorably earnest naïveté, they gave it a somewhat unfortunate name: "The Open Door."

Eager citizens got busy supplying everything The Open Door might need. In fact, some of those citizens seemed a little too eager. One fellow, Captain Richard Williams, offered the use of a building free of charge; the coordinators turned down his offer, saying the building was too large to be suitable, but their real reason may have had more to do with the captain's reputation: He was known around town as "Slippery Dick."

Fortunately, offers from less disreputable citizens came thick and fast — donations of kitchen equipment, furniture, linens. Soon The Open Door had a location, at 25 North Fifth Street, just off Burnside. A house matron, Mrs. Lucy Morgan, was hired and moved in. And by late spring, The Open Door was ready to receive its first Fallen Woman.

Now all was in readiness for Phase 2 of the reformers' plan: A city-wide crackdown on dens of iniquity.

To the great amusement of the jaded newshounds at the *Oregonian* and the *Telegram*, a reluctant constabulary was now sent forth to collect suspected prostitutes and bring them to justice. Time and again, the horse-drawn police wagon rumbled forth and returned creaking under a heavy burden of unrepentant Fallen Womanhood.

Interestingly, many of the women arrested were the city's most upscale entrepreneuses. Della Burris and Lida Fanshaw, CEOs of the most exclusive and elegant parlour-houses in the city, were among the first arrested. Dozens of their employees and colleagues were nicked too.

The cops had been, if we can believe Stewart Holbrook's account of the action, somewhat reluctant and skeptical about the whole thing at first. But once they started arresting the ladies, they seem to have had a change of heart. Portland police officers suddenly threw themselves into the effort. Soon the city's police-court docket was full of suspected Bad Girls.

The first to face prosecution was Della Burris, up on a charge of Operating a Bawdy House. Della coolly pleaded Not Guilty; the prosecution asserted

JUST PLAIN SEX.

Downtown Portland as seen looking south from the tower of the Kamm Building, located on Pine Street between Front and First, in 1886. The murder of Emma Merlottin occurred six blocks down and two blocks to the right of where the artist was standing when this image was made.

that everybody KNEW she was running a brothel; and the judge promptly dismissed the case.

"Common fame and general reputation are not sufficient evidence to convict anyone of keeping a bawdy house," he remarked.

The next defendant got pretty much the same treatment. And the next. And the next.

It turned out the cops, in bringing the ladies in, had simply been arresting them, collecting no evidence. The district attorney was simply filing charges against them, making no investigations. Without evidence, there could be no convictions. And this happened again and again.

The most likely explanation for this uncharacteristically cavalier attitude toward law enforcement was articulated very neatly by the editor of the *Morning Oregonian* on its editorial page on April 10:

"The District Attorney gets $5 for every arrest; $7.50 for trial; and $15 for convictions," the editor wrote tartly. "In each case, having taken pains to draw all the indictments separately, if there are no convictions, he will make from $500 to $600. The police justices and constables make about $12 out of each case, or as much more, and the county foots the bill. This is the total visible profit of the moral crusade so far — about $1,200 diverted from the pockets of taxpayers to those of officials."

In other words, some clever devil had figured out that the authorities were essentially working on commission. Reformers having demanded action from them, they'd realized that such pressure was like a license to print money — and who were they to refuse such a clear call to action from the citizenry, anyway?

But the law enforcement pressure did look like it was having its intended effect on Portland's Ladies of the Evening. One by one, the Rose City's Roxannes wandered into The Open Door and settled in, apparently ready to put away their makeup and embrace the clean and sober life. By late June, The Open Door was starting to look like a big success.

Then the logging camps shut down for the traditional "Fourth of July Drunk," and Portland was suddenly flooded with strapping young lads smelling of sawdust and pitch and whiskey, freshly paid and ready to "blow 'er in." And a funny thing started happening: The Wayward Women started melting away from The Open Door. They'd go out shopping and just never come back.

It turned out the opening of The Open Door had just happened to coincide precisely with the least lucrative time of the year for Portland prostitutes — the early summer season, when the loggers were all hard at work in the woods. They'd been happy to check in for a few weeks and enjoy free room and board. But now the boys were back in town, and it was time to go get some of their money.

Soon Mrs. Lucy Morgan was alone in the big empty house, listening to roaring-drunk loggers and Fallen Women cavorting around in the streets outside.

A few weeks later, the demoralized reformers gave up on the whole thing.

Sources and Works Cited:
- *"The Great Moral Crusade," an article by Stewart Holbrook published in the Aug. 2, 1936, issue of the* Portland Morning Oregonian;
- *"Vice in Portland," an article by Herbert Lundy published in the Aug. 2, 1939, issue of the* Portland Morning Oregonian;
- *"Confesses to a Portland Crime," an un-by-lined article in the April 28, 1896, issue of the* San Francisco Call.

THE SMUTTY ANARCHISTS.

The editors and writers of Anarchist-Communist newspaper *The Firebrand*, published in Portland and distributed nationwide from 1895 to 1897, surely expected to get some resistance from The Establishment. They may even have expected to be arrested, possibly even charged with sedition or treason.

But they surely didn't expect that when their publication was shut down, it would be for griping about marriage.

That's what happened, though. The wide-open town of Portland reacted to their strident advocacy of revolution and regime change with a collective yawn; but when they started advocating unmarried cohabitation, well, that was going just a little too far.

The *Firebrand* was a product of what may have been the worst depression in American history, as measured in per-capita human misery. This depression, usually referred to by the misleading moniker "Panic of 1893," got its start in February of that year when a revolution broke out in Argentina, the most prosperous and stable country in South America at the time. Spooked, European investors pulled their money out and, seeking a safe place to park it while they awaited further developments, started buying up dollars.

The U.S. Dollar was at the time rigidly pegged to gold. So the more dollars the Europeans bought up, the more scarce dollars became ... and the more valuable they got, and the more attractive they became to foreign investors. So, a self-reinforcing feedback loop was formed, a vicious circle of currency deflation.

At the same time, the rising dollar value made everyone who had a dollar less inclined to spend it, and debtors more likely to default on their mortgages.

One thing led to another, and by the end of that year, the U.S. was plunged into depression.

Very few people today realize how bad it was, that depression; the Great Depression of the 1930s absorbs most of the attention. But, the mid-1890s were the last time large numbers of American women living in urban areas were forced to choose between prostitution and starvation. Among other unemployed Americans, the lucky ones were able to trade their dignity for a meager meal at a soup kitchen once or twice a day or poach animals and fish; the unlucky ones died of illnesses their hunger-weakened bodies couldn't fight off.

To make matters worse, the unemployed and starving had to watch wealthy upper-class citizens strutting callously by as they suffered; situations of the worst and most grueling privation coexisted side by side with wealth and privilege. It was like the first few scenes from "Charlie and the Chocolate Factory," the book by Roald Dahl. Many well-off citizens tried to pretend the problem was one of morals rather than economics — that the unemployed were jobless because they were lazy — and the "robber barons" made no secret of the fact that they didn't care who lived or died. Naturally, these attitudes inspired some resentment.

By 1895, it had been so bad for so long that the American working class was a demographic powderkeg. Forces of reform grew stronger as the economy grew weaker: the free-silver movement sought to bolster the gold stocks, to stop the dollar's climbing value; Populist politicians sought to claw power away from the smoke-filled rooms with projects like the Oregon Initiative and Referendum System; and support for journalistic "muckrakers" exposing the corruption of the powerful was strong and growing.

But to the small group of dedicated journalists producing *The Firebrand* in Portland, all of that was useless — like performing cosmetic surgery on a patient dying of cancer.

Henry Addis and his tiny group of colleagues — lapsed Mennonite Abraham Isaak and his family, and the elderly ex-Quaker Abner J. Pope — called themselves "Anarchist-Communists," but the meaning of that term at the time was closer to what we know today as "libertarian."

The Firebrand was an interesting publication, because although Addis and his crew really didn't know what they were doing, they had been

JUST PLAIN SEX.

This political cartoon, by Thomas Nast, ran in Harper's Weekly in 1871. It nicely illustrates society's attitude toward those who advocated "free love" — in this case, Victoria Woodhull. (Image: OSU Libraries)

The masthead or flag of The Firebrand. (Image: Oregon Historical Society)

interested observers of previous anarchist movements and they'd learned a great deal from their mistakes. So although freelance articles poured in from radical writers across the country, those that advocated covert operations and sabotage, or authoritarian devotion to some charismatic leader, or the use of bombings and assassinations, were slipped quietly into the trash.

The Firebrand's political and editorial positions were fairly well defined by its masthead motto — "For the Burning Away of the Cobwebs of Ignorance and Superstition," superimposed on a graphic of the state capitol building and a church steeple connected by a spiderweb occupied by a fat spider holding a bag of money — and by the sarcastic definitions of pillars of Gilded Age society which it published: "CLERGY: The paid tools of the rich to keep the poor divided on religion and unanimous in their respect for the state. FRAUD: Shrewdness in business. MARRIAGE: Legalized prostitution and enslavement of the sexes. ARMY: Licensed murderers. CONGRESS: A body of men organized to break laws and make debts."

All of this probably resonated pretty well with working-class Portlanders, and it seemed also to play well in the crews of bachelors in the mining and logging camps across the state. But none of those people had much money to spare, and the "*Firebrand* Family" always had great difficulty getting enough to eat. They moved their operations into the country outside of

town where they could do some subsistence farming, keeping a cow and some chickens; they spent days in the Portland hills picking wild blackberries to can, to get them through the winter; they picked hops for a little seasonal side income; and they tried, and failed, to start a dairy farm.

Toward the end the plan was to acquire a small farm on the lower Columbia and set up a commune there. But before that could be done, the cops moved in.

It wasn't *The Firebrand's* political positions that brought on the trouble, though. It was the publishers' advocacy of what was then called "Free Love."

Free Love was an idea that covered a wide range, from "get the state out of the marriage business" to total sexual freedom. What all these positions had in common was, they violated the (patently unconstitutional) Comstock Laws, violations of which were punished with jail time.

The Firebrand had freely published articles arguing that marriage should be abolished, along with articles like "Plain Talks about the Sexual Organs" and "Teaching Sexual Truths to the Children."

One particular article, by writer Oscar Rotter, advocated "variety" in personal relations — meaning, of course, multiple sexual partners. This sparked a lively debate among advocates of monogamistic free love (basically, common-law marriage) and those who — like the editors of *The Firebrand* — felt that other people's choices to be slutty or chaste were nobody's business but their own and certainly not the state's. The debate went on for several months.

This may be what caught the attention of the postal authorities. In any event, something did, and one day in 1897 as Abner Pope was preparing what would be *The Firebrand's* last issue for mailing, a deputy U.S. marshal arrived and arrested all three of them.

The ensuing trial was rather a disaster, primarily because the defendants' attorney was extraordinarily incompetent. Judge C.B. Bellinger was so exasperated that, after the jury brought in a verdict of "guilty," he made a point of telling the defendants that he would support a request for a new trial.

Pope seemed determined to take as much of the "blame" as he could, and Addis and Isaak were happy to oblige. This, as historian Carlos Schwantes points out in his 1981 article in the *Oregon Historical Quarterly*, probably had a lot to do with the fact that the city jail was very comfortable compared with the accommodations the "*Firebrand* Family" had been making do with before his arrest. Remember, Pope was very old; and he had just gone from a winter of subsisting on grubbed-up roots, canned blackberries, and the occasional pot-shot squirrel, to three square meals a day in a building with steam heat and indoor plumbing.

In the end, Pope was sentenced to four months, and charges against the other two were dropped. But the paper was never restarted.

In the end, the "*Firebrand* family" must have been a little nonplussed to find that one could shout all day about revolution and regime change, but suggesting that the state should stop prosecuting people for unauthorized sexual activity got them sent straight to jail.

Well, in 1897, that was Portland.

Sources and Works Cited:
- "*Free Love and Free Speech on the Pacific Northwest Frontier: Proper Victorians vs. Portland's 'Filthy Firebrand,'*" an article by Carlos Schwantes published in the September 1981 issue of Oregon Historical Quarterly;
- "*The Firebrand,*" an article by William Cornett published on March 17, 2018, in The Oregon Encyclopedia *(oregonencyclopedia.org).*

THE REAL MEANING OF "BICYCLE FACE."

Many people today still think of bicycles as toys for children or tools for specialized hobbyists and exercise buffs — like hockey sticks or fencing foils. Others think of them as indispensable but unexciting tools for modern life. But for most of us, it's hard to imagine the bicycle as a cutting-edge modern wonder, or a socially revolutionary device.

But in the early 1870s, that's just what bicycles were: fast, exciting, dangerous things that could make an ordinary human fly like the wind. Even more revolutionary was the fact that on a bicycle, unlike basically every other physical activity known to the Victorian Age, a woman was no slower or less potent than a man.

And what the dashing auto racer or aeroplane flier was to any small boy in 1910, champion trick rider Carrie Moor was to 11-year-old Fred T. Merrill in 1870.

Little Fred's father had opened a riding rink in the town of Lynn, Massachusetts, where the Merrill family then lived, and stocked it with a few of the two-wheeled "velocipedes" that were then the state of the art in bicycles.

A velocipede in 1870 was a brutally crude thing, just a step removed from the notorious all-wood "boneshakers" of the 1850s. It featured a smaller wheel in the back and a bigger one in front, driven directly by pedals, like the front wheel of a modern toddler's tricycle. (The basic design would be refined over the following decade or so into the notorious and lethal

LOVE, SEX and MURDER in OLD OREGON

A satirical illustration from the magazine Puck, published in 1895, showing all the ways the "New

JUST PLAIN SEX.

Woman" might be expected to use her bicycle. (Image: Library of Congress)

high-wheel "Ordinary Bicycles" of the 1880s.) But Carrie Moor could make a velocipede dance like a ballerina, and young Fred — doubtless a little smitten with the dashing "scorcher" — found her fascinating.

"I took to watching her at every opportunity, and soon I was trying some of her fancy stunts," Merrill told Portland *Morning Oregonian* writer Stewart Holbrook many years later. "Long before we left for the Pacific coast, I was an expert rider, doing all the tricks Carrie knew and inventing some of my own."

The Merrill family moved across the country to San Francisco in 1873, and Fred continued his stunt riding. (Carrie seems to have moved there as well a year or two earlier; in 1871, she was the headline act at the Occidental Skating Academy, and later was named female roller-skating champion of the world.)

Fred apprenticed as an engraver, but soon found he could make far more money as a trick rider. On one memorable evening, he built a plank bridge a foot wide across the arena and pedaled his brand-new British-built high-wheel "ordinary bicycle" — the first one ever imported to America — across the bridge while his two baby brothers sat each on one of his shoulders. Had he slipped, there would have been a triple funeral; but he didn't fall, and the crowd loved it.

Soon, though, Fred started hearing about an Australian chap up north in Portland who was claiming to be the "finest trick rider in the world." This didn't sit well with Fred, who considered that title rightfully his. So off to Portland he went to settle the matter.

In Portland, the Aussie accepted Fred's challenge, but left town that very evening in the dark of night, never to be seen again. Meanwhile, Fred had discovered that he really liked Portland.

"I found the city a lively place," he said, "even when compared with San Francisco."

So he stayed, and in 1885 — now convinced that bicycles were destined to become a real mainstream thing — he opened the Northwest's first bicycle dealership, in a big tent built for him by legendary Portland neophile Henry Wemme (original founder of the White Stag clothing company and owner of Oregon's first automobile).

Fred was selling Columbia brand Ordinary bicycles — the penny-farthing kind, with a huge front wheel and a tiny trailing wheel. These were speedy and fun, but a little hard to get used to and rather dangerous to boot, especially going downhill; "taking a header" while perched atop a six-foot-high wheel was relatively common, and frequently fatal. (This is why the hipsters have not brought back penny-farthing bicycles. No manufacturer can afford the liability.)

JUST PLAIN SEX.

An engraving titled "The American Velocipede" by Theodore R. Davis, published in Harper's Weekly in December 1868. This is the type of machine on which Fred Merrill learned his trick-riding skills. (Image: Harper's Monthly)

So sales were slow, and Fred mostly was paying the bills with his trick riding.

But when, in the early 1890s, the "safety bicycle" was invented, Fred knew his time had come. The safety was, essentially, the modern bicycle — two equal-size wheels of moderate size, and a rear-wheel chain drive. It was easy to learn to use, fast, and fun. With a tool like this, bicycle riding was going to explode. Fred knew it — and he was ready when it did.

Fred quickly developed a reputation as the Tom Peterson of his time — an advertiser and promoter of legendary wizardliness. He talked to the telephone company, gave them some money and got permission to paint the words "RIDE A RAMBLER" (Rambler was his top-selling brand) in screaming red on all the telephone poles in town. And he staged events — daredevil riding exhibitions, races against thoroughbred horses, even a trick dog (the "Rambler Dog") that jumped off the roof of his building into a net.

And the craze continued. In the late 1890s, the state governor, Theodore Geer, was a passionate bicyclist, and in 1900 rode his bicycle from Salem to

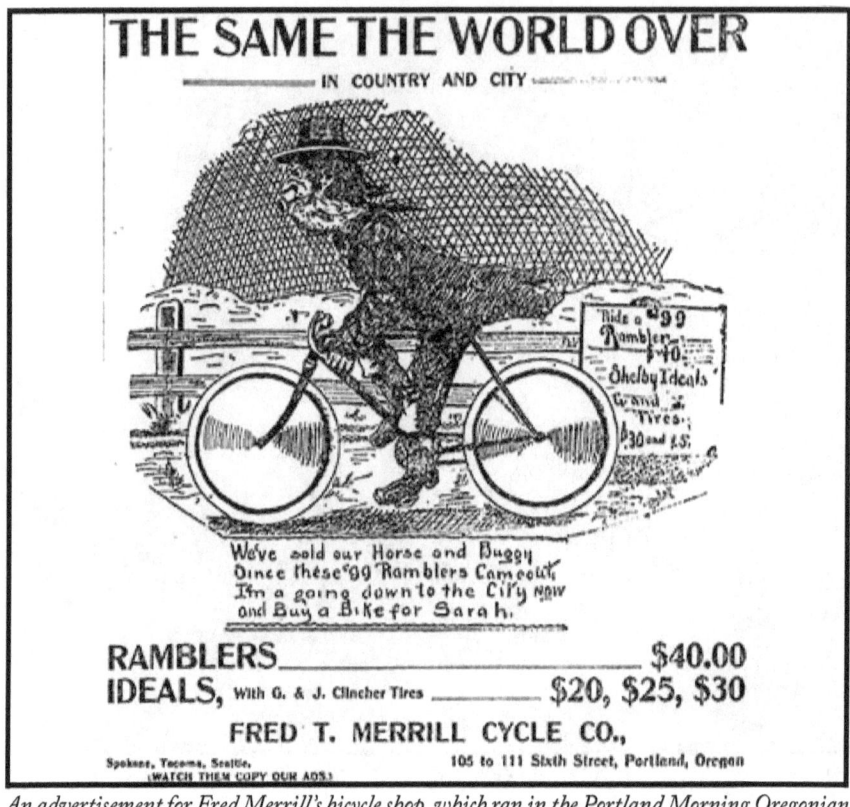

An advertisement for Fred Merrill's bicycle shop, which ran in the Portland Morning Oregonian on Feb. 26, 1899. (Image: Oregonian)

Champoeg to mark the location of the formation of Oregon's first territorial government in 1843.

Bicycles famously liberated the women of the "*Belle Epoque*" from the drawing room, giving them a means of getting around quickly that wasn't dependent on a brother or husband hitching up horses. Of course, many Oregon women of the time were perfectly capable of handling stock, but lots of others weren't, and a bicycle made it possible for them to go places and do things that had never been open to them previously. Plus, of course, on a bicycle they were just as fast and capable as a man; the difference in leg-muscle size and capability between men and women is virtually nonexistent. This, of course, disconcerted a lot of late-Victorian-age men.

"Pastors preached powerful sermons against any and all women who took to the deviltry of riding a wheel," Merrill recounted. "And if you know anything about the women, you will know that all of them who could get a wheel had one.... There were letters to the paper and editorials about the great menace to life, health and morals of the bicycle, and 'scorchers' (recklessly fast riders)

JUST PLAIN SEX.

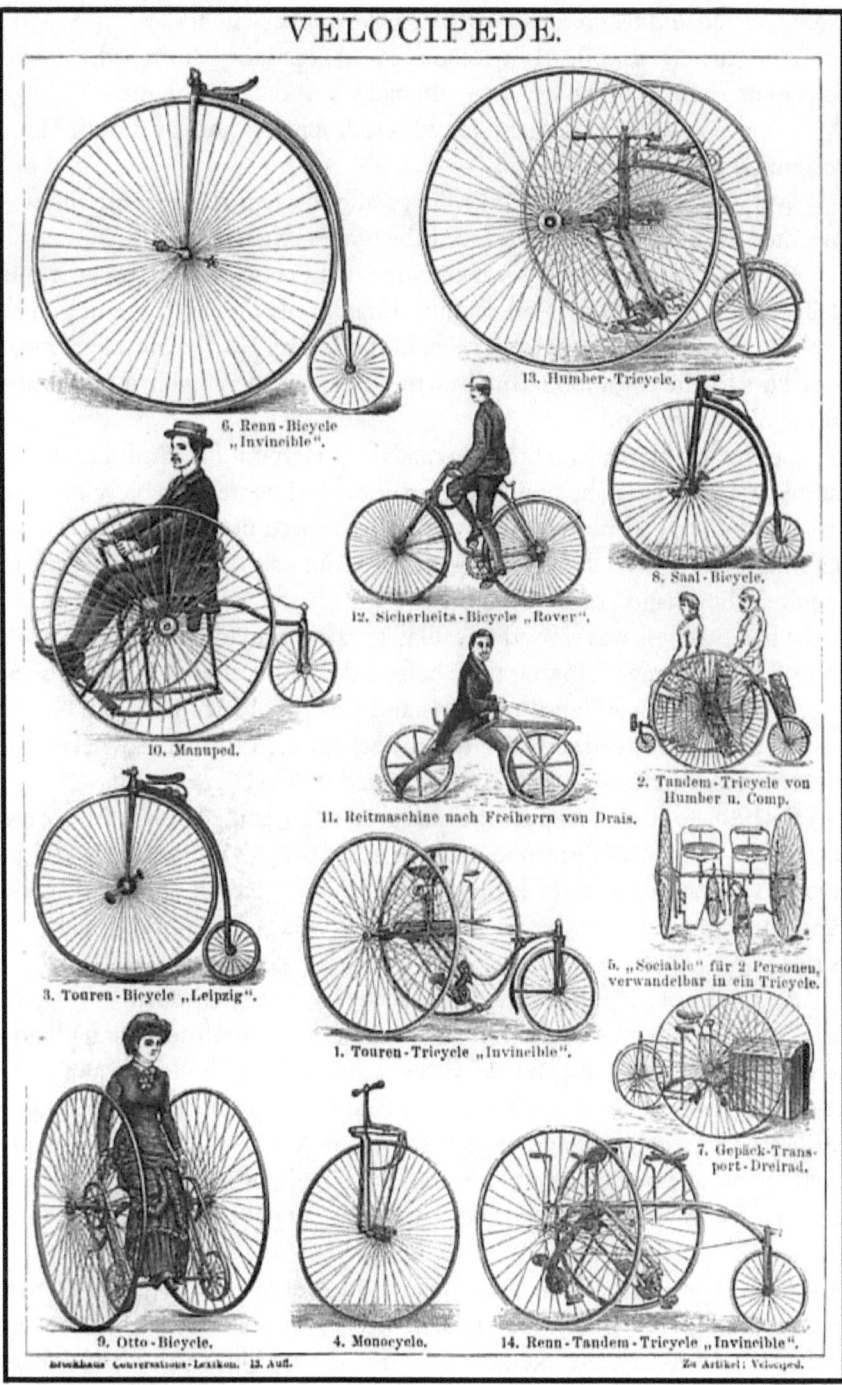

Drawing of various designs of velocipedes, including a couple very early versions of the modern "safety bicycle," from an 1887 German encyclopedia. (Image: Brockhaus' Conversations-Lexikon)

were arrested and taken to jail just as reckless drivers are today."

And then — after nearly a decade of wild popularity, during which Fred sold more than 50,000 bicycles — the fad went "out like a light."

"From 1900 on, the demand for wheels dropped month by month," Fred recounted.

Well, sure, you might think. That's about when the automobile was invented, right? So the car displaced the bicycle, right?

Wrong, says Fred. Remember, cars were expensive, temperamental, delicate things in the nineteen-oughts, suitable only for wealthy young men; the first Ford Model T was still years in the future. No, the bicycle fad was killed not by the automobile, but by a group of enterprising businesswomen in the old North End.

Legendary North End bordello madam "Liverpool Liz" Smith probably started it; in any case, she took it the farthest. She invested in a bicycle riding track and equipped her girls with brightly colored outfits and skirts with slits high enough to deploy as much leg as any situation might seem to require. They staged races around the track for the "gentlemen" to bet on, and when business was slow, they sallied forth around town on their wheels to troll for customers, ringing their bells and flashing their winning smiles.

"When Blanche Hamilton's girls and Liverpool Liz's girls and all the rest of them took to the wheel, the society girls got off their wheels and went afoot, or went back to the buggy," Fred recalled.

By 1903, for the most part, the only women pedaling around town were also, if you will, *peddling* around town — a fact that it's interesting to reflect upon when looking at historic photos of women on bicycles from that time. And it would be 30 years before bicycle riding would start coming back into favor.

As a side note, it's almost certain that the severe scowl known as "bicycle face" was cultivated by society bicyclistes as a means to differentiate themselves from their less "respectable" sisters, who of course smiled coquettishly at all the prospective customers they encountered as they rode. The ladies really liked their bikes, and gave them up only reluctantly. It also seems pretty good guess that a woman would feel like scowling after four or five random "gentlemen" have mistaken her for a prostitute, so there's that as well.

As for Fred, he went on to a wild and colorful career as a city politician (on the "Keep Portland Wide Open" ticket), auto dealer, roadhouse owner and sports promoter. He liked to say he'd made a million and a half dollars in Portland, and spent every cent of it.

Fred finally retired to a home on Stark Street across from Laurelhurst Park and died at the age of 84 in 1944.

Sources and Works Cited:
- *"The Life and Times of Fred T. Merrill,"* an article by Stewart Holbrook published in the March 8, 15, and 22, 1936, issue of the Portland Morning Oregonian;
- *"The Bicycle King,"* an article by J.D. Chandler published on Jan. 16, 2013, at *weirdportland.blogspot.com.*

THE HEIRESS WHISPERER.

Every now and then, one runs across a man who can sweet-talk absolutely anyone into anything.

Such a man was William "Diamond Bill" Barrett Jr., the black sheep of a solid, respectable family of Hillsboro pioneers.

As a character, Diamond Bill was like a twentieth-century version of George Wickham, the rakish Army officer in Jane Austen's novel *Pride and Prejudice*. Like Mr. Wickham, Diamond Bill was a dashing, handsome military man with a particular talent for persuading the daughters of wealthy families to elope with him.

Call him, if you will, "The Heiress Whisperer."

As a teenager growing up in Washington County in the first decade of the 1900s, Diamond Bill seems to have been a real handful for his father, state Senator William Barrett Sr. He was, in the vernacular of the day, a "fast young man" — a high roller and a big spender with a habit of running up hefty gambling debts that he lacked the wherewithal to pay; and, in the interest of avoiding scandal, his father would scurry around after him squaring his accounts.

Perhaps hoping that a military education would straighten him out, William Sr. sent the young rake off to the U.S. Naval Academy at Annapolis, and he did well there, graduating and taking a post as a midshipman. But very shortly thereafter, he and the Navy parted ways — most likely as a result of a 1911 incident in San Francisco that perhaps didn't entirely rise to the Navy's famous "officer and a gentleman" standard. This was the incident that earned him the moniker "Diamond Bill."

Ashore in San Francisco, Bill visited a jewelry store and, pretending to be a wealthy swell and turning on that legendary Diamond Bill charm, actually talked the proprietor into letting him borrow a $2,000 diamond ring (worth about $55,000 in 2019 money) to take home and "see if my wife likes it."

He then headed for a pawnshop, hocked the ring for $1,500, returned to the jewelry store, and arranged to pay for the diamond over four months with $500 monthly payments. He then made his first month's payment, and left with $1,000 in clear cash money.

He then started to work the same play on a second jewelry store, but by the time he did, the police had noticed the unusually large $1,500 pawnshop payment, and Diamond Bill was collared by a bluecoat and parked in the city joint on suspicion of being a diamond thief.

The cops assumed it was his intention to run, leaving the jeweler holding the bag for the $1,500 balance owed on the hocked ring; and that also appears to have been the Navy's take on the matter. But it's far more likely that the target of Bill's swindle was his father, who he must have expected to make good on his debt as he always did. Otherwise, he wouldn't have used his real name.

The judge threw the case out of court, observing acidly that no crime had been committed: Bill had bought the diamond on credit, but he wasn't behind on payments and he was perfectly within his rights to pawn his property if he wanted to. Senator Barrett hastily covered the debt, and the matter was forgotten, except that from that day forward, the young Mr. Barrett was saddled with the flashy nickname "Diamond Bill."

Diamond Bill's next big score came three years later, in 1914, when he wangled an introduction to Miss Kathleen Baillie of Tacoma, the daughter of one of the richest men in Washington State. Following a whirlwind romance, the couple eloped, married, and moved to New York.

It's not clear what happened with Diamond Bill's marriage to Kathleen, but something obviously did, because in roughly one year it was over, and Kathleen was suing for divorce.

Shortly thereafter, the Great War broke out, and Diamond Bill, instinctively identifying the Army Air Corps as the most dashing and romantic arm of the service, wangled his way into it. He served in France with

JUST PLAIN SEX.

This photo spread ran in the Feb. 5, 1922, issue of the Portland Morning Oregonian, illustrating an overview of the story of Alice Drexel's whirlwind romance, elopement, and bitter disappointment at the hands of rakish Army aviator Captain William "Diamond Bill" Barrett of Hillsboro, Oregon.

sufficient distinction to be promoted to the rank of Captain, and at the war's end he was proudly calling himself Captain Bill — not quite as colorful as Diamond Bill, but decidedly more respectable.

It was as Captain Bill Barrett that he then, in 1919, managed to work

LOVE, SEX *and* MURDER *in* OLD OREGON

This photo spread ran in the Society section of the Portland Morning Oregonian on Nov. 29, 1921, shortly after Oregon's "Diamond Bill" Barrett scandalized New York society by eloping with its most eligible debutante, Alice Drexel — whose profile is shown at the left side of this montage. (Image: UO Libraries)

his way into the good graces of Miss Alice Drexel — heiress to the John Drexel fortune, one of the biggest in New York.

In keeping with our *Pride and Prejudice* analogy, Alice Drexel apparently had about as much in common with Lydia Bennett as Captain Bill did with Mr. Wickham. She seems to have been a bit boy-crazy, and had four ardent suitors, of whom Captain Bill was one; and her mother, fearful that things would get too serious, was hastily arranging for a family trip to Europe. Before that could happen, though, Captain Bill convinced Alice to elope with him. They slipped away by night in an automobile to New Rochelle, got married in a little church, checked into a posh hotel on Fifth Avenue — and then Alice called her mother.

The conversation did not go well. The young couple was summoned to the family manse to continue the discussion; there, the conversation went even worse. The upshot was that the newlyweds headed off across the ocean for a tour of Europe without any financial support from the Drexels ... and Diamond Bill found himself having to try to maintain an heiress in the condition to which she was accustomed, on an Air Force captain's salary.

They bounced around a bit in three-star hotels and railroad apartments, and one imagines Alice getting more and more disillusioned with the whole affair. Then finally, one day — Diamond Bill just bounced. He vanished from their room, leaving her flat broke and pregnant to boot, and hustled home to America.

It would be a while before Alice learned why he left when he did. It had to do with her friend, Sydia "Sidi" Wirt Spreckels, dashing showgirl wife of a San Francisco sugar magnate's son. Bill, it seems, had run into Sidi in London, to which city he'd traveled for some business reason, leaving his new wife in their shabby digs in France. He and Sidi were already acquaintances from the old days when he'd been a man-about-town in San Francisco and she a local Vaudeville star.

Sidi was in London by herself; she and her new husband had quarreled on their honeymoon, and he'd ditched her and run off to Norway; she was left wondering if he planned to return, and if not, how much money she could get out of the $120,000 string of pearls that he had given her as a wedding prezzie.

"Alone as you are, in this big city, I should think you would be afraid to wear those beautiful pearls in public," Diamond Bill told her. "But, of course, you have them insured?"

"No, I have not," Sidi replied.

"You should neglect that no longer," said Diamond Bill. Then, he paused for a second, as if he'd just been struck by a thought. "Why not let me have them?" he asked suddenly. "I'll take them and have them insured. It will save you the trouble and it will guard against possibility of substitution, because I can spend the whole day at the matter and see to it that when they are appraised there will be no underhand work."

Sidi, delighted by this kind offer by her dear friend's husband, immediately removed the pearls and handed them over.

She never saw them again. The next day, Diamond Bill Barrett hopped on a fast steamer bound for the U.S., leaving his young pregnant wife and her too-trusting friend behind in Europe, and disappeared.

The abandoned Alice appealed to her parents for help, and they came to her rescue; after her baby was born, she quietly secured a divorce. The baby died in infancy ten months later.

Naturally, the police in London and the U.S. got busy trying to track down Diamond Bill. Eventually the cops in Los Angeles found him, living there under a pseudonym and working now in the movie industry — or, rather, trying to; he was, as historian Ken Bilderback puts it in his book *Law and Order at the End of the Oregon Trail*, "waving around wads of cash, trying to arrange a movie to produce." Brought in for interrogation, Bill deployed his legendary charm, claiming that he knew nothing about Sidi's pearls, although she'd shown them to him and he had admired them. And as for the alias he was living under, well, he explained, he'd adopted the pseudonym not to dodge the arm of the law, but merely in order to get solidly into character for a movie he was working on.

The Diamond Bill charm worked like it usually did, and, when the London police were a little slow in issuing a warrant, the L.A. cops let him go — much to Sidi's subsequent disgust. Because, of course, he then promptly disappeared again.

Not much is heard from Diamond Bill after this. In 1932 he was arrested in Brazil for counterfeiting, and sentenced to a six-year prison stretch. By that time he was, of course, a little too old to be sweeping wealthy debutantes off their feet, and apparently the "printing business" was his attempt to find a new racket.

It must not have worked for him, because by the time he died of old age in 1963, he was flat broke and living on his Army pension and Social Security benefits. He was buried with full military honors in Arlington National Cemetery.

Looking back over his life, it's hard not to think the biggest mistake Diamond Bill ever made was burning his bridges with Sidi Wirt Spreckels, who was clearly his soul mate. Sidi's romantic resumé is even wilder than Bill's. While a student at the University of Kansas, she got engaged to marry a Brazilian nobleman; but then she ran out on him on their wedding day, and got married to a newspaper reporter in an automobile while literally running from her angry ex-fiancé and his family — apparently the preacher was in the passenger seat. This marriage ended just a few days later, and after that she went into show business as a cabaret singer. It was around this time that she first met Diamond Bill Barrett.

In 1918 she swept sugar-fortune heir Jack Spreckels off his feet, married him — very much against the wishes of his family — and received the $120,000 string of pearls from him as a wedding gift.

The marriage quickly soured, which is why she found herself alone in London when she met Diamond Bill there; and she filed for divorce shortly after that, after returning alone to the U.S. to pursue Diamond Bill and her stolen pearls.

But Jack died in a car wreck before the divorce could be finalized.

A year or two later, Sidi married a Turkish prince, and apparently finished her remarkable career as an Anatolian princess.

But, this is perhaps the most interesting part of the whole story: What if the two of them actually *were* in cahoots? The pearls that Diamond Bill nicked were not paid for, and Tiffany's of London made several unsuccessful attempts to hold Sidi responsible for their disappearance. Eventually they collected the $80,000 balance owing on them from the Spreckels family; but if they hadn't been stolen from her, Sidi would probably have had to give them back.

So: Did she and Diamond Bill really "just happen to meet" in London? Or did Diamond Bill actually journey to London especially to meet her, to do a mutually profitable favor for an old friend and partner-in-crime?

As clever as those two clearly were, we'll never know the real story for sure. But Sidi's protestations of anger and bitterness against Bill in subsequent newspaper articles have the distinct flavor of a lady who, methinks, doth protest, perhaps, just a little too much.

Sources and Works Cited:
- Law and Order at the End of the Oregon Trail, *a book by Ken and Kris Bilderback published in 2015 by Ken and Kris Bilderback;*
- Portland Morning Oregonian *archives: 1911, 1920-1922, and 1932)*

PART IX:

COLD CASES.

In the early years of Oregon's history as a state, law enforcement was thin and unskilled. It wasn't uncommon for a suspicious death to take place and never be properly investigated. Evidence would grow cold, and people would move on.

Less common, but more interesting, were those cases in which the authorities thought they had the case solved — but looking back through the historical records, we can see that they really didn't. Glaring out from between the lines of the old newspaper articles and jailhouse diaries and witness testimonies, we can glimpse the possibilities of what the true story may have been. In some cases, those possibilities are really chilling.

Here are a few of them.

SEE PORTLAND AND DIE.

Joseph E. Swards was 16 years old when he left his native Philadelphia as a brand-new apprentice seaman on the barque *Geo. F. Manson*, bound for Astoria and Portland. He would turn 17 at sea, in July of 1878.

By the time he was 18, he would be doing life without parole for a crime he didn't commit.

The facts of Joseph's story are clearly laid out in the Portland newspapers, and they read like a nineteenth-century cautionary tale — the oddly merciless kind of children's story ending in fatality that Victorian-age writers wrote to demonstrate the dangers of playing with matches, disobeying Mother, socializing with "gypsies," etc.

I haven't been able to learn why young Joseph shipped out — whether it was for the romantic idea of adventure at sea (still a thing in the late 1870s, although fading fast) or to escape from something unpleasant at home. Nor do I know how he was treated on this, his first deepwater voyage, although as an apprentice he would have been very low on the pecking order, so it's likely it wasn't comfortable. But however lousy his life had been before his arrival, it probably was a palmy paradise by contrast with what awaited him in Oregon.

After he arrived in Portland, Joseph does not seem to have even considered going back to sea. Of course, he didn't think about much of anything at first. He was young and free with money in his pockets, loose in a wild and hard-partying city. Surely he was looking forward to an epic blowout.

He almost immediately met up with a man named Martin Tracy, who kept a grocery store on First Street. Tracy, standing at the door of his store, invited the lad in for a beer as he walked by, and Joseph naively took him up on it.

"I drank a glass and a half and then 'went away'; I was tight," Joseph testified, at a subsequent inquest. "He must have put something in it. Then we went to bed."

It's hard to tell for sure, through the filter of Victorian sensibilities and the fog of 150 years, if this meant what it sounds like to the modern ear — that Joseph was drugged and sexually exploited on his first day in Portland. But it probably did, because later that night, Tracy's wife caught Tracy "pouring something on me in bed, or trying to" — and, it seems, kicked him out.

So Tracy and young Joseph left together, going to a boardinghouse, where they stayed for several nights and met another drifter by the name of James Johnson.

A few days later, Joseph said, Tracy "left for the mountains" — an 1870s colloquialism for going on the lam, which seems a strange thing for a storeowner to do — and the lad was once again at loose ends.

"Johnson asked me what I was going to do," Joseph testified later. "I told him I was going to work; he said he was going to hunt work too, and told me to stay with him and we would board in the Norton house .... I told him I had no money except a dollar and a quarter; he said never mind, that he had money and would pay my board."

The two of them stayed at the Norton house for a few days, skipped on the board bill, then stayed in a hotel for two nights in order to steal some blankets. Then they met up with another drifter by the name of Archie Brown; the three of them "borrowed" a rowboat, crossed the river and walked up the railroad tracks to Oregon City.

When they got there, Johnson and Brown made Joseph stay and guard their camp while they looked for work — at least, that's what they said they were doing. Actually, they were trying to rob the post office. But they were watched so closely that they thought the better of it and returned to camp.

So the three of them headed back to Portland again, setting up their camp just outside town, and Joseph heard his two adult companions talking about pawnshops. Still in need of work, and subsisting on potatoes and turnips stolen from gardens by night, they had decided to pawn the stolen hotel blankets — or so they said.

On August 20, the three of them left their camp and went to Portland to pawn the blankets.

COLD CASES.

This early photo of the Gem Saloon and the Oro Fino Theater dates from 1876, two years before Joseph Swards arrived in Portland. These businesses were located on First Street between Stark and Oak; the grocery store at which Swards started his tragic spree was also on First Street, probably farther north. (Image: Oregon Historical Society)

It was a day Joseph would remember — and lament — for the rest of his life. Which, as an indirect result of the events of that day, would be considerably shortened.

"When we got to Second Street, where Mr. O'Shea's shop is, they told me to wait on the corner, and they went into the store," Joseph said. "They were about ten minutes, and I went down to see what they were doing."

Joseph didn't know it, but when he opened the door of O'Shea's pawnshop, he was not only walking into a store — he was also walking into the penitentiary. Because Johnson and Brown were not there to pawn blankets. They were there to rob the place. Had he stayed on the corner as instructed, no one would ever have known he was connected with the robbers in any way. But now he was dawdling in the shop, waiting for them to get done with their transaction so they could all leave together.

While he waited, standing near the front window, he noticed two boys across the street looking at him, and he smiled, winked and wagged his finger at them. They thought this was odd, so they continued to watch him.

Then suddenly there was a flurry of movement behind him, and a sickening thump.

347

"After I heard the first groan, I looked and saw Brown strike O'Shea again," Joseph said. "He struck him with a piece of iron ... it was about 18 inches long and about three-quarters of an inch round."

Now, too late, Joseph tried to run for it — but nothing doing.

"Johnson told me I had got myself in trouble by coming in there, and told me to stand at the counter and pushed me away from the door," he said.

Meanwhile, the boys Joseph had wagged his finger at were figuring out what was going on. They ran to get a nearby police officer — and the chase was on.

The three bandits broke out a back window and fled, hampered by several pounds of gold, jewelry and pocket watches. The cop was unarmed, but fast gaining on them. Brown pulled his pistol, a big .44-caliber cap-and-ball Colt Navy revolver that he'd probably just stolen from the pawnshop, and turned and sent a bullet zipping past the cop's ears.

Brown didn't mean to hit the policeman; he just wanted to scare him off enough to gain a little distance. And, in fact, he didn't hit the policeman. The bullet from the revolver flashed past the cop —

— and lodged in the heart of 14-year-old Louis Joseph, a local youngster who'd come to see what the fuss was about.

"I'm shot!" gasped Louis, and collapsed to the ground, and died a few seconds later.

As a distraction, this unhappy event seems to have worked. The three bandits got away clean, stealing a wagon and racing off into the woods outside of town.

Outrage swept the city. A $250 reward was promptly offered, then increased to $500. The three fugitives did the best they could to avoid capture and leave the area, but every eye was peeled for them. Even the baddest bad guy in town, shanghaier Jim Turk, joined in the hunt for the murderers.

Young Swards, the most naïve of the bunch, was captured the very next day. Brown, whose real name was Avery, was taken at gunpoint by the landlord of a boardinghouse he'd checked into. Johnson was the only one of the three who was smart enough to leave town immediately, but it didn't do him much good; word of the killing spread fast, and he was soon captured in Los Angeles.

The trials of the three got under way in December, and in January they were all found guilty. Johnson and Brown were sentenced to hang, and Swards, convicted of second-degree murder, drew a life sentence in the state penitentiary.

The *Morning Oregonian*, for one, thought the unhappy teenager was getting off easy.

"It is not easy to see why Swards ... is not as criminal as his associates, who are under sentence of death," the paper opined in an editorial. "But various considerations, among which are the youth of the prisoner and the probability that he was not the originator of the scheme of robbery which led to the murder, seem to have inclined the jury to leniency."

In the end, though, it amounted to the same thing. Swards caught tuberculosis in prison, and it took just a year or two for the disease to wear him down and kill him.

Sources and Works Cited:
- Portland Morning Oregonian *archives, August 1878 through January 1879.*

BALCH FAMILY VALUES.

On the afternoon of Nov. 8, 1858, 48-year-old Danford Balch stood on the deck of the Stark Street Ferry, holding a double-barreled shotgun. Both barrels were still smoking. At his feet in a widening crimson puddle lay the body of his son-in-law, Mortimer Stump.

This was the crime that would lead, early the following year, to the first public execution in Portland's history. And it happened so long ago — it's so shrouded in the mists of time and of rough-and-ready frontier record-keeping — that it's hard to know exactly what happened, or why.

But the information we do have points to some very dark possibilities.

Danford Balch had come to Oregon in 1847 on the Oregon Trail with his wife, a pretty young widow with two children, whom he'd married around 1842 when he was about 31 years old. They crossed the continent in the usual covered-wagon way with their several children — "hers and ours," as it were. Upon arrival, they staked a claim that included most of what today is the Northwest Heights neighborhood and much of what's now Forest Park — some of the most valuable real estate in the entire state. At the time, though, it was pretty remote, and mostly thickly forested.

But as a decade passed and Portland grew from a cluster of shacks into the preeminent city in the Oregon Territory, Balch found he had grown into

A drawing of the first house to be built in Portland, a log cabin built at what would soon become Front and Washington streets in 1844. Three years later, Danford Balch arrived. (Image: Joseph Gaston)

a pretty important fellow. And that may be at least part of the reason he reacted so poorly when the son of a less-prominent neighbor asked for his daughter's hand in marriage.

The would-be bridegroom was a strapping lad named Mortimer, a son of the Stump family from the east side of the Willamette. Young Mortimer had been staying with the Balches as a hired hand, and during his time there he and the eldest of the nine Balch children, 15-year-old Anna, had fallen for each other. So, in keeping with the patriarchal custom of the time, Mortimer asked her father for his permission to marry her.

Old Man Balch, apparently deeply offended by the request, rebuffed Mortimer forcefully and then fired him and ordered him off the property.

But a few days later, Anna stole away and met up with Mortimer, and together they secretively eloped across the Columbia to Vancouver to marry.

Danford Balch did not take the news well.

"The night I came home and found the girl gone, it struck a pain to my heart, like a knife cutting me," he wrote later, in his jailhouse diary. "I ate a little supper and went to bed, but did not sleep a wink all night. In the morning, at once after getting up, I started for town, and it seemed as if my stomach would burst from anxiety and grief, which were more than I can express."

Keeping in mind that Balch had eight other children and a wife at home, the question of why he reacted in such an extreme way is the central mystery of his story. His vivid description of emotional desolation introduces a really disturbing note into the narrative. Historian Diane Goeres-Gardener comes right out and says what you are probably already thinking right now: "The description he gave of his emotional, physical and psychological state sounded more like a man describing the loss of a lover than a daughter," she writes, in *Necktie Parties*.

Her observation, and the implication that Balch may have been secretly using young Anna as a sex toy, gains a lot of plausibility from the fact that Anna was probably Danford's stepdaughter — not related to him by blood. The dates are fuzzy, but remember, Mary Jane Balch had two children already when Danford married her in '42. Was Anna one of those? It's impossible to say for sure, but she was the oldest child in the Balch home in 1858 when all this happened. So the math works.

Balch also, by all accounts (including his own), had started drinking heavily several years before this incident.

Downtown Portland in 1854, four years before the murder. This is the era in which Portland became known for the whitewashed stumps that dotted its streets. (Image: Oregon State University Archives)

The Stark Street Ferry in the 1880s. The ferry on which the murder of Mortimer Stump took place was a different boat; in fact, it was mule-powered — a mule on a treadmill drove a paddlewheel, and the ferryman urged it on by throwing rocks at it. (Image: Oregon Historical Society)

So on that fateful November day, Balch apparently was in Portland having a drink at a saloon when the newlyweds came to town to buy supplies so that they could set up housekeeping. A confrontation ensued in front of the store kept by Multnomah County Sheriff and former Portland mayor Addison Starr.

Here's what Balch had to say about that encounter:

"He [the elder Stump, Mortimer's father] cursed a great deal and said I was making a great fuss about my child; that she was an ordinary little bitch, and [he] did not know what [unknown expletive] I wanted of her," Balch wrote. "There was more said. I do not recollect saying another word."

After this encounter, Balch apparently ran for home, poured himself another big drink, grabbed his double-barreled shotgun, and hustled back to town with it. He later claimed his plan was to use it to demand the return of his "stolen property" — viz., Anna. Obviously, he was not thinking very clearly, and witnesses to the incident that followed confirm he was by then quite drunk.

The Stumps almost escaped from his clutches. They were on James Stephens' mule-powered Stark Street ferry, ready to take off across the river, when Balch ran up with his shotgun and dispensed the contents of both barrels directly into his new son-in-law's face.

Balch was, of course, very roughly taken into custody on the spot by outraged fellow passengers, and lodged in the rickety rented building that the new city was using as a jail. He promptly escaped and was on the lam for a while, hiding out in the woodsy part of his land, but a few months later he was recaptured by Portland's new city marshal, James Lappeus.

At his trial, to his evident astonishment, Balch was convicted and sentenced to hang. Several people testified at his trial that they'd heard him threaten to kill Mortimer Stump; apparently he was in the habit of going to Portland saloons, drinking to the point of blackouts and then making belligerent verbal threats that he didn't remember the next day. His confession, written just before his hanging when it wouldn't do him any good at all to lie, is full of bewilderment at all the Portland residents who testified at his trial to deadly drunken pledges that he didn't remember making.

Balch was hanged on Oct. 18, 1859, ten months to the day after his crime. His was the first legal execution in the history of the city of Portland.

As a side note, there were rumors — fairly credible ones — that Marshal Lappeus had offered to let him escape from the city jail for a $1,000 bribe, which the widow had been unable to raise; these rumors haunted Lappeus for the rest of his law-enforcement career.

At the hanging, Portlanders were shocked to see a dry-eyed Anna Balch Stump there with her in-laws. They were there to watch Danford die. And they did.

The reporter from the Portland *Oregonian* was aghast.

"The idea of a daughter, by her own volition, attending the execution of a father upon a gallows, is a disgrace to the intelligence of the age, and to every principle of filial affection manifested or exhibited by every species of the brute creation, in the sea or upon the earth," he wrote in the following week's paper. "This fact is of a character that we cannot pass unnoticed, and must meet with the surprise, reprobation and detestation of the whole community."

This surely seemed like a reasonable inference. But then, maybe the *Oregonian* reporter just didn't know the whole story. And that's probably all that should be said about that.

Sources and Works Cited:
- *"The Hanging of Danford Balch," an episode of the* Kick Ass Oregon History

Podcast *by Doug Kenck-Crispin and Andy Lindberg (Vol. 1, No. 4);*
- Necktie Parties: Legal Executions in Oregon 1851-1905, *a book by Diane L. Goeres-Gardner published in 2005 by Caxton Press;*
- *"Execution of Balch," an un-by-lined article in the Oct. 22, 1859, issue of the* Portland Weekly Oregonian.

BONEYARD MARY.

This is the story of Portland's coldest cold-case file — a suspicious death in the worst neighborhood of the old Stumptown waterfront, almost lost in the mists of time, 140 years ago. Was it an accident? Or a murder?

We'll never know for sure. But there are good reasons to be suspicious.

Our story begins in a smoky, lamp-lit saloon in the rough part of Portland, back in early February of 1878. W.H. Harrigan, one of the tough, hard-working longshoremen who worked the docks in early Portland, was having a drink or two with his friend Thomas McMahon — known to friends and enemies alike as "Mac."

Mac was a scow operator on the river, in charge of one of the large flat-bottomed boats that helped shuttle cargo among ships in the harbor, and he lived in a cabin on board the scow. Mac's scow was usually kept tied up to the dock by the Oregon Steam Navigation Company's "boneyard" — a dilapidated and labyrinthine marina of sorts, where the company docked its worn-out steamboats while they were waiting to be dismantled or scavenged for parts.

Mac wasn't his usual free-spirited self that evening. In fact, Mac told Harrigan he was flat-out scared. He explained that he'd gotten in a fight with a man named Jack Abrahagen a week or two before, and Abrahagen had beaten him badly and then pulled a knife. Abrahagen was, at that moment, under arrest in the city jail awaiting trial for this deadly assault, and McMahon was worried that Abrahagen would come for him and finish the job, so that he couldn't testify against him. Would Harrigan be willing to come spend the night at his place, for protection?

Harrigan said he would. But as the night went on, the two of them set out to drink Portland dry. Harrigan did such a thorough job of this that he was arrested for public drunkenness and thrown into the drunk tank for the night.

It was the last time Harrigan would ever see McMahon alive.

The next day, Harrigan stopped by McMahon's scow to check on him, and found no sign of the man anywhere.

Alarmed, Harrigan kicked in the door of the scow's cabin. There was no sign of Harrigan, but all his belongings were still there in the scow — including, most alarmingly, $4.50 (about $110 worth, in modern currency) in cash.

"I then started for up town," Harrigan said, during the coroner's inquest that followed a few weeks later, "and after I had passed the house of Boneyard Mary she called to me and said McMahon had fallen in the river; that she saw him swimming; that she thought he had got out as someone struck a light in the scow."

"Boneyard Mary" was the nickname of a woman named Eliza Bunets, who lived either on one of the old riverboats in the boneyard, or in a boardinghouse next door to it. Aesthetically, the boneyard was kind of like a combination of a junkyard and a haunted mansion, the whole thing floating on an occasionally evil-smelling river at the foot of Flanders Street, decrepit by day and, in those pre-streetlight days, positively sinister by night.

McMahon's scow was anchored right next to the boneyard, so he and Boneyard Mary were neighbors — but, it seems, not friends.

Boneyard Mary gave her occupation as "laundress," and, well, maybe she was. A careful reading of the newspaper accounts, though, suggests she derived most of her income in other ways.

Harrigan had no reason to disbelieve Boneyard Mary. He moved on, trying to convince himself that McMahon had simply gone on the lam to avoid being called as a witness against Abrahagen. But something about the whole thing bothered him, especially the money. Why would Mac leave his money behind?

The notorious Oregon Steam Navigation Company "boneyard," covering the waterfront at the north end of the North End and stocked with old and dilapidated steamboats, as it appeared in an 1892 commemorative publication by the Portland Morning Oregonian. (Image: City of Portland Archives)

Two weeks later, Harrigan's worst fears were realized. A young boy fishing off a nearby dock hooked and reeled in the unfortunate McMahon's corpse.

At the coroner's inquest, Harrigan told his story, and then it was Boneyard Mary's turn. She said the evening Harrigan was arrested, she was there when he arrived home for the night.

"I went inside the house and told (neighbor) Mr. Nelson and his wife that McMahon was very drunk," she testified. "I then stepped out on the wharf, and in a few minutes heard a splash in the water. I ran to the edge of the wharf and looked down in the river and saw an object in the water which I thought was him."

Boneyard Mary then went back to the house and notified the Nelsons that McMahon had fallen in the drink. Nelson promptly came out to help.

"Mr. Nelson went immediately on board the scow," Bunets said, "and found a hat saturated with water, and Mr. Nelson said he thought he had gone in the cabin and was all right."

A few other interesting things developed out of Bunets' testimony, though. First, Jack Abrahagen — the man arrested for beating and knifing McMahon — was, as it turned out, more than just her friend. He'd been living with her for several weeks before the fight broke out. She'd been smuggling letters to him in jail, slipped inside newspapers. And the two of them were engaged to be married.

Furthermore, she told the court, "I think the fight between (Abrahagen) and McMahon was about some bad words being said by McMahon about me."

Also, after McMahon disappeared, Bunets smuggled a letter to Abrahagen "stating that he need not be afraid now as 'Mc' had gone away."

Could it be that Eliza "Boneyard Mary" Bunets had something to do with McMahon's drowning that night?

Certainly Bunets had the motivation to do the job. She was 40 years old — an age at which a "working girl" in the 1870s couldn't look forward to many more years of plying the trade. She'd met a man who wanted to marry her — to make her a "respectable" married woman. Now that whole dream was being threatened by the prospect of attempted-murder charges. If Abrahagen were hauled off to the penitentiary, it was likely those wedding bells would go forever unrung.

The only way that could be prevented with absolute certainty, would be for McMahan to "disappear" before he could testify. And it's not hard to spin a not-too-fanciful theory about how she might accomplish such a thing.

Let's say, theoretically, that she sees Mac coming home drunk that night, and sees her chance. She slips over to his scow with a bottle, a smile, and maybe a little extra something to put in his drink — or maybe she just drinks with him and goads him into having more than he should, and he passes out. It would be the work of a few minutes to slip the unconscious McMahon into the river to quietly drown.

Then she dips his hat in the water, plants it on the boat and trots up the wharf to the Nelson house to fabricate an alibi. "Mac is very drunk tonight," she remarks, as if just making chit-chat, and then wanders back out again. She dawdles outside for two or three minutes, then hustles back in.

"Help!" she shrieks. "Mac fell in the water! Help me get him out!"

Nelson runs down to the scow and, as Boneyard Mary had planned (in our hypothetical scenario) finds the wet hat.

"Oh good," Boneyard Mary remarks innocently. "He must have gotten out."

The two of them talk it over and decide McMahon must have run off to Washington Territory to avoid testifying against Abrahagen, and they all go to bed. Boneyard Mary has her witness and her alibi. The currents of the river (it's February, remember) seem likely to carry the body out to sea and no one will be the wiser. And everything is going right according to plan ... until that pesky meddling kid fishes up McMahon's corpse and gets the cops involved.

COLD CASES.

So ... could this have been what happened that night?
Maybe. Certainly it would explain why there was a wet hat on the scow even though McMahon never made it back aboard.
But we'll never really know. Because the Coroner ruled the death an accident, and that was the end of that.

Sources and Works Cited:
- Portland Weekly Oregonian *archives, February 1878.*

THE BORDELLO MURDER.

At around 2 p.m. on a sunny Monday afternoon in August 1911, Klamath Falls resident John Hunsaker was driving past the Oak Avenue Canal when he saw something in it — something that looked like a man.

Now, this canal was the waterway that carried the pioneer city's untreated sewage out to the Link River. So although some things were occasionally observed floating in it, they usually weren't people. Hunsaker took a closer look.

It was a man, all right. Or, rather, the body of a man.

There was no mystery as to how he had died. The right side of his head showed two massive wounds, apparently inflicted with an ax. But as to where this had happened, and by whom — that was another story.

The body, as it turned out, belonged to a man named Charles Lyons. Lyons was a logger working in a camp at Stukel Mountain, just a few miles outside Klamath Falls. On the previous Friday morning, three days before his body was found, Lyons had drawn his pay — a whopping $80 in cash, the equivalent of about $2,100 today — and headed for town to "blow 'er in" with Ben Robbs, his buddy from work at the logging camp.

The two of them arrived in Klamath Falls and checked into a hotel before sallying forth to paint the town.

A hand-tinted postcard image of downtown Klamath Falls as it appeared around 1911, when the murder of Charles Lyons took place. (Image: OSU Archives)

They first stopped at a watering hole called The Road House, where they got the night started off with a few drinks, and Lyons had the house barber give him a shave — he clearly wanted to look and smell his best for the ladies later that night.

And oh, yes, there would be ladies. Lyons and Robbs were on their way to the swankiest, fanciest, swingin'est bordello Klamath Falls had to offer: Faye Melbourne's "Red House," located near the Oak Avenue Canal at the foot of a small bridge known to locals as the "Bridge of Sighs."

The Bridge of Sighs was named in a joking reference to the famous *Ponte dei Sospiri* in Venice, the covered and fortified bridge across the Rio di Palazzo canal which connects what was once Venice's prison with the interrogation rooms in the Doge's palace. The condemned, being conveyed across the bridge, supposedly got one last chance to peer out through the stone-barred windows at the beauty of Venice before being hustled down the hall to their execution or imprisonment.

Klamath Falls' Bridge of Sighs, on the other hand, crossed from the city's thriving red-light district on one side of the canal to the city jail on the other. The name is a joking reference to the frequency with which city cops escorted drunken, rowdy revelers across the bridge to be lodged in the city joint.

Lyons and Robbs now hurried across that bridge in the other direction, eager to get to Miss Melbourne's place and continue the party. They got there around 7 p.m.

The evening wore on and the two furloughed loggers burned through their money.

By midnight, Robbs had had enough and was ready for bed. Lyons, though, was just getting started. He was drunk, but not dead drunk, and not yet ready to call it a night.

So Robbs left him there in the care of the friendly ladies of the Red House and headed for the hotel.

He never saw Charles Lyons alive again.

WOMEN ORDERED TO LEAVE CITY

POLICE CHIEF'S EDICT IS FOR DISORDERLY HOUSES TO CLOSE—FOUR MALE VISITORS ARE CAUGHT—TWO EXILED

Chief of Police Samuel L. Walker last night visited the four disorderly establishments on Oak street, ordering the proprietresses and inmates to leave town, as well as arresting four visitors, two of whom as well were ordered to quit the town.

There are a score or more women who have, it is said, been living in the places, and the mysterious killing of Charles Lyons last August, as well as the robbery of J. W. Rosier at an early hour last Thursday morning, both near the houses in the undesirable district, as well as other incidents in connection with the "badlands," have stirred the authorities to the determination that there must be less disorder in the city, and as they believe the immoral settlement to be responsible for much of the trouble that has been going on, they have decided to have the district simply cleaned up.

One feature of the situation that has puzzled the authorities is the fact that the women who run the resorts own the property, and just how to go about the matter has been something of a conundrum. It is understood that the authorities now have a way in which they can proceed which will take care of this horn of the dilemma.

City Attorney Horace M. Manning, when asked if it was through his advice that the district was raided, stated to the Herald that he would rather not speak on the subject.

"You may say, however, that in any steps the police take for the abolition of the disorderly houses they will have the backing of the city attorney's office just as far as it can be given," said Mr. Manning.

A story from the Nov. 15, 1911, issue of the Klamath Falls Evening Herald illustrates the impact the unsolved murder of Charles Lyons had on the town. It was this vice clampdown that resulted in the charges against Faye Melbourne. (Image: UO Libraries)

The famous Bridge of Sighs (Ponte dei Sospiri) in Venice, after which the bridge connecting Klamath Falls' red-light district with the city jail was jokingly named. (Image: Aqwis/Wikipedia)

At first, authorities thought perhaps the drunken Lyons had simply fallen off the Bridge of Sighs into the unsanitary water of the canal and drowned. This theory, however, lasted only until the body was lifted from the water and they saw the massive wounds on his head.

Such wounds would have let out quarts of blood. But police scrounged all along the banks of the canal for clues, and on the bridge, and — they found nothing.

Police ran a fine-toothed rake along the bottom of the canal, hoping to find the weapon. An unfortunate assistant was drafted to dive to the bottom of the filthy waterway every time they snagged something, and bring it to the surface. But again, nothing.

The unsolved murder of a logger near the red-light district intensified public pressure for the city to do something about the brothels; after all, prostitution was supposed to be illegal.

Another highly publicized incident in December at another openly-secret bordello, the Comet Lodging House, whipped the public up even more. It happened just before Christmas, and it involved the arrest of the town's most notorious septuagenarian, a disreputable and disorderly Civil War vet popularly known as Old Man Haley.

"Several nights ago in the Comet Lodging House, Old Man Haley ... was making Rome howl," the Klamath Falls Evening Herald reported. "He was disrobed, in bed, full [drunk], and waving a $10 bill in his hand."

Apparently all the Comet's employees had declined to earn Old Man Haley's $10, and he'd taken offense; so the Comet had called the cops to escort him and his $10 across the Bridge of Sighs to spend the night in the drunk tank. A generally happy outcome; but the optics, for the bordello business, were not particularly good. Did Klamath Falls want to be the kind of town where sex parlors draw in drunks and dirty old men for wild, noisy, disorderly parties every night, drinking and fighting and occasionally getting murdered?

The answer from the town's respectable citizens was a resounding "no."

Prodded by the citizens, City Hall ordered all the ladies of the evening to close up shop. They, of course, ignored the edict. And so it was that in January 1912, Miss Faye Melbourne found herself in the dock, facing charges of operating a bawdy-house.

Now, this was not a new situation for Miss Faye. In that era, Oregon was full of bordellos pretending to be something else, and their proprietresses frequently had to face charges. Usually, it was part of the cost of doing business — a way to transfer some of their income over to City Hall while giving the impression of rigorous law enforcement.

But something was different this time. For one thing, Miss Faye's lawyer, in court, accused Police Chief Samuel Walker of collaborating with and shielding the town's bordellos in exchange for a cut of the take. Walker was actually forced to admit that Miss Faye had solicited his advice about where to build the Red House. Clearly, the gloves were off.

The verdict in the trial was a hung jury: eight to four. A new trial would have to be scheduled.

Posting $200 in bail money, Miss Faye walked out the door ... and was never seen again.

Behind her she left her palatial, richly furnished real estate — which, unlike most bordello madams, she actually owned outright. She left her mail piling up at the post office. She even left her lawyer in the lurch for his court fees. The newspapers concluded that she'd skipped town to avoid prosecution.

But, prosecution for prostitution — an offense worth, at most, a month or two in jail? Why would she do a thing like that?

Lake County historian Melany Tupper suggests it might have been because she'd learned she was about to be indicted as an accessory to the murder of Charles Lyons. After all, it was her parlor in which he'd last been seen; could that have been where he was murdered?

It's an intriguing theory: Lyons, after getting really drunk, tries to force himself on one of the girls; in defense, one of the other employees steps up behind with an ax and lets him have it, right behind the ear; Miss Faye's terrified employees quickly mop up the blood, wrap Lyons in a blanket, hustle his body out onto the Bridge of Sighs and drop him in, hoping he'll sink out of sight . . . .

Well — maybe. But there is a darker possibility — darker and, given that Miss Faye clearly had some dirt on several powerful people in Klamath Falls, probably more likely. It involves a blackjack, and a shallow grave somewhere in the woods outside of town.

But, of course, we'll probably never know.

Sources and Works Cited:
- *The Trapper Murders, a book by Melany Tupper published in 2013 by Central Oregon Books;*
- *Portland Morning Oregonian archives, August 1911;*
- *Klamath Falls Evening Herald archives, November 1911.*

www.ingramcontent.com/pod-product-compliance
Lightning Source LLC
Chambersburg PA
CBHW020938180426
43194CB00038B/225